The principal objective of THE MATHESON TRUST is to promote the study of comparative religion from the point of view of the underlying harmony of the great religious and philosophical traditions of the world. This objective is being pursued through such means as audio-visual media, the support and sponsorship of lecture series and conferences, the creation of a website, collaboration with film production companies and publishing companies as well as the Trust's own series of publications.

The Matheson Monographs cover a wide range of themes within the field of comparative religion: scriptural exegesis in different religious traditions; the modalities of spiritual and contemplative life; in-depth mystical studies of particular religious traditions; broad comparative analyses taking in a series of religious forms; studies of traditional arts, crafts and cosmological science; and contemporary scholarly expositions of religious philosophy and metaphysics. The monographs also comprise translations of both classical and contemporary texts, as well as transcriptions of lectures by, and interviews with, spiritual and scholarly authorities from different religious and philosophical traditions.

PATHS THAT LEAD TO THE SAME SUMMIT
AN ANNOTATED GUIDE TO WORLD SPIRITUALITY

सत्यान्नास्ति परो धर्मः

There is no dharma higher than Truth.

Maxim of the Maharajas of Benares
Mahābhārata, CE 1, 69, 24

PATHS
THAT LEAD
TO THE SAME SUMMIT

An Annotated Guide
to World Spirituality

by

Samuel Bendeck Sotillos

THE MATHESON TRUST
For the Study of Comparative Religion

© The Matheson Trust, 2020

This first edition published by
The Matheson Trust
PO Box 336
56 Gloucester Road
London SW7 4UB, UK

www.themathesontrust.org

ISBN: 978 1 908092 20 5

*All rights reserved. No part of this publication
may be reproduced, stored in a retrieval system,
or transmitted in any form or by any means, electronic,
mechanical, photocopying, recording, or otherwise,
without the prior written permission of the Publisher.*

British Library Cataloguing-in-Publication Data.
A catalogue record for this book is
available from the British Library.

Typeset by the publishers in Baskerville 10 Pro

Cover illustration and design by Susana Marín.

Contents

Preface xi
Introduction: The Path and the Perennial Philosophy . 1

I The Hindu Tradition   17
1. *Introduction to Hindu Dharma* by the Jagadguru of Kanchi 18
2. *The Original Gospel of Rāmakrishna* 28
3. *Timeless in Time: Sri Ramana Maharshi* by A.R. Natarajan 46
4. *The Essential Śrī Ānandamayī Mā* 55
5. *Eastern Light in Western Eyes* by Marty Glass 74

II The Taoist Tradition   83
6. *An Illustrated Introduction to Taoism* by Jean C. Cooper 84

III The First Peoples Religion and their Shamanic Traditions   93
7. *The Spiritual Legacy of the American Indian* 94
8. *Black Elk, Lakota Visionary* by Harry Oldmeadow . . . 99

IV The Buddhist Tradition   109
9. *Uncompromising Truth for a Compromised World* by
   Samdhong Rinpoche 110
10. *Honen the Buddhist Saint* 119

V The Jewish Tradition   122
11. *Universal Aspects of the Kabbalah and Judaism* by Leo
    Schaya 123

VI The Christian Tradition   132
12. *The Rationale Divinorum Officiorum* by Durandus . . 133
13. *Meister Eckhart on Divine Knowledge* by C.F. Kelley . . 141
14. *Christianity and the Doctrine of Non-Dualism* by A
    Monk of the West (Elie Lemoine) 151

VII The Islamic Tradition   154
15. *What Does Islam Mean in Today's World?* by William
    Stoddart. 155
16. *Know Yourself: An Explanation of the Oneness of Being* . 161
17. *The Sufi Doctrine of Rumi* by William C. Chittick . . . 168
18. *A Spirit of Tolerance* by Amadou Hampaté Bâ 177
19. *Introduction to Sufi Doctrine* by Titus Burckhardt . . 185

VIII Other Themes in World Spirituality   190
20. *The Underlying Religion* 191
21. *Pray Without Ceasing: The Way of the Invocation in
    World Religions* 196
22. *The Essential René Guénon* 205
23. *Touchstones of the Spirit* by Harry Oldmeadow. . . . 211

CONTENTS

24. *The Mystery of Individuality* by Mark Perry 216
25. *Men of a Single Book* by Mateus Soares de Azevedo . 234
26. *Of the Land and the Spirit: The Essential Lord Northbourne* 240
27. *On the Origin of Beauty* by John Griffin 243
28. *Beads of Faith* by G. Henry & S. Marriott. 251
29. *Death as Gateway to Eternity* by Hans Küry 257
30. *Invincible Wisdom* by William Stoddart. 271
Acknowledgments 275
Bibliography. 280

Preface

The initial idea for this monograph came from Robert D. Crane (b. 1929), who after reading several of my reviews suggested that I compile them into a book as they would "make an excellent annotated bibliography for the whole field of perennial wisdom." The reader may ask, why purchase a book of previously published reviews? After all, it is not common to find a book consisting solely of reviews. The significance and value of such a collection is that each review provides a "crib sheet" or draws upon what is essential to understand and reflect upon regarding religion and what the religions say about each other, to provide the reader with a glimpse into a religious and spiritual universe of a particular faith tradition, while at the same time seeing how it differs from and parallels other traditions of the world. The collection provides a map of the terrain and a reference point on how to make sense of religious pluralism in today's world, in order to recognize what the great art historian of the twentieth century Ananda K. Coomaraswamy (1877–1947) termed "Paths That Lead to the Same Summit".[1]

As many of the spiritual themes overlap in this monograph, the reader will find unavoidable repetitions, yet rather than being viewed as a limitation, they can be viewed as a boon. Remembering that traveling the spiritual path itself is not only a continuous unfolding of the divine Mystery, but time and

---

[1] See Ananda K. Coomaraswamy, "Paths That Lead to the Same Summit: Some Observations on Comparative Religion," *Motive*, Vol. 4, No. 8 (May 1944), pp. 29–32, 35.

time again returning to the present moment and examining the limits of what was thought to be known, realizing that there is yet again a deeper and more integral perspective that transcends and assimilates the former point of view. Ongoing practice and repetition then become essential for deepening one's awareness of the essential themes and how to travel the spiritual path in light of the fact that supraformal Truth is inexhaustible.

It was difficult to select which reviews were going to be included in this monograph as there was insufficient space to include all of them. It is thus essential to discern which themes were covered and how to limit the replication of the themes presented as much as possible. The book reviews that comprise this collection nonetheless speak in their own unique way to the timeless and universal wisdom found in all times and places and known as the perennial philosophy.

Some may recall the extensive collection of book reviews and articles by the French metaphysician René Guénon (1886–1951),[2] the many book reviews compiled by the distinguished Thomist metaphysician Bernard Kelly (1907–1958),[3] or those of the leading perennialist author William Stoddart (b. 1925), largely unpublished, all of whom inspired the creation of this current anthology.

Many of the saints and sages of the world's religions have emphasized the limitations of relying solely on books for spiritual realization, as Śrī Rāmakrishna (1836–1886), the Paramahamsa of Dakshineshwar, notes here: "You may read thousands of volumes, you may repeat verses and hymns by hundreds, but if you cannot dive into the ocean of Divinity

---

[2] See René Guénon, "Reviews of Books and Articles," in *Studies in Hinduism* (Ghent, NY: Sophia Perennis, 2001), pp. 105–232.

[3] See Scott Randall Paine (ed.), *A Catholic Mind Awake: The Writings of Bernard Kelly* (Brooklyn, NY: Angelico Press, 2017).

with extreme longing of the soul, you cannot reach God";[4] or "One cannot realize Divinity by reading books."[5] True knowledge and the human being's return to the Divine are not dependent on book learning, but rather on what Plato calls *anamnesis* (recollection or remembrance), that is a knowledge obtained by recalling the truths latent within the human soul. From this point of view learning is possible because it already exists within, and for this reason the Spirit is both transcendent and immanent. Śrī Ānandamayī Mā (1896-1982) emphasizes: "If someone really wants God, and nothing but God, he carries his book in his own heart. He needs no printed book."[6]

With this taken into consideration, books can nonetheless provide a significant support for those seeking and those on the Path, especially in the present-day when authentic spiritual teachers are very few and far between and given the myriad confusions around spiritual matters. Coomaraswamy discusses the importance of books in regard to the phase of the temporal cycle in which we find ourselves in the contemporary world, and gives the following advice to the serious seeker in order to realize "paths that lead to the same summit":

> Constant reading of all the traditional literature and learning to think in those terms [rather than "thinking for yourself"].... I would say you have to read the "100 best books"...all of Plato, Philo, Plotinus, Hermes, Dionysius, Eckhart, Boehme; some of John Scotus Erigena, Nicholas of Cusa, St Thomas Aquinas (eg, at least the first volume of the *Summa* in translation), St Bernard; *The Cloud of*

---

[4] Śrī Rāmakrishna, "God and the Scriptures," in *The Original Gospel of Rāmakrishna: Based on M.'s English Text, Abridged*, eds. Swāmī Abhedānanda and Joseph A. Fitzgerald (Bloomington: World Wisdom, 2011), p. 151.

[5] *Ibid.*

[6] Śrī Ānandamayī Mā, quoted in *The Essential Śrī Ānandamayī Mā: Life and Teachings of a 20th Century Indian Saint*, trans. Ātmānanda, ed. Joseph A. Fitzgerald (Bloomington: World Wisdom, 2007), p. 5.

> *Unknowing*. Also some of the American Indian origin myths; all of Irish mythology; and the *Mabinogion*. Folklore generally. From the East, all of Rumi, Attar and other Sufi writings including Jami's *Lawaih*; the *Bhagavad Gita* (in various versions, until you know it almost by heart); the *Satapatha* and the other Brahmanas—and you know what of Chinese and Japanese yourself. When you have assimilated all this and begin to act accordingly, you will have got somewhere and will find that much of the internal conflict—"which shall rule, the better or the worse, inner or outer man"—will have subsided.[7]

Due to the abnormal conditions and spiritual crisis in our midst, Marty Glass points out that, "In our life in the spirit we have to keep reading.... The traditional guru relationship is not available to the overwhelming majority..."[8] He continues,

> Books, in other words, in our times, are equivalent to that "society of the holy" which tradition is unanimous in declaring indispensable. So reading is necessary. But not sufficient.... We need to go directly to the Teacher. To the source. And in devotional meditation, that's Who we are going to: The Teacher. He is within us, and He alone can definitively, so we'll never doubt it again, impart the Truth, the Truth which He is. He can reveal the Truth because He is the Truth. "I am the Teacher of all teachers," says Krishna in the *Bhagavatam*. The books we read—I use the classic image—are fingers pointing at Him.[9]

The task of reading all the books contained in this volume may be arduous for the curious or even challenging for the seeker given the lack of time and complexity of the present-

---

[7] Ananda K. Coomaraswamy, "Letter to Helen Chapin, Oct. 21, 1945," in *Selected Letters of Ananda K. Coomaraswamy*, eds. Alvin Moore, Jr. and Rama P. Coomaraswamy (Oxford University Press, 1988), p. 325.

[8] Marty Glass, "Ask the Teacher," in *Eastern Light in Western Eyes: A Portrait of the Practice of Devotion* (Hillsdale, NY: Sophia Perennis, 2003), p. 136.

[9] *Ibid.*, p. 137.

day. It is the intent of this collection to function like a guide to aid the seeker with taking a pilgrimage through the distinct religious and spiritual universes and to convey and remember what is at the heart of each of the revealed sapiential traditions, the one Truth hidden in all the forms. Our aim is conveyed in the words of St. John of the Cross (1542–1591) who, when providing instruction on the spiritual path wrote, "those who read this book will in some way discover the road they are walking along, and the one they ought to follow if they want to reach the summit."[10] We recall the words of the *hadīth qudsī* that speak to the symbolic meaning of the manifestation of the cosmos: "I was a hidden treasure, and I wanted to be known; hence I created the world." At the summit where all paths converge in the transcendent Unity, the seeker and the sought, appearing as subject-object also coincide and become One, as the Divine alone exists, and this is the dominating paradox of the human condition. Without seeking, the Self cannot be found, and yet seeking also prevents finding the Self, as only the Self can know the Self. The human being that embarks on the spiritual path initially identifying as an "I" or empirical ego, envisioning itself as separate, at the end of the journey sees that this was always an illusion. The pure Subject as the Self realizes the object within itself which is inseparable from Ultimate Reality or the Absolute.

Samuel Bendeck Sotillos

---

[10] St. John of the Cross, quoted in the Prologue to "The Ascent of Mount Carmel," in *John of the Cross: Selected Writings*, ed. Kieran Kavanaugh (Mahwah, NJ: Paulist Press, 1987), p. 60.

Introduction
The Path and the Perennial Philosophy

Across the world, throughout the four directions and encompassing all times and places including the diverse societies and civilizations, is the recognition that the human being was and is inseparable from Spirit and that there are many paths to realize this unanimous Truth. There are many names for this universal and timeless wisdom known as the perennial philosophy. Aldous Huxley (1894–1963) is responsible for popularizing the term in recent times with his anthology *The Perennial Philosophy* (1944).

It was in the early twentieth century when several key figures, later regarded as the perennialist or traditionalist school of comparative religious thought, became associated with the perennial philosophy. Some of these luminaries are René Guénon (1886–1951), Ananda K. Coomaraswamy (1877–1947), Frithjof Schuon (1907–1998) and Titus Burckhardt (1908–1984).[1] Yet they also include many others such as Marco Pallis (1895–1989), Lord Northbourne (1896–1982), Martin Lings (1909–2005), Whitall N. Perry (1920–2005), Joseph Epes Brown (1920–2000), William Stoddart (b. 1925) and Seyyed Hossein Nasr (b. 1933).

---

[1] Frithjof Schuon emphasized that the perennialist or traditionalist school has two "originators," Guénon and Schuon, and two "continuators," Coomaraswamy and Burckhardt. See William Stoddart, "Frithjof Schuon and the Perennialist School," in *Remembering in a World of Forgetting: Thoughts on Tradition and Postmodernism*, eds. Mateus Soares de Azevedo and Alberto Vasconcellos Queiroz (Bloomington: World Wisdom, 2008), pp. 51–66.

Within Hinduism this teaching is known as the *sanātana dharma* (eternal religion), and in Islam as *al-ḥikmat al-khālidah* (eternal wisdom; *jāwīdān-khirad*, in Persian), or also *al-dīn al-ḥanīf* (primordial religion). Other Latin phrases that are also used to articulate the perennial philosophy are: *sophia perennis* (perennial wisdom), *religio perennis* (perennial religion) and *religio cordis* (religion of the heart). It is sometimes known as the transcendent unity of religions, the underlying religion, Great Chain of Being, Primordial Tradition or simply as Tradition. Coomaraswamy has additionally referred to this metaphysical doctrine as the "Universal and Unanimous Tradition"[2] or "*Philosophia Perennis et Universalis*".[3]

Although the perennial philosophy is not a monolith and has innumerable variations and expressions so that no single individual or school can claim for itself this timeless and universal metaphysics, this does not mean that there are multiple or divergent forms of the perennial philosophy.[4] It is paramount to clarify also that this does not mean that all religions are the same or that one religion or spiritual path is viewed from this perspective as being superior to another religion or path. To assume this is to mistake what the perennial philosophy signifies. This again is because "Truth is one, and it is the same for all who, by whatever way, come to know it."[5] In the same way that "there can be only one

---

[2] Ananda K. Coomaraswamy, "The Nature of Mediaeval Art," in *Christian and Oriental Philosophy of Art* (New York: Dover Publications, 1956), p. 144.

[3] "*Philosophia Perennis et universalis* must be understood, for this 'philosophy' has been the common inheritance of all mankind without exception" (Ananda K. Coomaraswamy, "Eastern Wisdom and Western Knowledge," in *The Bugbear of Literacy*, Middlesex, UK: Perennial Books, 1979, p. 68).

[4] "The Philosophia Perennis... embodies those universal truths to which no one people or age can make exclusive claim," Ananda K. Coomaraswamy, *Hinduism and Buddhism*. New York: Philosophical Library, 1943, p. 4.

[5] René Guénon, "Eastern Metaphysics," in *Studies in Hinduism*, p. 87. "There is a unity at the heart of religions" (Huston Smith, "Introduction" to Frithjof

metaphysics,"[6] correspondingly, "There is only one 'Perennial Philosophy'."[7] The perennial philosophy, like metaphysics, cannot be the exclusive property of any individual or school, as is made clear in the following: "The truths just expressed are not the exclusive possession of any school or individual: were it otherwise they would not be truths, for these cannot be invented, but must necessarily be known in every integral traditional civilization."[8] Guénon powerfully states:

> If an idea is true, it belongs equally to all who are capable of understanding it; if it is false, there is no credit in having invented it. A true idea cannot be "new", for truth is not a product of the human mind; it exists independently of us, and all we have to do is to take cognizance of it; outside this knowledge there can be nothing but error.[9]

When we speak here of "philosophy" as it is associated with the perennial philosophy, we mean the ancient understanding of *philo-sophia* or the "love of wisdom" grounded in a way of life to achieve its goal of wisdom and assimilating the primacy

---

Schuon, *The Transcendent Unity of Religions* [Wheaton, IL: Theosophical Publishing House, 1993], p. xxiii).

[6] Ananda K. Coomaraswamy, "Śrī Ramakrishna and Religious Tolerance," in *Coomaraswamy, Vol. 2: Selected Papers, Metaphysics*, ed. Roger Lipsey (Princeton University Press, 1977), p. 38. Hereafter cited as *Coomaraswamy. Metaphysics*.

[7] Ananda K. Coomaraswamy, "Recollection, Indian and Platonic," in *Coomaraswamy. Metaphysics*, p. 65.

[8] Frithjof Schuon, "Preface," to *The Transcendent Unity of Religions*, p. xxxiii. "There can be no property in ideas. The individual does not make them, but finds them; let him only see to it that he really takes possession of them, and his work will be original in the same sense that the recurrent seasons, sunrise and sunset, are ever new although in name the same" (Ananda K. Coomaraswamy, "Understanding the Art of India," *Calcutta Review*, Vol. 55, Nos. 1–3 [April/June 1935], p. 3).

[9] René Guénon, *The Crisis of the Modern World* (Hillsdale, NY: Sophia Perennis, 2004), pp. 56–57.

of Truth[10]—in order to "put [everything] in its rightful place"[11] and—to learn "how to think".[12] It is the doctrines and methods found across the religions that provide discernment between the Real and the illusory or the Absolute and the relative, together with the concentration on the Real as a means to return to the One.

Perhaps no other theme is more perplexing to the contemporary mind than religion and how to understand religious pluralism in today's world amidst all of the confusion that surrounds these matters. Due to the militant secularism and skepticism in these times, an integral framework for building bridges between the religions is imperative. This is especially necessary at a time when "the outward and readily exaggerated incompatibility of the different religious forms greatly discredits, in the minds of most of our contemporaries, all religion."[13] Without the integral framework of the perennial philosophy authentic bridge-building between the religions cannot take place.

While the word *religion* has become off-putting and is less used today than *spirituality*, it is necessary to remember that the etymological root of the English word "religion" is the Latin *religare*, meaning "to re-bind," or "to bind back", by implication to the Divine or the Supreme Identity that is at once transcendent and immanent. The etymological significance of the term religion itself alludes to its powerful connotation in restoring the integral human condition that has become estranged and besieged with myriad ill-fated

---

[10] See Pierre Hadot, *Philosophy as a Way of Life: Spiritual Exercises from Socrates to Foucault* (Oxford: Blackwell Publishers, 1999).

[11] René Guénon, *The Crisis of the Modern World*, p. 42.

[12] Frithjof Schuon, quoted in James S. Cutsinger, *Splendor of the True: A Frithjof Schuon Reader* (Albany, NY: State University of New York Press, 2013), p. xxxii.

[13] Frithjof Schuon, "Preface," to *The Transcendent Unity of Religions*, pp. xxxiii-xxxiv.

diagnostics. Nonetheless religion is both paramount for both the individual and the human collectivity as it is the unitive force of humanity.

The perennialist critique of the modern and postmodern world is concerned with the loss of the sense of the sacred and the spiritual crisis that has developed in its wake. Although this crisis emerged in post-medieval Western Europe, it has since spread throughout the world, becoming a global phenomenon, and the human collectivity is now grappling with its destructive consequences. The perennial philosophy views the "secularizing and desacralizing tendencies"[14] to be at the heart of the crisis of modernism and postmodernism. The consequences of the eclipse of the sacred have had catastrophic effects on the contemporary West.

A fundamental divide and no less a conflict exists between the tenets of modernism and Tradition. Nasr underscores the essential distinction between Tradition and the ideology of modernism, "that which is cut off from the transcendent, from the immutable principles which in reality govern all things and which are made known to man through revelation in its most universal sense."[15] This outlook culminates in the now famous phrase and false thesis of the "Clash of Civilizations",[16] which has been aptly debunked as the "Clash of Ignorance".[17] The "clash" is in many ways aggravated by the extremism

---

[14] Seyyed Hossein Nasr, *The Need for a Sacred Science* (Albany, NY: State University of New York Press, 1993), p. 159.

[15] Seyyed Hossein Nasr, "Reflections on Islam and Modern Thought," *Studies in Comparative Religion*, Vol. 15, Nos. 3 & 4 (Summer/Autumn 1983), p. 164.

[16] Bernard Lewis coined the term "clash of civilizations" before Samuel P. Huntington. See Bernard Lewis, "The Roots of Muslim Rage," *The Atlantic Monthly*, Vol. 266, No. 3 (September 1990), pp. 47–60; Samuel P. Huntington, "The Clash of Civilizations?" *Foreign Affairs*, Vol. 72, No. 3 (Summer 1993), pp. 22–49.

[17] See Edward W. Said, "The Clash of Ignorance," *The Nation*, Vol. 273, No. 12 (October 22, 2001), pp. 11–14.

of anti-religious secularism and religious fundamentalism. When considered in a larger context, the rise of modernism which gave birth to secularism has created a void in the human collectivity which has heavily impacted the religions themselves. This vacuum has created an imbalance which religious fundamentalism and New Age spirituality attempt to fill. Religious fundamentalism, which emerged to defend itself from the threats of anti-religious secularism, has totally lost sight of what religion is, and it is in fact a betrayal of religion.[18] The loss of the sense of the sacred has created an unbalanced human psyche which has become myopic and almost impermeable to the invisible or unseen world that is of a higher order of reality.

While a deep immersion into the sapiential traditions is needed to comprehend what they say about each other, to recognize their uniqueness and even the necessary and providential nature of these differences, the goal is to simultaneously understand these differences and how they reconcile and meet one another in the divine Unity. This does not in any way minimize the formalistic practice of religion, as each orthodox faith tradition provides the fullness of truth through its doctrines and methods. When the religions are understood through metaphysics, they are no longer viewed as a limitation, but rather as a necessity leading to the doorway of the supra-formal: "Forms are doors to the essences"[19] rather than obstacles. These spiritual or "traditional forms… are keys to unlock the gate of Unitive Truth."[20]

Each of these exclusive truth claims, while necessarily

---

[18] See Joseph E.B. Lumbard (ed.), *Islam, Fundamentalism, and the Betrayal of Tradition: Essays by Western Muslim Scholars* (Bloomington: World Wisdom, 2009).

[19] Frithjof Schuon, *Survey of Metaphysics and Esoterism* (Bloomington: World Wisdom Books, 1986), p. 11.

[20] Marco Pallis, "Foreword," to *A Treasury of Traditional Wisdom*, ed. Whitall N. Perry (New York: Simon and Schuster, 1971), p. 10.

differing with each other in their exoteric or outer dimensions, since each faith tradition is the only valid and true religion for that particular individual or human collectivity, does not present contradictions or irreconcilable differences within their esoteric or inner dimension, as there is what has been termed a "transcendent unity of religions". This is clarified further here:

> Our starting point is the acknowledgment of the fact that there are diverse religions which exclude each other. This could mean that one religion is right and that all the others are false; it could mean also that all are false. In reality, it means that all are right, not in their dogmatic exclusivism, but in their unanimous inner signification, which coincides with pure metaphysics or, in other terms, with the *philosophia perennis*.[21]

If each Revelation differentiates itself from others, it is because of its supra-formal essence which cannot be reduced to its formal manifestation.

The perennial philosophy, while timeless and universal, is not in any way advocating a religion or tradition of its own, a common misconception. There cannot be a "supra-religion" or "meta-religion" that places one religion above all others, as the diverse religions correspond to the diverse human beings and derive from the Absolute. Each faith tradition is sufficient for the return or reintegration into the Divine and requires diverse means of facilitating this function. There cannot be a "supra-religion" or "meta-religion" that replaces all the sapiential traditions because this would distort the intrinsic meaning of the perennial philosophy that all the religions are unique manifestations of Absolute.

---

[21] Frithjof Schuon, quoted in Deborah Casey, "The Basis of Religion and Metaphysics: An Interview with Frithjof Schuon," *The Quest: Philosophy, Science, Religion, the Arts*, Vol. 9, No. 2 (Summer 1996), p. 75.

It is also important to keep in mind that: "No new religion can see the light of day in our time for the simple reason that time itself, far from being a sort of uniform abstraction, on the contrary alters its value according to every phase of its development. What was still possible a thousand years ago is so no longer."[22] As the perennial philosophy acknowledges the "transcendent unity of religions", it can sometimes be erroneously confused with New Age pseudo-spirituality, which is syncretic in nature and is a parody of integral spirituality. Let us be clear: the perennial philosophy has nothing to do with New Age counterfeit-spirituality.

A defining symbol that is used to describe the perennial philosophy and the diverse spiritual paths is the *circumference and the center* of a circle, and correspondingly the *mountain and the summit*. Regarding the circumference and the center, the outer dimensions of the religions are situated along the points of the circumference while the inner or mystical dimensions of the religions are the radii leading from the circumference to the center. The center is itself the Absolute where the diverse religions originate and consequently where they return. "We must be capable of the cardinally important intuition that *every religion*—be it Christianity, Hinduism, Buddhism, or Islam—*comes from God and every religion leads back to God.*"[23] The "transcendent unity of religions" is analogous to the center as described here: "Centre where all the radii meet, the summit which all roads reach. Only such a vision of the Centre," Nasr continues, "can provide a meaningful dialogue

---

[22] Frithjof Schuon, "No Activity Without Truth," in *The Sword of Gnosis: Metaphysics, Cosmology, Tradition, Symbolism*, ed. Jacob Needleman (London: Arkana, 1986), p. 33.

[23] William Stoddart, "Religious and Ethnic Conflict in the Light of the Writings of the Perennialist School," in *Remembering in a World of Forgetting*, p. 32.

between religions, showing both their inner unity and formal diversity."[24] Martin Lings comments:

> Our image as a whole reveals clearly the truth that as each mystical path approaches its End, it is nearer to the other mysticisms than it was at the beginning. But there is a complementary and almost paradoxical truth which it cannot reveal, but which it implies by the idea of concentration which it evokes: increase of nearness does not mean decrease of distinctness, for the nearer the centre, the greater the concentration, and the greater the concentration, the stronger the "dose".[25]

From this we can logically deduce that in aligning oneself with an authentic spiritual form, one can by similitude know other traditions and where they converge—as radii traveling from the periphery of the circle to its center.

The symbol of the mountain and the summit illustrates the diverse religions and at the same time the "transcendent unity of religions". At the bottom or the base of the mountain the distance between the various religions or paths up the mountain appear to be wide and incompatible, yet at the summit there is the unanimity of the One or Ultimate Reality. As Lord Northbourne explains, "Paths that lead to a summit are widely separated near the base of the mountain, but they get nearer together as they rise."[26] Lings summarizes this doctrine in a powerful way:

> Religions may be likened in their outward or exoteric aspects to different points on the circumference of a circle

---

[24] Seyyed Hossein Nasr, "Islam and the Encounter of Religions," in *Sufi Essays* (Albany, NY: State University of New York Press, 1973), p. 150.

[25] Martin Lings, *What is Sufism?* (Berkeley, CA: University of California Press, 1977), pp. 21-22.

[26] Lord Northbourne, "Religion and Tradition," in *Religion in the Modern World*, ed. Christopher James 5th Lord Northbourne (Ghent, NY: Sophia Perennis, 2001), p. 4.

and in their esoteric or mystical paths to radii leading from these points to the one centre which represents the Divine Truth. This image shows exoterism as the necessary starting point of mysticism, and it also shows that whereas the different exoterisms may be relatively far from each other, the mysticisms are all increasingly near and ultimately identical, converging upon the same point.[27]

Stoddart utilizes what he has termed the "mountain-climbing metaphor" to articulate the perennial philosophy and the spiritual path:

> The doctrine of the transcendent or esoteric unity of the religions is not a syncretism, but a synthesis. What does this mean? It means that we must *believe* in all orthodox, traditional religions, but we can *practice* only one. Consider the metaphor of climbing a mountain. Climbers can start from different positions at the foot of the mountain. From these positions, they must follow the particular path that will lead them to the top. We can and must believe in the efficacy of all the paths, but our legs are not long enough to enable us to put our feet on two paths at once! Nevertheless, the other paths can be of some help to us. For example, if we notice that someone on a neighboring path has a particularly skillful way of circumventing a boulder, it may be that we can use the same skill to negotiate such boulders as may lie ahead of us on our own path. The paths as such, however, meet only at the summit. The religions are one only in God.[28]

Nasr observes this ascent of the spiritual path within the human being: "The human spirit is One only at the summit of

---

[27] Martin Lings, *Ancient Beliefs and Modern Superstitions* (Cambridge, UK: Archetype, 2001), p. 65.
[28] William Stoddart, "Religious and Ethnic Conflict in the Light of the Writings of the Perennialist School," in *Remembering in a World of Forgetting*, pp. 30–31.

the human soul. Therefore, means must be found for men to climb to this summit of their own being."[29]

What this means for those who change their religion is very informative, as Stoddart explains:

> While it is a grave matter to change one's religion, the mountain-climbing metaphor nevertheless illustrates what takes place when one does. One moves horizontally across the mountain and joins an alternative path, and at that point one starts climbing again. One does not have to go back to the foot of the mountain and start again from there.[30]

Schuon astutely comments from the esoteric or mystical perspective that, "to practice one religion is implicitly to practice them all."[31] This is because "a given religion in reality sums up all religions, and all religion is to be found in a given religion, because Truth is one."[32] This vastly differs from endless dabbling in the various religions or mystical practices, as it is decisive that one path be taken and traveled until its end. This non-committal way of approaching religion is very deceptive and ultimately goes nowhere, as Shaykh al-Darqāwī (1743–1823) makes clear: "They are like a man who tries to find water by digging a little here and a little there and [who] will die of thirst; whereas a man who digs deep in one spot, trusting

---

[29] Seyyed Hossein Nasr, *The Need for a Sacred Science*, p. 49.

[30] William Stoddart, "Religious and Ethnic Conflict in the Light of the Writings of the Perennialist School," in *Remembering in a World of Forgetting*, p. 31.

[31] Frithjof Schuon, "Diversity of Revelation," in *Gnosis: Divine Wisdom, A New Translation with Selected Letters*, ed. James S. Cutsinger (Bloomington: World Wisdom, 2006), p. 20. "To have lived and experienced any religion fully is in a sense to have experienced all religions" (Seyyed Hossein Nasr, *The Need for a Sacred Science*, p. 159).

[32] Frithjof Schuon, "To Refuse or To Accept Revelation," in *From the Divine to the Human* (Bloomington: World Wisdom Books, 1982), p. 147.

in the Lord and relying on Him, will find water; he will drink and give others to drink."[33]

As human diversity mirrors religious pluralism, in the same way "the underlying truth is one... because man is one."[34] The many ways to the Divine belong to the diversity of human types, as the Sufi adage upholds, "There are as many paths to God as there are human souls."

Contemporary ecumenical or interfaith dialogue, although often well intentioned in accepting other faiths as legitimate, and advocating tolerance towards other faiths, radically falls short and does not truly plumb the depths of the religions to understand how authentic bridges may be established between them. Present-day ecumenical or interfaith dialogue, often without necessarily realizing it, ends up concluding that no one religion can possibly possess the fullness of the Truth: since they are all the same and each facilitates a part of the Truth, it is implied that each religion is an imperfect receptacle of Truth. It goes without saying that no amount of tolerance equates with understanding and, while tolerance is much needed, it is limited to say the least. This perspective unequivocally restricts the full scope of what religion signifies, and therefore it cannot facilitate a true understanding and authentic meeting between the diverse religions. Again, each religion possesses the fullness of the Truth, which is sufficient for salvation or the return to the Divine, as each is an expression of the one Truth originating in a common metaphysical essence. It cannot be forgotten that "Traditional norms... provide the criteria of culture and

---

[33] Shaykh al-Darqāwī, *Letters of a Sufi Master*, trans. Titus Burckhardt (Louisville, KY: Fons Vitae, 1998), pp. 61–62. "You can't chase two rabbits at the same time" (quoted in Francis Dojun Cook, *How to Raise an Ox: Zen Practice as Taught in Zen Master Dogen's Shobogenzo* [Los Angeles, CA: Center Publications, 1978], p. 77).

[34] Frithjof Schuon, "Understanding Esoterism," in *Esoterism as Principle and as Way*, trans. William Stoddart (Bedfont, Middlesex, UK: Perennial Books, 1990), p. 16.

civilization. Traditional orthodoxy is thus the prerequisite of any discourse at all between the traditions themselves."[35]

What is needed is to build bridges between the religions based on an "esoteric ecumenicism"[36] that transcends sectarian boundaries, is rooted in metaphysics, and is an expression of the universal and timeless wisdom of the perennial philosophy that is "neither of the East nor of the West" (Qur'ān 24:5).

The expositors of the perennial philosophy in no way attempt to alter or update the religions and their mystical dimensions, as this would be unnecessary and even mistaken, but rather allow the traditional sources and their saints and sages speak for themselves on their own terms, in order to present the universal and timeless wisdom to contemporaries seeking the one Truth hidden in all the forms.

What is of essential importance in this topsy-turvy and radically confused time is to adhere to an authentic religious form and to practice it with all of one's heart and mind. Yet this commitment cannot be imposed from without and needs to come directly from the person themselves, as we are reminded: "There is no compulsion in religion" (Qur'ān 2:256).

> Tradition speaks to each man the language he can understand, provided he be willing to listen; this reservation is essential, for tradition, we repeat, cannot become bankrupt; it is rather of man's bankruptcy that one should speak, for it is he who has lost the intuition of the supernatural and the sense of the sacred.[37]

While religion derives from a supra-formal order, human beings need forms to travel the spiritual path in order to return

---

[35] Bernard Kelly, "Notes on the Light of the Eastern Religions," in Scott Randall Paine (ed.) *A Catholic Mind Awake: The Writings of Bernard Kelly*, p. 33.

[36] See Frithjof Schuon, *Christianity/Islam: Essays on Esoteric Ecumenicism* (Bloomington: World Wisdom Books, 1985).

[37] Frithjof Schuon, "No Initiative without Truth," in *The Play of Masks* (Bloomington: World Wisdom Books, 1992), p. 77.

to the Spirit. Forms themselves are the disclosure of the supra-formal order, as "form is a revelation of essence."[38] Human beings live in the world of forms and analogously require them for their return to the Divine: "To say man is to say form,"[39] and likewise, "to say man is to say spirit."[40] Spiritual forms correspond to both human diversity and religious pluralism as: "Truth is situated beyond forms, whereas Revelation, or the Tradition which derives from it, belongs to the formal order, and that indeed by definition; but to speak of form is to speak of diversity, and so of plurality."[41]

Even though each religion is a "relative absolute", human beings require a spiritual form to travel one of the revealed paths up the mountain to its summit, or analogously to travel from the circumference of the circle to its center. The principal difficulty in reconciling the particular tensions and antagonisms that arise from the exclusive truth claims of the world's religions has been succinctly framed by Nasr:

> The essential problem that the study of religion poses is how to preserve religious truth, traditional orthodoxy, the dogmatic theological structures of one's own religion and yet gain knowledge of other traditions and accept them as spiritually valid ways and roads to God.[42]

The resolution to this ever-perplexing issue is none other than the universal metaphysics that has existed at all times and in all places, known as the perennial philosophy. What

---

[38] Meister Eckhart, quoted in Whitall N. Perry (ed.), *A Treasury of Traditional Wisdom*, p. 673.

[39] Frithjof Schuon, "Understanding Esoterism," in *Esoterism as Principle and as Way*, p. 29.

[40] Frithjof Schuon, "Outline of a Spiritual Anthropology," in *From the Divine to the Human*, p. 76.

[41] Frithjof Schuon, "Diversity of Revelation," in *Gnosis: Divine Wisdom*, trans. G.E.H. Palmer (Bedfont, Middlesex, UK: Perennial Books, 1990), p. 25.

[42] Seyyed Hossein Nasr, "Islam and the Encounter of Religions," in *Sufi Essays*, p. 127.

is needed in order to restore the myopic condition of human consciousness is "To see all things in the yet undifferentiated, primordial unity,"⁴³ or as exemplified in the *Heart Sutra* (*Prajñāpāramitā-hridaya-sūtra*): "Form is emptiness; emptiness is form. Emptiness is not other than form; form is not other than emptiness."⁴⁴ What is necessary to understand for any serious seeker on the path is that not all facets of religion will be comprehended at once and that these matters are not dependent on human will as "He guides whomsoever He will to a straight path" (Qur'ān 10:25), but derive from a higher source, from what is above: "The point I am making is correct, but if you cannot grasp it then let it be, until God himself helps you to understand."⁴⁵ Each human being again is a reflection of the diverse and unique religions and spiritual paths that lead to the same summit. According to Ibn 'Arabī, "If he knew what Junayd said—that the water takes on the color of the cup—he would let every believer have his own belief and he would recognize God in the form of every object of belief."⁴⁶ As Coomaraswamy writes in his foundational article "Paths That Lead to the Same Summit," by ascending a single spiritual path to its conclusion the wayfarer will reach the single and unanimous summit found at the heart of all of the religions:

> There are many paths that lead to the summit of one and the same mountain; their differences will be the more apparent

---

⁴³ Lao Tzu, quoted in Jean C. Cooper, *An Illustrated Introduction to Taoism: The Wisdom of the Sages* (Bloomington: World Wisdom, 2010), p. 37.

⁴⁴ The Heart Sūtra, quoted in Donald S. Lopez, Jr., *The Heart Sutra Explained: Indian and Tibetan Commentaries* (Albany, NY: State University of New York Press, 1988), p. 57.

⁴⁵ "Chapter 34," in *The Cloud of Unknowing and The Book of Privy Counseling*, ed. William Johnston (New York: Doubleday, 1996), p. 80.

⁴⁶ Ibn al-'Arabī, quoted in William C. Chittick, *The Sufi Path of Knowledge: Ibn al-'Arabi's Metaphysics of Imagination* (Albany, NY: State University of New York Press, 1989), p. 344.

the lower down we are, but [they] vanish at the peak; each will naturally take the one that starts from the point at which he finds himself; he who goes round about the mountain looking for another is not climbing.[47]

---

[47] Ananda K. Coomaraswamy, "Paths That Lead to the Same Summit," p. 35.

Part I

The Hindu Tradition

1
*Introduction to Hindu Dharma**

Ekam sat viprā bahudhā vadanti.
(It is the one truth, which the sages call by different names.)

Rigveda 1:164:46

This recent work brings to light over four thousand discussions of the axial sage His Holiness Jagadguru Shankaracharya Shri Chandrashekarendra Saraswati Swamigal, the 68th Jagadguru of Kanchi (1894–1994). His spiritual lineage is traced to an unbroken chain of succession back to Ādi Śaṅkarācārya (509–477) who established the philosophical school of *Advaita Vedānta* (non-dualism). The Jagadguru of Kanchi was installed as pontiff in Kanchi at the young age of thirteen, meaning that he spent eighty-seven years of his life dedicated to preserving and perpetuating the Hindu *dharma*. When opening this book the reader will find that the first pages and the back cover are full of testimonies devoted to the 68th Jagadguru of Kanchi by kings, prime ministers, scholars and a spiritual paragon of the twentieth century—Śrī Ramana Maharshi (1879–1950), who responded the following when asked about the Jagadguru: "When were we separate...? We are always together." There is also a statement of gratitude

---

* *Introduction to Hindu Dharma: Illustrated*, by the 68th Jagadguru of Kanchi, Introduction by Arvind Sharma, edited by Michael Oren Fitzgerald, Bloomington: World Wisdom, 2008, 168 pp.

and blessing from the Kānchi Kāmakoti Pītha or spiritual hermitage of the Jagadguru with regards to this laborious and noteworthy publication.

Despite the reverence and acknowledgment from such renowned and distinguished individuals, it is curious that little is known about the 68th Jagadguru of Kanchi in the West, particularly with the growing interest in non-dual spirituality. It is for this reason that this book is of vital importance, for it not only stands as an irreplaceable introduction to Hinduism through the spiritual legacy of one of the most beloved and honored spiritual authorities (*āchāryas*) of the twentieth century, but it also illuminates the quintessential necessity of religion in a world that has disowned itself from its spiritual heritage. The ramifications of the split between the spiritual and secular worlds are now blatant, disclosing its mark of disarray throughout the four directions of the earth. This book thus functions as a call to spiritual life for all people of all nations: whatever their religious orientation may be, it is a call to remember their own spiritual heritage.

It should also be remembered that the Jagadguru did not write these teachings contained in the text; they were conveyed to his disciples by the traditional method of oral transmission, which esoterically speaking means not orally transmitted *per se*, but transmitted *via* the direct presence of an *āchārya*—known as "heart to heart". This form of transmission is exemplified by the term *Upanishad*, "to sit down near to", which describes one of the central methods by which most, if not all, spiritual traditions have been passed down throughout time. As sacred art is characteristic of India's spiritual traditions, it is fitting that this book is filled with sacred images (*murtis*) of the 68th Jagadguru, including the current and past *Āchāryas* of the Kānchi Kāmakoti Pītha, Hindu deities and many other images referenced throughout the text, giving the reader not only a written, but also a visual pilgrimage (*tīrtha-yātrā*) into the sacred dimension of this axial sage.

The Jagadguru clarifies the misnomers attributed to the terms "Hindu" and "Hinduism" as these terms were given to the Indian people by foreigners and not by the Indian people themselves. They were used to refer to the land adjacent to the Sindhu (*Indus*) River that they called "Indus" or "Hind" and it is from this name that the religion of India became known as Hinduism. The Jagadguru states that originally no name was given to the Indian religion because it was the ancient religion that was found everywhere extending beyond India and the Indian subcontinent. This is why it has been referred to as the *sanātana dharma* or "primordial, eternal code of conduct". It is from the perspective of the *sanātana dharma* that the Jagadguru confirms that all spiritual paths lead to the same summit—*Paramātman* or "Transcendent Unity":

> The temple, the church, the mosque, the *vihāra* (a Buddhist monastery; a residence for meditation) may be different from one another. The idol or the symbol in them may not also be the same and the rites performed in them may be different. But the *Paramātman* (Transcendent Unity) who grants grace to the worshipper, whatever be his faith, is the same. The different religions have taken shape according to the customs peculiar to the countries in which they originated and according to the differences in the mental outlook of the people inhabiting them. The goal of all religions is to lead people to the same *Paramātman* according to the different attitudes of the devotees concerned (p. 8).

The Jagadguru of Kanchi also acknowledges the unanimity of the divine messengers and teachers in spite of religious and social distinctions:

> ... great *jñānins* have arisen in the world, from time to time, no matter what religion they professed. All these prophets and saints proclaimed the same Truth, each in his own way, and if they happened to come back to life now and meet together, there would be perfect unity in

their messages. It is the followers that have put into their mouths more than what they said and wrangle with others, freezing the original teachings, mangled in their hands into institutional forms, which foster narrowness and bigotry (p. 139).

The Jagadguru openly discusses controversial topics that are perceived heresies in the current era, such as the caste system (*varnadharma*) or the role of women in Indian culture. There is perhaps nothing more fervently attacked and criticized within "Hinduism" or *sanātana dharma* than the caste system. In today's world Westerners are not alone in this critique. There are even many Indians who have begun to share this modern outlook that not only questions their spiritual heritage, but in many ways denies or negates its implicit authority. The Jagadguru reminds the reader of the often forgotten virtues of this integral system: "Greed and covetousness were unknown during the centuries when *varna dharma* [caste system] flourished. People were bound together in small, well-knit groups, and they discovered that there was happiness in their being together" (p. 22). The Jagadguru explains further:

> That was the tradition for ages together in this land—there was oneness of hearts. If every member of society does his duty, does his work, unselfishly and with the conviction that he is doing it for the good of all, considerations of high and low will not enter his mind. If people carry out the duties common to them, however adverse the circumstances be, and if every individual performs the duties that are special to him, no one will have cause for suffering at any time (p. 25).

The misunderstandings of the caste system extend into the role of women in Indian culture which are assumed to be, by Western standards, inherently discriminated against, treated unfairly or degraded, "The vocations have to be properly divided for the welfare of mankind. If everybody paid attention to this fact, instead of talking of rights, it would be realized that the *śāstras* [scriptures] have not discriminated against women or any of the *jātis* [a sub-division of caste]" (p. 95). The Jagadguru also clarifies that "Those who complain that women have no right to perform sacrifices on their own must remember that men too have no right to the same without a wife. If they knew this truth they would not make the allegation that Hindu *śāstras* look down upon women. A man can perform sacrifices only with his wife" (p. 95).

Regarding marriage (*saha-dharma-cāriṇī-samprayoga*), which is perceived as a union for the practice of *dharma* and wedding ceremonies, the Jagadguru categorically denies the extravagances that have become a norm in the current era. He also denies the notion of the dowry: "All the ostentation at weddings, the dowry and other gifts given to the groom's people have no sanction in the *śāstras*" (p. 97). And again "Above all the custom of dowry must be scrapped" (p. 97).

The Jagadguru of Kanchi also discusses with great detail and precision traditional government that integrates spiritual authority and temporal power. He asserts that "true secularism" is not that "the State should be completely detached from all religions. On the other hand a State, instead of being supportive of a particular religion, should support all the religions" (p. 134), even to the degree that "The State should support all religions with equal concern and help in their growth, without mutual ill-will" (p. 134).

Another misunderstanding is the notion that the Brahmin caste somehow imposes a tyrannical system upon the non-Brahmins (i.e. *Śūdras*) and is therefore able to acquire wealth and comfort at the expense of other castes. Although this scenario did take place in the wake of the British occupation of India, it was not a traditional *de jure* facet of the social makeup, but a *de facto* error. It is through this idea that ill feelings have arisen between the Brahmins and non-Brahmins.

To bring light to such mentality the Jagadguru states, "As a matter of fact, even by strictly adhering to this *dharma* the Brahmin is not entitled to feel superior to others. He must always remain humble in the belief that 'everyone performs a function in society; I perform mine'" (p. 29), and elsewhere he confirms, "A Brahmin ought not to keep even a blade of grass in excess of his needs" (p. 105). The Jagadguru does not create a scapegoat so to speak of the Brahmins for "It is the duty of these others [non-Brahmins] to make Brahmins worthy of their caste" (p. 99). The author sums up about the caste system with the following words, "No civilization can flourish in the absence of a system that brings fulfillment to all. *Varna dharma* brought fulfillment and satisfaction to all" (p. 25). In contrast to traditional society and its integral foundations, the Jagadguru states the following in regard to the postmodern West and its so-called "freedom":

> There is much talk today of freedom and democracy. In practice what do we see? Freedom has come to mean the license to do what one likes, to indulge one's every whim. The strong and the rough are free to harass the weak and the virtuous. Thus we recognize the need to keep people bound to certain laws and rules. However, the restrictions must not be too many. There must be a restriction on restrictions, a limit set on how far individuals and society can be kept under control. To choke a man with too many rules and regulations is to kill his spirit. He will break loose and run away from it all (p. 76).

The Jagadguru discontentedly acknowledges that there are not enough authentic spiritual teachers in the present age (*yuga*) and this is a distressing reflection of the state of the *dharma*. In identifying the current decline of the *dharma*, coupled with the influx of interest in non-dualism (*advaita*), the Jagadguru underscores the pitfalls of neo-advaita or neo-vedānta that have become commodities in the spiritual marketplace of today's world, "those who want to take the path of *jñāna*, without being prepared for it through *karma*" (p. 57). Yet, as the Jagadguru reminds the reader, it is by means of the spiritual doctrine and method that one can potentially realize the non-dual nature of reality: "... the deities must be worshipped, but again with the conviction of arriving at the point where we will recognize that the worshipper and the worshipped are one" (p. 60), and even then it is not that the spiritual forms are discarded *per se*, it is that there is no longer a dualism (*dvaita*) of subject-object separateness, "When you come to this state there will be no need for the Vedas too for you: this is stated in the Vedas themselves" (p. 61). Those who interpret non-dualism to be a "dropping" or getting rid of spiritual doctrines and methods are quite mistaken, as the founder of this philosophical school, Śaṅkarā, says: "Chant the Vedas every day. Perform with care the sacrifices and other rites they enjoin upon you" (p. 51). In many ways the innovative notion of "evolutionary" spirituality that has become common place in the current era bear resemblance to what the Jagadguru cautions directly against:

> If we tried to create a new dharma for ourselves it might mean trouble and all the time we would be torn by doubts as to whether it would bring us good or whether it would give rise to evil. It is best for us to follow the dharma practiced by the great men of the past, the dharma of our forefathers (p. 2).

The 68th Jagadguru of Kanchi encapsulates the quintessence of Ādi Śaṅkarācārya's metaphysics whose lineage he is the direct spiritual succession and representative of:

> Briefly put, this is the concept of *Bhagavatpāda* (Śankara): ultimately everything in the phenomenal world will be seen to be *Māyā* (cosmic illusion). The One Object, the One and Only Reality, is the *Brahman*. We must be one with It, non-dualistically, without our having to do anything in the same way as the *Brahman*. I, who bear the name of Śri Śankara,

keep speaking about many rights, about *pūjā* (sacrificial offerings), *jāpā* (invocatory prayer), service to fellow men, etc. It is because in our present predicament we have to make a start with rites. In this way, step by step, we will proceed to the liberation that is non-dualistic. It is this method of final release that is taught us by Śrī Krishna *Paramātman* and by our *Bhagavatpāda* (Śankara). At first *karma*, works, then *upāsana* or devotion and, finally, the enlightenment called *jñāna* (p. 113).

The Jagadguru invites the reader—even those not of Indian origin—to return to their respective spiritual traditions. It is through returning to one's respective tradition, while acknowledging that there is only one *Paramātman*, that the spiritual illness that filters into one's psychological and social life can be cured. It must be remembered that "it is religion that develops the mental health" (p. 134). In the Jagadguru's teachings there is no notion of "conversion" as such for—"its [the *sanātana dharma*'s] canonical texts do not contain any rite for conversion" (p. 8). His position is transparent and lucid: "there is no need to abandon the religion of your birth and embrace another" (p. 7). He continues to elaborate on this point:

> My wish is indeed that people following different religions ought to continue to remain in their respective folds and find spiritual fulfillment in them. I do not invite others to embrace my faith. In fact I believe that to do so is contrary to the basic tenets of my religion. Nothing occurs in this world as an accident (p. 21).

In fact the notion of conversion is irrelevant to the *sanātana dharma* for "Our catholic outlook is revealed in our scriptures which declare that whatever the religious path followed by people they will finally attain the same *Paramātman*. That is why there is no place for conversion in Hinduism" (pp. 14–16).

And perhaps we can put to rest this idea of conversion with these words, "The goal must be unity, not uniformity" (p. 9).

The 68th Jagadguru of Kanchi confirms that it is through the completion of the individual and collective duties that social harmony and prosperity as a norm can prevail. We are called to remember the words of the Jagadguru "A man can be fortunate in many ways. But there is nothing that makes him more fortunate than the opportunity he has of serving others" (p. 127). Love is inseparable from the spiritual path—"if there is no love there is no meaning in life" (p. 132). It is the same voice that guides the terrestrial world that "We must learn to look upon the entire universe as the *Paramātman* and love it as such (p. 132).

The Jagadguru strangely enough brings elucidation to a troubled and broken age by affirming that there are certain benefits to living in the *Kali-Yuga* which were unavailable to human individuals of earlier ages:

> Vyāsa himself says: 'The age of *Kali* is in no way inferior to the other ages...' In other *yugas* or ages Bhagavān is attained to (Self-realization) with difficulty by meditation, austerities, and *pūjā*, but in *Kali* He is reached by the mere singing of His names. (pp. 106–107)

It is in the repetition (*japa*) of the Divine Names that human individuals living in the age of *Kali* can practice the *dharma*, as it is a spiritual method available to all regardless of social status or spiritual aptitude: "He may think of god even on the bus or the train as he goes to his office or any other place" (p. 5). The Jagadguru even states that should there be an absence of priests: "in the future everyone should be able to perform Vedic rites himself" (p. 30). And yet the Jagadguru also confirms his concerns regarding the current state of an untraditional world: "I am also extremely concerned about the fact that, if the Vedic tradition which has been maintained like a chain from generation to generation is broken, it may not be possible to create the tradition all over again" (p. 37).

This book is an invaluable contribution to the treasury of traditional wisdom that has paradoxically become more accessible in the present era due to the breakdown of the numerous traditional civilizations. It will be of considerable significance for the varied seekers of truth as the Jagadguru speaks as a pontiff *par excellence*, acknowledging both the need *in divinis* for the participation in an authentic spiritual tradition, and at the same time emphasizing its transcendent function that is universal and unanimous—the *sanātana dharma*. It is in the light of such a work that modern seekers can better understand the pre-modern or traditional world in order to recognize and comprehend the inherent biases that are already ingrained and conditioned into the modernist outlook. We will conclude this review with the discerning and humbling words of the 68th Jagadguru of Kanchi, "Setting an example through one's life is the best way of making others do their duty or practice their dharma" (p. 77).

2

*The Original Gospel of Rāmakrishna**

> God is Truth, the world is untruth; this is discrimination. Truth means that which is unchangeable and permanent, and untruth is that which is changeable and transitory. He who has right discrimination knows that God alone is the Reality; all other things are unreal.
>
> Śrī Rāmakrishna[1]

Amidst the spiritual confusion that besieges the contemporary world with its counterfeits, Śrī Rāmakrishna is an authentic luminary of a forgotten era, who brings crystalline clarity to the modern and postmodern malaise, reminding the sincere wayfarer of what is required for those on the path of Self-Realization. Śrī Rāmakrishna (1836–1886), the Paramahamsa of Dakshineshwar, was the living embodiment of the perennial philosophy, the *sanātana dharma* or "eternal religion", as he not only emphasized the transcendent unity of religions in its theoretical tenets, but lived and experienced its pluralism directly and as a personification of its universality. Reductionist attempts to psychologize the saints and sages,

---

* *The Original Gospel of Rāmakrishna: Based on M.'s English Text, Abridged*, revised by Swāmī Abhedānanda, edited and abridged by Joseph A. Fitzgerald. Foreword by Alexander Lipski, Introduction by Swāmī Vivekānanda. Bloomington: World Wisdom, 2011, 260pp.

[1] *Ibid.*, p. 33.

such as Rāmakrishna, cannot by their very nature yield insights into their inner lives due to their profane point of view. Due to the rise in secularism, some have considered the saints and sages to be suffering from mental illnesses or psychopathologies, as illustrated in the following excerpt from Stanislav Grof:

> Psychiatric literature contains numerous articles and books that discuss what would be the most appropriate clinical diagnoses for many of the great figures of spiritual history. St. John of the Cross has been called "hereditary degenerate," St. Teresa of Avila dismissed as a severe hysterical psychotic, and [Prophet] Mohammed's mystical experiences have been attributed to epilepsy. Many other religious and spiritual personages, such as the Buddha, Jesus, Ramakrishna, and Shri Ramana Maharshi have been seen as suffering from psychoses, because of their visionary experiences and "delusions."[2]

Because the domain of the human psyche or psychology is always subordinate to the spiritual domain and not the other way around, so reductionism in whatever form can never transcend its own limits, just as the human psyche cannot leap beyond itself.

Interest in neo-Advaita and in the doctrine of "non-duality" is proliferating in the present-day, especially in its commonality with modern science. Neo-Advaita, while appearing to be a legitimate expression of *Advaita Vedānta*, has more in common with New Age spirituality, having

---

[2] Stanislav Grof, "Spirituality and Religion," in *Psychology of the Future: Lessons from Modern Consciousness Research* (Albany, NY: State University of New York Press, 2000), p. 215. "Medical materialism finishes up Saint Paul by calling his vision on the road to Damascus a discharging lesion of the occipital cortex, he being an epileptic. It snuffs out Saint Teresa [of Avila] as an [sic] hysteric, Saint Francis of Assisi as an [sic] hereditary degenerate" (William James, "Religion and Neurology," in *The Varieties of Religious Experience*, New York: Penguin Books, 1985, p. 13).

largely departed from the traditional understanding of Hindu spirituality.³ Selecting doctrines and practices based on personal preferences contradicts all true forms of religion and spirituality. It is not for human beings to decide these things, but the Divine. This phenomenon of subjectivized religiosity is indicative of a fundamental misunderstanding of what religion and spirituality are in their truest sense.

In the same way, there has been a rise of false spiritual masters who attract seekers by the manifestation of certain psychic powers, but such powers have been illustrated by numerous spiritual authorities to have nothing to do with the realization of the Absolute (*Brahman*): "The realization of God is not the same as psychic power" (p. 147). In fact, psychic powers are inferior and even dangerous for those traveling the spiritual path and should be avoided, "There is, indeed, great danger in possessing psychic powers" (p. 147). There have also been attempts by contemporary *gurus* or so-called spiritual masters to forge a spiritual lineage that links directly back to Śrī Rāmakrishna or another spiritual giant, Śrī Ramana Maharshi, in order to obtain legitimacy, when there was no authenticated lineage to be had or recognized.

With the death of great masters like these and others, their legacy is vulnerable to being coopted and rewritten to benefit the agenda of New Age counterfeits. There is the case of a so-called American-born *avatāra* who asserts that he is the incarnation of both Swāmī Vivekānanda and Rāmakrishna in the modern West. The impostor seized on the following statements by Rāmakrishna—"Today I have

---

³ See René Guénon, *Introduction to the Study of the Hindu Doctrines* (Ghent, NY: Sophia Perennis, 2001), pp. 232–235; Frithjof Schuon, "Vedānta," in *Spiritual Perspectives and Human Facts: A New Translation with Letters* (Bloomington: World Wisdom, 2007), pp. 99–129; Rama P. Coomaraswamy, "The Desacralization of Hinduism for Western Consumption," *Sophia: The Journal of Traditional Studies*, Vol. 4, No. 2 (Winter 1998), pp. 194–219; Harry Oldmeadow, *Journeys East: 20th Century Western Encounters with Eastern Religious Traditions* (Bloomington: World Wisdom, 2004).

given you my all and I am now only a poor fakir, possessing nothing."[4] and "My Divine Mother has also shown me that I shall have to come back again and that my next incarnation will be in the West" (p. 199)—and erroneously interpreted them to substantiate his own claim to be the incarnation of both Vivekānanda and Rāmakrishna. This was further complicated by the fact that the *avataric* manifestation would not be recognized by the masses, as stated by Rāmakrishna himself: "When an avatar comes, an ordinary man cannot recognize him—he comes as if in secret."[5] This phenomenon suggests that any *avataric* manifestation in theory could be utilized by the less scrupulous to abusively claim spiritual authority. It goes without saying that such assertions need to be approached with a large dose of skepticism, mindful that religion and spirituality in the *Kali-Yuga* take on innumerable abnormalities.

Rāmakrishna was aware of these dangers and wrote the following regarding the inability of false teachers to adequately provide spiritual guidance to the seeker, as well as the possible harm that could occur:

> He cannot get realization himself and he tries to show the way to others. It is like the blind leading the blind. In this way more harm is done than good. When God is realized the inner spiritual sight opens and it is then that the true teacher can perceive the sickness of the soul and can prescribe the proper remedy (p. 75).

Śrī Rāmakrishna in large part became known in the West through the book *The Gospel of Sri Ramakrishna*, translated by Swāmī Nikhilānanda (1895–1973). What is generally unknown

---

[4] Śrī Rāmakrishna, quoted in *The Gospel of Ramakrishna: Originally recorded in Bengali by M., a disciple of the Master*, trans. Swami Nikhilananda (New York: Ramakrishna-Vivekananda Center, 1977), p. 72.

[5] Śrī Rāmakrishna, "March 11, 1883 – Section 2, Chapter 3," in Mehendranāth Gupta, *Srī Srī Rāmakrishna Kathāmrita, Vol. 2* (Chandigarh, India: Sri Ma Trust, 2002), p. 28.

is that there was an earlier version of the *Gospel* that predates the better-known 1942 translation by Nikhilananda, yet it does not help that the earlier edition was published under the same title as the later edition; however, the earlier edition published in 1907 is considered to be the "Authorized Edition". Both these editions stem from the Bengāli work entitled *Srī Srī Rāmakrishna Kathāmrita* or "Words of Nectar of Srī Rāmakrishna" recorded by householder disciple "M." or Mehendranāth Gupta (1854–1932). From its inception, the *Kathāmrita* continued to expand during "M.'s" life, and in its final version consisted of five volumes. What makes this new volume of *The Original Gospel of Rāmakrishna* unique and important is that it was translated from Bengāli into English in part by Mehendranāth Gupta himself who gave Swāmī Abhedānanda, also a direct disciple of Rāmakrishna, permission to edit it and translate some parts from the original Bengāli. Hence, this volume is an edited and abridged version of the original 1907 English edition. Until recently the "Authorized Edition" of 1907 was difficult to obtain, but is now, after more than sixty years, made available again.

Rāmakrishna was born as Gadādhara (a name of Vishnu) in the village of Kāmārpukur, in the Hooghly District of West Bengal, India, into an orthodox Brahmin family. Before his birth his parents experienced signs about the significance of his birth. From an early age people were drawn to him and wanted to spend time in his presence. At the age of six, he was well-versed in the sacred Hindu scriptures such as the *Purānas*, the *Rāmāyana*, the *Mahābhārata*. As the pilgrim route to Purī was near his village he came into contact with ascetics and wandering monks whom he spent time with, discussing facets of the Hindu *dharma* and listening to tales of their journeys. The following captures an early glimpse into Rāmakrishna's inner world through an ecstatic experience he had as a young boy:

> At the age of six or seven Gadadhar had his first experience

of spiritual ecstasy. One day in June or July, when he was walking along a narrow path between paddy-fields, eating the puffed rice that he carried in a basket, he looked up at the sky and saw a beautiful, dark thundercloud. As it spread, rapidly enveloping the whole sky, a flight of snow-white cranes passed in front of it. The beauty of the contrast overwhelmed the boy. He fell to the ground, unconscious, and the puffed rice went in all directions. Some villagers found him and carried him home in their arms. Gadadhar said later that in that state he had experienced an indescribable joy.[6]

Rāmakrishna's universal outlook on the religions of the world was a striking and extraordinary dimension of his teaching: "all religions are like paths which lead to the same common goal" (p. 201). And yet traditional paths, while essential, must not be mistaken for the goal; he states: "all religions are paths, but the paths are not God" (p. 6). In fact arguments about religion and spirituality were discouraged: "As long as a man argues about God, he has not realized Him."[7]

The tale commonly known as "The Elephant in the Dark", known in various religious traditions, is a fitting example of mistaking the part for the whole and is especially significant regarding the theme of religious pluralism and what has been termed the transcendent unity of religions. Rāmakrishna retells this tale entitled "Parable of the Elephant and the Blind Men":

> "Four blind men went to see an elephant. One touched a leg of the elephant and said: 'The elephant is like a pillar.' The second touched the trunk and said: 'The elephant is like a thick club.' The third touched the belly and said: 'The elephant is like a huge jar.' The fourth touched the ears and said: 'The elephant is like a big winnowing-basket.' Then

---

[6] Swami Nikhilananda, "Introduction," to *The Gospel of Ramakrishna*, p. 4.
[7] Śrī Rāmakrishna, "With the Devotees in Calcutta," *ibid.*, p. 735.

they began to dispute among themselves as to the figure of the elephant. A passer-by, seeing them thus quarreling, asked them what it was about. They told him everything and begged him to settle the dispute. The man replied: 'None of you has seen the elephant. The elephant is not like a pillar, its legs are like pillars. It is not like a big water-jar, its belly is like a water-jar. It is not like a winnowing-basket, its ears are like winnowing- baskets. It is not like a stout club, its trunk is like a club. The elephant is like the combination of all these.' In the same manner do those sectarians quarrel who have seen only one aspect of the Deity. He alone who has seen God in all His aspects can settle all disputes" (p. 7).[8]

Similarly, all the Divine Names are distinct ways of expressing the underlying Reality. Rāmakrishna affirms this point: "Vaishnavas, Mohammedans, Christians, and Hindus are all longing for the same God; but they do not know that He who is Krishna is also Shiva, Divine Mother, Christ, and Allah. God is one, but He has many names" (p. 5).

The ability of Rāmakrishna to remain firmly rooted within a single religion, that of Hinduism, and at the same time to

---

[8] Cf. other versions: "Some Hindus had brought an elephant for exhibition and placed it in a dark house. Crowds of people were going into that dark place to see the beast. Finding that ocular inspection was impossible, each visitor felt it with his palm in the darkness. The palm of one fell on the trunk. 'This creature is like a water-spout,' he said. The hand of another lighted on the elephant's ear. To him the beast was evidently like a fan. 'I found the elephant's shape is like a pillar,' he said. Another laid his hand on its back. 'Certainly this elephant was like a throne,' he said" (Rūmī, "The Elephant in the Dark," in A. J. Arberry, *Tales from the Masnavi* [Surrey, UK: Curzon, Press, 1994], p. 208). "It is as if some blind men, hearing that an elephant had come to their town, should go and examine it. The only knowledge of it which they can obtain comes through the sense of touch; so one handles the animal's leg, another his tusk, another his ear, and, according to their several perceptions, pronounce it to be a column, a thick pole, or a quilt, each taking a part for the whole" (Abū Ḥāmid Muḥammad al-Ghazzālī, *The Alchemy of Happiness*, [Armonk, NY: M.E. Sharpe, 1991], p. 20).

remain universal in his orientation allowing him to travel other spiritual paths, is illustrated here:

> There is something in Ramakrishna that seems to defy every category: he was like the living symbol of the inward unity of religions; he was in fact the first saint to wish to enter into foreign spiritual forms, and in this consisted his exceptional and in a sense universal mission—something allying him to the prophets without making him a prophet in the strict sense of the word; in our times of confusion, distress, and doubt, he was the saintly "verifier" of forms and the "revealer" as it were of their single truth.... [His] spiritual plasticity was of a miraculous order.[9]

A further elaboration of Rāmakrishna's "spiritual plasticity" or universality is provided in the following excerpt:

> Nothing, perhaps, so strangely impresses or bewilders a Christian student of Saint Ramakrishna's life as the fact that this Hindu of the Hindus, without in any way repudiating his Hinduism, but for the moment forgetting it, about 1866 completely surrendered himself to the Islamic way, repeated the name of Allah, wore the costume, and ate the food of a Muslim. This self-surrender to what we should call in India the waters of another current of the single river of truth resulted only in a direct experience of the beatific vision, not less authentic than before. Seven years later, Ramakrishna in the same way proved experimentally the truth of Christianity. He was now for a time completely absorbed in the idea of Christ, and had no room for any

---

[9] Frithjof Schuon, "Vedānta," in *Spiritual Perspectives and Human Facts*, pp. 122, 127. "To be sure, there have been rare individuals such as Ramakrishna, who lived in the nineteenth century in India, who have actually tried to climb the different paths to give experiential proof of these paths leading to the same summit, but even in such cases there has been an a priori intellectual certitude that the paths did actually do so" (Seyyed Hossein Nasr, "Reply to Huston Smith," in *The Philosophy of Seyyed Hossein Nasr*, [Chicago, IL: Open Court, 2001], p. 160).

other thought. You might have supposed him a convert. What really resulted was that he could now affirm on the basis of personal experience,[10] "I have practiced all religions—Hinduism, Islām, Christianity—and I have also followed the paths of the different Hindu sects.... A lake has several ghāts. At one the Hindus take water in pitchers and call it 'jal'; at another the [Muslim] take water in leather bags and call it 'pāni'. At a third the Christians call it 'water'."[11]

Rāmakrishna again in no way repudiates or brings into question his participation in Hinduism, but affirms the universality of all sapiential traditions, while abiding within the fold of his own faith tradition.

Given the modern loss of receptivity to the sacred, the forms of spiritual practice (*sādhanā*) of previous ages, where the palpable sense of the sacred dominated, have not been as accessible as they once were for the common person. In addressing the connection between the *Kali-Yuga* or "Dark Age" and the changes in the human receptivity to the Divine, he stated: "Truthfulness in speech is the *tapasyā* of the Kaliyuga.... By adhering to truth one attains God."[12] "The fact is that in the Kaliyuga one cannot wholly follow the path laid down in the Vedas."[13] Rāmakrishna unequivocally affirms that the most effective spiritual practice in the *Kali-Yuga* is the Invocation of the Divine Name, or *japa-yoga* as it is known in Hinduism:

> The holy name has saving powers, but there must be earnest longing with it. Without earnest longing of the heart no

---

[10] Ananda K. Coomaraswamy, "Śrī Ramakrishna and Religious Tolerance," in *Coomaraswamy. Metaphysics*, p. 34.

[11] Śrī Rāmakrishna, quoted in *The Gospel of Ramakrishna*, p. 35.

[12] Śrī Rāmakrishna, "The Master's Reminiscences," in *The Gospel of Ramakrishna*, p. 749.

[13] Śrī Rāmakrishna, "Instruction to Vaishnavas and Brāhmos," *ibid.*, p. 297.

one can see God by mere repetition of His name. One may repeat His name, but if one's mind be attached to lust and wealth, that will not help much. When a man is bitten by a scorpion or a tarantula, mere repetition of a *mantram* will not do; a special remedy is necessary (p. 4).

Far from being empty phrases, the distinct names of the Divine are synonymous with the Divine, as Rāmakrishna himself affirms, "God and His name are identical".[14] The practice of *japa-yoga* is found in both *jnāna* and *bhakti*, as Shankara affirmed in one of his hymns: "Control thy soul, restrain thy breathing, distinguish the transitory from the True, repeat the holy Name of God, and thus calm the agitated mind. To this universal rule apply thyself with all thy heart and all thy soul."[15] The Invocation is not to be undertaken with blind adherence but with the fullness of our hearts and minds: "It is necessary to have absolute faith in the name of the Lord" (p. 70).

While this spiritual practice is intended to be accessible to all in an age when authentic spiritual forms are increasingly more difficult to access, the seeker must have a sincere longing for the Divine to make it effective.

> In this age (*Kali yuga*) the path of devotion and love (*bhakti yoga*) is easy for all. The practice of...*bhakti* is better adapted to this *yuga*. One should repeat the holy name of the Lord and chant His praises and with earnest and sincere heart, pray to Him, saying: 'O Lord, grant me Thy divine wisdom, Thy divine love. Do Thou open my eyes and make me realize Thee.' (p. 108)

The futility of relying solely on human effort to attain liberation (*moksha*) or realization of the Self (*Ātmā*) overlooks

---

[14] Śrī Rāmakrishna, "The Master with the Brāhmo Devotees," *ibid.*, p. 222.

[15] Śrī Śaṅkarācārya, quoted in *Pray Without Ceasing: The Way of the Invocation in World Religions*, ed. Patrick Laude (Bloomington: World Wisdom, 2006), p. 69.

the true enactor of all activity in the phenomenal world. All sapiential traditions challenge the notion that the empirical ego is the enactor of all activity, "I am the doer" (Bhagavad-Gītā 3:27). The empirical ego is in fact not the doer. Due to the misidentification with the empirical ego, the human being wrongly attributes agency to him or herself, forgetting that "God is the real Actor, others are actors in name only" (p. 106). "A man may make thousands of attempts, but nothing can be accomplished without the mercy of the Lord" (p. 23). Likewise, "Everything depends upon His grace" (p. 36). In the Christian tradition this same truth is recognized: "with God all things are possible" (Matthew 10:27). And similarly within Islamic spirituality: "In His hands is to be found the dominion (*malakūt*) of all things" (Qur'ān 26:83). When seekers came to Rāmakrishna to ask him how to help the world, he recommended that they first help themselves by confronting the disorder within before attempting to help others. As long as the self identifies with, and is consumed by, the empirical ego, the possibilities of selfless service are challenged: "You talk glibly of doing good to the world...who are you to do good to the world? First practice devotional exercises and realize God. Attain to Him. If He graciously gives you His powers (*shakti*), then you can help others, and not till then" (p. 75).

It is not through book-learning alone that the seeker can realize the Absolute (*Brahman*), in fact, nothing short of inner longing and abiding in the Divine alone will grant the seeker the Real: "You may read thousands of volumes, you may repeat verses and hymns by hundreds, but if you cannot dive into the ocean of Divinity with extreme longing of the soul, you cannot reach God" (p. 151), or "One cannot realize Divinity by reading books" (p. 35).

Divine transcendence is beyond all things in the phenomenal world, yet Divine immanence is within all things in the phenomenal world. Thus, the Divine is also to be found within the human body: "The Lord dwells in the temple of the human body" (p. 26), or "Thou appearest as a human being, but in reality Thou art the Lord of the universe" (p. 193). True human identity is inseparable from the Divine, but due to forgetfulness, our psyche remains deluded by the world of appearances: "The soul in its true nature is Absolute Existence, Intelligence, and Bliss, but on account of *māyā* or the sense of 'I', it has forgotten its real Self and has become entangled in the meshes of the various limitations of mind and body" (p. 19). This immanent Self is expressed in Islamic spirituality in the following terms, "We are nearer to him than the jugular vein" (Qur'ān 50:16), and again, "He is with you wherever you are" (Qur'ān 57:4). When responding to a devotee's questions about how to meditate on God, Rāmakrishna responds: "The heart is the best place. Meditate on Him in your heart" (p. 89). This is also confirmed within the broader Hindu tradition: "I am seated in the hearts of all" (Bhagavad-Gītā 15:15). Similarly Divine immanence is expressed in the Christian tradition as: "The kingdom of God is within you" (Luke 17:21).

Through right discrimination both the uniqueness and similarity of human diversity becomes evident, as well as its essential core, its transpersonal nature: "You should love everyone; no one is a stranger; God dwells in all beings" (p. 11). However, this prescription does not therefore mean that we should dispense with discernment (*viveka*) for "although God resides in all human beings, still there are good men and bad men, there are lovers of God and those who do not love God" (pp. 12–13); nonetheless, one must remember that "God is walking in every human form and manifesting Himself alike through the sage and the sinner, the virtuous and the vicious" (p. 37). With this said, even with the best intentions to help others, some attempts can be futile when hearts have become hardened and unresponsive to the influence of the Divine: "Those who are thus caught in the net of the world are the *baddhas*, or bound souls. No one can awaken them. They do not come to their senses even after receiving blow upon blow of misery, sorrow, and indescribable suffering" (p. 16).

Rāmakrishna also affirms that the Divine is not to be found in the hereafter, but where we are, in this very moment, in the world: "this world is the kingdom of God" (p. 37). Rāmakrishna makes no distinction between householder and non-householder, both can equally realize the Divine given their different circumstances: "He who has found God here has also found Him there.... He can then live both in God and in the world equally well" (p. 40). Likewise, "Whether you live in the world or renounce it, everything depends upon the will of Rāma. Throwing your whole responsibility upon God, do your work in the world" (p. 39). The spiritual seeker can realize the Divine within the busy-ness of contemporary life. The seeker does not need to flee the responsibilities of the world in order to fulfil ones spiritual obligations: "You can attain to God while living in the world" (p.152) for "God can be realized even at home" (p. 153). For Rāmakrishna, like other saints and sages, the Divine is to be found everywhere. We recall the often-quoted words of the Qur'ān, "Wherever you turn, there is the Face of God" (2:115), and also, "Everything is perishing but His face" (28:88). Likewise for Rāmakrishna, the Divine is clothed in the world of phenomena:

> I saw a woman wearing a blue garment under a tree. She was a harlot. As I looked at her, instantly the ideal of Sītā appeared before me! I forgot the existence of the harlot, but saw before me pure and spotless Sītā, approaching Rāma, the Incarnation of Divinity, and for a long time I remained motionless. I worshipped all women as representatives of the Divine Mother. I realized the Mother of the universe in every woman's form (p. 92).

God, the object of his contemplation, was so utterly fused in his mind with the object of his vision, that in a state of ecstasy or God-consciousness (*samādhi*), Rāmakrishna transcended the normal subject-object relations, even the ordinary dichotomies of male and female as is conveyed here: "At that time I felt so strongly that I was the maidservant of my Divine Mother that I thought of myself as a woman.... My mind was above the consciousness of sex" (p. 93). To the ill-informed such experiences may initially appear to be signs of mental illness, when they are quite the opposite, being gifts of a Realized soul: "At one-time I had this madness. I used to walk like a madman, seeing the same Spirit everywhere and recognizing neither high nor low in caste or creed. I could eat even with a *pariah*. I had the constant realization that *Brahman* is Truth and the world is unreal like a dream" (p. 103). Rāmakrishna makes an important point on God-intoxicated states: "These states are not for those who are living in the world and performing the duties of the world, but for those who have absolutely renounced internally and externally" (p. 103). It is also important to clarify that no amount of authentic spiritual practice will lead the psychologically balanced seeker to be unbalanced: "He who is mad after God can never became unbalanced or insane" (p. 112).

While Rāmakrishna regarded himself as a *bhakta*, he also understood the disposition of the *jnāni*: "There are various paths which lead to the realization of the Absolute *Brahman*. The path of a *jnāni* is as good as that of a *bhakta*. *Jnāna yoga* is true; so is *bhakti yoga*" (p. 50). Again, Rāmakrishna asserts that all paths lead to the Divine: "Innumerable are the paths. *Jnāna, karma, bhakti* are all paths which lead to the same goal" (p. 123). He recognized that the transpersonal dimension of the Intellect (*buddhi*) "can be realized by the purified intellect (*buddhi*)" (p. 172). The ordinary mind or reason is not synonymous with *buddhi* as is often assumed, but transcends normal boundaries of cognition: "The small intellect of a man cannot grasp the whole nature of God" (p. 159). Rāmakrishna thus illustrates the vantage point between both *bhakta* and *jnāni*: "A *bhakta* wishes to enjoy communion with his Lord and not to become one with Him. His desire is not to become sugar, but to taste of it" (p. 66).

While yoga has become a popular commodity for mass consumption in the contemporary West, it is important to contextualize it within the broader scope of Hindu spirituality in order to understand that, though it can bring about certain physical and psychological benefits, for its full benefits to be experienced yoga needs to be connected to the spiritual practice of the Hindu *dharma*. The limitations of yoga to transcend the psychophysical domain are presented here by Rāmakrishna:

> *Hatha yoga* deals entirely with the physical body. It describes the methods by which the internal organs can be purified and perfect health can be acquired... these powers are only the manifestations of physical *prāna*. So the practice of *hatha yoga* will bring one control over the body, but it will carry one only so far (p. 125).

Hindu metaphysics takes into consideration both the manifest and the unmanifest domains of Reality, which correspond to the relative and the Absolute: "to think of Him as the formless Being [*Brahma nirguna* or "unqualified"] is quite right, but do not go away with the idea that that alone is true and that all else is false. Meditating upon Him as a Being with form [*Brahma saguna* or "qualified"] is equally right" (p. 25). On qualified non-dualism, Rāmakrishna emphasizes:

> No doubt we reason at the outset that the all-important thing is the kernel—not either the shell or the seeds. In the next place, we go on reasoning that the shell and the seeds belong to the same substance to which the kernel belongs. At the first stage of the reasoning we say, 'Not this, not this.' Thus the Absolute (*Brahman*) is not the individual soul. Again, it is not the phenomenal world. The Absolute (*Brahman*) is the only Reality, all else is unreal. At the next stage we go a little farther. We see that the kernel belongs to the same substance as that to which the shell

and the seeds belong; hence the substance from which we derive our negative conception of the Absolute *Brahman* is the identical substance from which we derive our negative conceptions of the finite soul and the phenomenal world. Our relative phenomena (*līlā*) must be traced to that Eternal Being which is also called the Absolute. (pp. 173-174)

Hindu metaphysics teaches that manifestation or *prakriti* is made up of qualities or *gunas*. Rāmakrishna explains how each human being is composed in varying degrees of the three *gunas*: "All men look alike, but they differ in their nature. In some the *sattva* quality is predominant, in others *rajas*, and in the rest *tamas*" (p. 74), likewise, "People's character can be divided into three classes—*tamas*, *rajas*, and *sattva*" (p. 157). The quality which dominates will determine the nature of the person:

> Those who belong to the first class [*tamas*] are egotistic; they sleep too much, eat too much, and passion and anger prevail in them. Those who belong to the second class [*rajas*] are too much attached to work.... Those who belong to the third class [*sattva*] are very quiet, peaceful, and unostentatious; they are not particular about their dress; they lead a simple life and earn a modest living, because their needs are small; they do not flatter for selfish ends; their dwelling is modest (p. 157)

Identification with the empirical ego remains until the soul is reabsorbed into the Divine: "Egoism does not leave until one has realized God" (p. 107), or "When 'I' is dead, all troubles cease" (p. 19). This mistaken identification with the empirical ego is perpetuated by the dominant *tamasic* quality, "Egotism is the quality of *tamas* arising from ignorance" (p. 157). The Divine cannot be realized until the qualities of *rajas* and *tamas* are reintegrated into the Spirit: "God cannot be realized until the *sattva* qualities, such as devotion, right discrimination, dispassion, and compassion for all, prevail" (p. 108). Ultimately, Spirit transcends *prakriti* and the three *gunas*: "God is beyond the three gunas—*sattva, rajas, and tamas*."[16]

Because of the inverted nature of today's world in the *Kali-Yuga*, seekers need to remember the traditional adage, "Man shall not live by bread alone, but by every word that proceedeth out of the mouth of God" (Matthew 4:4). In the *Kali-Yuga*, this looks strikingly different from the earlier temporal conditions due to it being more removed from the spiritual domain. Paradoxically, in the present-day: "In this age our life depends upon material food; if you cannot get anything to eat for a day, your mind will be turned away from God" (p. 153).

> In the Kaliyuga the life of a man depends entirely on food. How can he have the consciousness that Brahman [the Absolute] alone is real and the world illusory? In the Kaliyuga it is difficult to have the feeling, 'I am not the body, I am not the mind, I am not the twenty-four cosmic principles; I am beyond pleasure and pain, I am above disease and grief, old age and death.'[17]

While there remains a spiritual void within the contemporary world, there are endless attempts made to fill it with everything under the sun except what can bestow ultimate peace and contentment to the soul. The one thing needful according to all sapiential traditions is to: "Perform all your duties with your mind always fixed on God" (p. 28); "Thou shalt love the Lord thy God with all thy heart, and with all thy soul, and with all thy mind" (Matthew 22:37).

The Original Gospel of Rāmakrishna is essential reading for those interested in the world's religions, especially Hindu

---

[16] Śrī Rāmakrishna, "The Master and Vijay Goswami," in *The Gospel of Ramakrishna*, p. 176.

[17] Śrī Rāmakrishna, "The Master and Vijay Goswami," in *ibid.*, p. 172.

spirituality. It reflects the teachings of one of India's greatest saints, who embodies the *sanātana dharma*. This volume, deemed the "Authorized Edition", contains a text which has been virtually unavailable for more than sixty years. Through stories, parables, conversations and teachings offered during the last four years of his life, readers can capture the fragrance of what it was like to sit at the feet of one of India's great spiritual masters, the Paramahamsa of Dakshineshwar, Śrī Rāmakrishna. At a time when meaningful and integral forms of ecumenical dialogue or religious pluralism are evermore necessary, Śrī Rāmakrishna is a quintessential testament of how to be firmly rooted in one's own faith tradition while simultaneously upholding the legitimacy and truth of other faiths. It is through Rāmakrishna's example that an integral and universal understanding of what religion and spirituality are may be realized, without erring in either New Age syncretism or exclusivist claims that only one's own religion is true. The remarkable nature of Rāmakrishna's spiritual realization becomes known through his own self-disclosure of the One manifesting in all the distinct forms: "He who was Rāma, who was Krishna, Buddha, Christ, and Chaitanya, has now become Rāmakrishna" (p. 198).

3

*Timeless in Time: Sri Ramana Maharshi**

> Under whatever name and form one may worship the Absolute Reality, it is only a means for realizing It without name and form. That alone is true realization, wherein one knows oneself in relation to that Reality, attains peace and realizes one's identity with it.
>
> Śrī Ramana Maharshi[1]

Śrī Ramana Maharshi (1879–1950), known as the Sage of Arunachala, was a spiritual paragon of the twentieth century. He was revered by millions of people around the world as someone whose teachings transcend all forms of religious exclusivism and are not limited to Hindu spirituality, and people of all faiths and walks of life came to sit in his presence. He assisted individuals to inquire into the deepest truths and did so using very few words. His teachings were many times given in silence. This was often his preferred method of instruction in order to transmit to the human being in his company the essence of non-duality or Advaita Vedānta. He embodied what is known as the *sanātana dharma* or "eternal

---

* *Timeless in Time: Sri Ramana Maharshi*, by A.R. Natarajan. Foreword by Eliot Deutsch. World Wisdom, 2006, 160pp.

[1] "Forty Verses," in *The Collected Works of Ramana Maharshi*, ed. Arthur Osborne (Boston, MA: Weiser Books, 1997), pp. 72–73.

religion" that is found at the heart of each of the world's religions.

This book by A.R. Natarajan combines biographical material gathered from direct sources and the essential teachings of Ramana Maharshi. Also included in this volume is a Foreword by Eliot Deutsch, a leading authority on Hindu thought. The reader can find therein one hundred and sixty photographs documenting the span of Ramana Maharshi's lifespan.

The Sage of Arunachala was born as Venkataraman Iyer, in what is now Tiruchuli, Tamil Nadu, India, into an orthodox Hindu Brahmin family. On July 17, 1896, at the age of sixteen, Venkataraman for no apparent reason was overwhelmed by a sudden, violent fear of death. He provided the following description of this event:

> I stretched myself like a corpse, and it seemed to me that my body had actually become rigid—"I" was not dead—"I" was on the other hand conscious of being alive, in existence. So the question arose in me, "What was this 'I'?" I felt that it was a force or current working, despite the rigidity or activity of the body, though existing in connection with it. It was that current or force or center that constituted my personality, that kept me acting, moving etc. The fear of death dropped off. I was absorbed in the contemplation of that current. So further development or activity was issuing from the new life and not from any fear (p. 13).

From this event emerged his true identity as the Self (*Ātmā*) that is beyond birth and death (*saṃsāra*) and prompted his self-enquiry (*ātma-vichāra*) of "Who am I?"

> Who can understand the state of the one
> Who has dissolved his ego and
> Is abiding always in the Self?
> For him the Self alone is.
> What remains for me to do?

Nearly six weeks later, on August 29, 1896, Venkataraman left his uncle's home in Madurai, and traveled to the holy mountain Arunachala, in Tiruvannamalai. Since his arrival to the holy mountain on September 1, 1896 he remained there for the rest of his life. He emphasizes that this process was not of his own ego-bound will, but rooted in the Divine Will, being as he considered it an act, "in obedience to his command".

In needs to be emphasized that while Ramana Maharshi left home and became a renunciate at an early age he did so with the highest regard and love for his parents and credits them for his spiritual search:

> As mother and father both, you gave birth to me and tended me. And before I could fall into the deep sea called *jaganmaya*, and get drowned in the universal illusion, you came to abide in my mind, you drew me to yourself. O Arunachala, you whose being is all Awareness. What a wonderful work of art your Grace has wrought, my Mother-Father-Lord! (p. 7)

In fact, Ramana Maharshi's mother, Azhagammal or Alagammal (1864–1922), followed her son to live on the holy mountain with him during the last years of her life and was very devoted to him. The Matrubhuteswara Temple was built over her burial place and daily worship continues to be carried out until this day. Ramana Maharshi in no uncertain terms emphasized that "liberated women are on a par with liberated men" and viewed all women as being his mothers. At the *ashram*, according to Ramana Maharshi, "All are equal here."

Upon arriving in Tiruvannamalai he initially stayed at the Arunachaleswara Temple, and while he subsequently stayed at various sites on the sacred mountain, he is reported to have stayed the longest period in the Virupaksha Cave for seventeen years from 1899 to 1916. He in no way downplayed the householder life as he viewed it as being equal with a renunciate life. He adds, "There is no difference between domestic life and that of hermits. Just as you avoid the cares of home when you are here, go home and try to be equally unconcerned and unaffected at the circumstances amidst home life."

This early period of Ramana Maharshi's *sādhanā* or spiritual practice occurred in a remarkable fashion and demonstrated his total and utter surrender to the path for he underwent many physical and psychological austerities:

> Days and nights would pass without my being aware of their passing. I entertained no idea of bathing or cleaning of teeth or other cleansing activities even when I had defecated and had no baths. The face got begrimed, the hair had become one clotted mass like wax and the nails grew long. When anyone thought that I should have food, I would stretch a hand and smoothing would drop on my hand. My hands were not useful for any other purpose. I would eat and rub my hand on my head or body and drop again into my continuous mood. This was my condition for some years from the time of my arrival (p. 24).

Because of his non-dual point of view, he denied having engaged in any form of spiritual practice as it would affirm the insurmountable split of duality which was itself an illusion (*māyā*). It could be alternatively viewed as spontaneous penance, as he affirms, "I have never done any *sādhanā*." For Ramana Maharshi there was no otherness—no devotee or pilgrim—coming to visit him or asking questions, as this would again denote a fundamental duality and would further perpetuate the notion of separateness, when in reality there is only the Absolute or non-dual Essence. According to Hindu metaphysics the notion of the spiritual aspirant (*sādhaka*) and the realized, the enlightened and the unenlightened or *moksha* and *saṃsāra* are illusory, as they perpetuate this duality that is imaginary in nature. From the relative point of view, duality is all that exists, but from that of the Absolute such constructs are unreal. This is reflected in his dialogues with visitors and devotees, when he expressed: "What you seek is that which is already at hand, ever existent." Likewise, "Is there any way of adoring the Supreme who is all, except by abiding firmly as That!"

Ramana Maharshi emphasized, like many other saints and sages before him, that "the Guru is always within you,"[2] a powerful non-dual teaching which has been fundamentally misinterpreted and distorted. While this teaching is undoubtedly true and orthodox according to the different ways that immanence is expressed throughout the sapiential traditions, without prior transcendence there is no immanence. Meaning that without there first being an external *guru* it is improbable that the seeker will come to know the internal *guru*. For Ramana Maharshi, his relationship with the holy mountain of Arunachala took on the disciple-guru relationship. He describes this remarkable bond in the ensuing:

> O Arunachala, you who stand and shine before me in the form of my *guru*, destroy utterly my faults, cure me and convert me, and as your servant govern me.
>
> Look at me! Think of me! Touch me! Make me fit, ripen me! Then be my Master, govern me, O Arunachala.
>
> Oh Lord in the form of hill,
> You are the remedy for the endless chain of births.
> For me your feet alone are the refuge.
> Your duty it is to remove my mother's suffering and govern her.
> O Conqueror of Time!
> Your lotus feet are my refuge,
> Let them protect my mother from death.
> What is death if scrutinized?
> Arunachala, blazing fire of knowledge,
> Burn away the dross.
> Absorb my sweet mother in you,
> What need would there be then for cremation?

---

[2] Ramana Maharshi, "The Guru," in *The Teachings of Ramana Maharshi in His Own Words*, ed. Arthur Osborne (New York: Samuel Weiser, 1978), p. 102.

Arunachala, dispeller of *Maya's* veil,
Why then the delay in curing my mother's delirium?
O Mother of those who seek refuge in you,
Is there a better shield than you from fate's blows? (p. 68)

Ramana Maharshi discusses the traditional sources documenting the sacredness of Arunachala as the embodiment of Shiva:

> There is an *aitikya* (tradition) that this hill is *linga swarupa*, that is to say, that this hill itself is God. This *aitikya* is not to be found anywhere else. That is the cause of the glory of this place. The tradition of this place is that this hill is the form of God and that in its real nature it is full of light. Every year the Deepam festival celebrates the real nature of the mountain as light itself. Authority for this is found in the *Vedas*, the *Puranas*, and in the *stotras* (poems) of devotees. Because this tradition maintains that the hill is Siva *swarupa*, the practice of *giripradakshina*, walking clockwise around the mountain as an act of reverence or worship, has risen, I also have faith in *giripradakshina* and have had experience of it (p. 38).

He encouraged seekers that visited to walk around the sacred mountain, which is a custom that is common to many of the world's religions, known in Sanskrit as *pradakshina*. Ramana Maharshi describes the function of circumambulation for the spiritual aspirant:

> For every body it is good to do *pradakshina*. It does not matter if one has faith in the *pradakshina* or not. Just as fire will burn on touching it, whether they believe or not the hill will do good to all those who go around it (p. 45).

Ramana Maharshi clarifies the mistaken belief that he never had a teacher: "I have never said that there is no need for a guru." He affirms that while he had a guru, it was not a human guru in the traditional sense. He states this here, "a Guru need not always be in human form."[3] Yet this does not mean that other seekers can follow in his footsteps as his Spiritual Realization was due to his unique disposition and the *jñānic* nature that allowed him to attain deliverance or liberation (*moksha*) without the traditional requirement of initiation (*diksha*), which likens him to what is referred to in Islamic esoterism as a *fard*, a "solitary" or someone who awakens spontaneously and outside the normal channels of tradition. He elaborates further on the mistaken notion that he had not had a *guru*:

> That depends on what you call a *guru*. He need not necessarily be in the human form. Dattatreya had twenty-four *gurus*—elements, etc. That means that every form in the world was his *guru*. A *guru* is absolutely necessary. The Upanishads say that none but a *guru* can take a man out of the jungle of mental and sense perceptions, so there must be a *guru* (p. 40).

The Sage of Arunachala welcomed all and everyone who visited the *ashram*. He received Hindus, non-Hindus or even the non-religious in the same manner, for he did not want to withhold his *darshan* from anyone who desired it. However, this should not be then taken to suggest that to have a religion was unnecessary; on the contrary, for having a religion and committing oneself to it may very well have provided individuals with the framework needed to assimilate his teachings in a more integral way.

Ramana Maharshi's compassion and blessing extended to all of creation. All sentient beings were in their essential nature the Self and the notion of "other" or "otherness" was again non-existent and illusory (*māyā*). He had special relationships with squirrels, peacocks, and there was the well-known and highly esteemed Cow Lakshmi who came to the *ashram* as a

---

[3] A. Devaraja Mudaliar, *Day by Day with Bhagavan* (Tiruvannamalai, India: Sri Ramanasramam, 2002), p. 33.

calf in 1926 until her awakening or *mukti* in June 1948. When asked if the Cow Lakshmi had indeed been liberated, Ramana Maharshi confirmed that she had been. He emphasizes that happiness is the longing and natural state of all sentient beings:

> Every living being longs always to be happy, untainted by sorrow: and everyone has the greatest love for himself, which is solely due to the fact that happiness is his real nature. Hence, in order to realize that inherent and untainted happiness, which indeed he daily experiences, when the mind is subdued in deep sleep, it is essential that he should know himself. For obtaining such knowledge the enquiry "Who am I?" in quest of the Self is the best means (p. 48).

The Sage of Arunachala recognized the transcendent unity of all faith traditions. He went so far as stating that of all the non-dual Vedāntic statements none could match the one found within the Old and New Testaments:

> Of all the definitions of God, none is indeed so well put as the Biblical statement "I AM THAT I AM" in Exodus (chap. 3). There are other statements, such as *Brahmaivaham*, *Aham Brahmasmi* and *Soham*. But none is so direct as the name JEHOVAH = I AM. The Absolute Being is *what* is—It is the Self. It is God. Knowing the Self, God is known. In fact God is none other than the Self.[4]

A noteworthy parallel has been made between Śrī Ramana Maharshi and Shaykh Ahmad Al-'Alawī (1869–1934), two leading spiritual lights in the contemporary world.[5] This is

---

[4] Śrī Ramana Maharshi, *Talks with Sri Ramana Maharshi* (Tiruvannamalai, India: Sri Ramanasramam, 1996), p. 102.

[5] "Sri Ramana Maharshi of Tiruvannamalai, whose teaching was essentially the same as his own [Shaykh al-'Alawī]" (Martin Lings, *A Sufi Saint of the Twentieth Century: Shaykh Aḥmad Al-'Alawī, His Spiritual Heritage and Legacy* [Cambridge, UK: Islamic Texts Society, 1993], p. 80).

also an example of how two analogous spiritual traditions manifest themselves distinctly within the temporal cycle, one within Hinduism, a religion that traces itself back to the beginning of the *Manvantara* or the temporal cycle known as the *Krita-Yuga* or *Satya-Yuga* (Golden Age), and the other Islam, which represents the closing of the current temporal cycle known as the *Kali-Yuga* (Iron Age).

Ramana Maharshi provides an astute and sobering instruction on how to benefit others and the world when questioned on this point, "Help yourself, you will help the world." Likewise, he taught to live and abide always in the now or present moment, "Do what is right at a given moment and leave it behind."

This book depicting the life and teachings of one of the most celebrated spiritual luminaries of the twentieth century, the Sage of Arunachala, Ramana Maharshi, conveys the magnitude of his teachings in an era that has become increasingly disconnected from the sacred and finding itself in a continued and alarming state of disarray. A.R. Natarajan has done a commendable job in presenting these timeless teachings in a manner that makes them relevant and accessible for contemporary seekers. Throughout the book there are wonderful photographs that provide a *darshan*-like experience of being in the presence of this remarkable sage. It is the unborn and eternal essence within all sentient beings known as the Self that Ramana Maharshi unshakably identified with as his memorable words capture so eloquently: "Where can I go? I am here."

4

*The Essential Śrī Ānandamayī Mā: Life and Teachings of a 20th Century Indian Saint**

> True realization...[is when] one is fully enlightened as to all faiths and doctrines, and sees all paths as equally good. This is absolute and perfect realization."
>
> Śrī Ānandamayī Mā[1]

Śrī Ānandamayī Mā (1896–1982) was one of the great spiritual luminaries of the 20th century. She was the embodiment of the Divine Mother within traditional Hindu spirituality and while less known, she rightly belongs alongside spiritual giants such as Śrī Rāmakrishna (1836–1886), Śrī Ramana Maharshi (1879–1950), Swāmī Ramdas (1884–1963), and the 68th Jagadguru of Kanchi (1894–1994). She has inspired millions of people around the world from all walks of life and of diverse faiths. Some of her admirers include Mahatma Gandhi, Indira Gandhi, Jawarharlal Nehru, former Canadian Prime Minister Pierre Elliott Trudeau, Queen Frederika of Greece, and the first Indian President Rajendra Prasad.

---

* Biography by Alexander Lipski, words of Śrī Ānandamayī Mā (translated and compiled by Ātmānanda), edited by Joseph A. Fitzgerald. Bloomington: World Wisdom, 2007, 152pp.

[1] *Ibid.*, p. 130.

This volume consists of two books edited as a single volume: the first provides a biography titled *Life and Teaching of Śrī Ānandamayī Mā* by Alexander Lipski, and the other is an anthology of discourses titled *Words of Śrī Ānandamayī Mā*, translated and compiled by Ātmānanda. This edition contains one hundred and twenty-five photos and illustrations taken throughout the span of the Divine Mother's life providing a compressed and detailed portrayal of the seminal events and teachings. Additionally, included in this edition are selections from her teachings previously unpublished outside India.

Ānandamayī Mā or Mātājī, as she was known to her devotees, was born on April 30, 1896 in Kheorā, a small village in the interior of East Bengal (present-day Bangladesh), and was given the name Nirmalā Sundarī (Immaculate Beauty). Her mother Mokṣadā Sundarī and father Bipin Bihārī Bhattācārya were devout *vaiṣṇavas* or worshipers of Viṣṇu, the preserver and sustainer of the universe, and were strict observers of caste regulations. Her mother counted many scholars or teachers (*pandits*) among her ancestors and the father came from a distinguished *brāhman* family, and when he was not working he spent most of his time in spiritual practice.

Though Ānandamayī Mā attended school for less than two years, she possessed a sharp mind. She recalls having what could be regarded as an intuitive intelligence, "Somehow or other, I invariably happened to look up the very questions the teacher would ask, and consequently he always found me well prepared even after long absences. The meaning of unknown words would occur to me spontaneously..." (p. 4). For her, as for many other saints and sages of the world's religions, true knowledge was not dependent on book learning. She stated, "If someone really wants God, and nothing but God, he carries his book in his own heart. He needs no printed book" (p. 5).

When Ānandamayī Mā was almost thirteen years of age, after a careful search, her parents arranged for her marriage with Ramani Mohan Cakravartī (later known as Bholānātha, a name for Śiva) on February 7, 1909. Bholānāth had no idea who he was married to and what an unusual marriage it was to be. It is reported that upon approaching her physically, he received a violent electric shock. The marriage was in fact never physically consummated. Her relationship with her husband was complex; she was spiritually his superior and later became his spiritual teacher (*guru*), yet she also played the traditional role of his obedient wife. She skillfully molded her husband-disciple to deal with many of life's challenges until he was ready to face them. In early December 1922, Ānandamayī Mā initiated Bholānāth into the spiritual path, which marked another break with the conventions of her time. When her younger sister Surabalā died at the age of sixteen, Ānandamayī Mā, perceiving the unity of all existence without birth or death, stated: "Come what may, what does it matter?" (p. 19) While such a statement may appear as outwardly unsympathetic or lacking in compassion, it characterizes her Advaitic understanding that the phenomenal world possesses a transcendent eternal dimension. Reviewing the events of her own life, she saw them as a Divine Play (*līlā*), and she was never separated from her transpersonal nature from the earliest moments of life:

> Let me tell you that what I am, I have been from my infancy. But when the different stages of *sādhanā* were being manifested through this body there was something like superimposition of *ajñāna* (ignorance). But what sort of *ajñāna* was that? It was really *jñāna* (knowledge) masquerading as *ajñāna*... (p. 12)

She had a remarkable ability to adjust her spiritual instruction to the particular needs of the human individual, varying it according to the aspirant's religious framework. A disciple, Brahmacāri Vijayānanda (b. 1915) remarked about this:

> A *vedāntist*, for example, when talking to Mother for the first time, will feel convinced that She is a pure *advaita* (non-dualist) *vedāntin*; a *śākta* (worshiper of the Divine Mother) may very likely say that She is an incarnation of the Divine Mother, advocating the cult of *śakti* (divine energy personified as feminine; the Divine Mother); while a *vaiṣṇava* will see in Her a great *bhakta* (follower of the devotional path). It is only after having known Her fairly closely and for a long time that one becomes aware of Her innumerable facets (p. 53).

In the same way that Rāmakrishna embodied a "spiritual plasticity"[2] intrinsic to the *sanātana dharma* (eternal religion), so too Ānandamayī Mā had a remarkable ability to transcend and cross religious boundaries to provide spiritual direction to people of other faiths without in any way repudiating her own tradition of Hinduism. She felt equally at home with each of the distinct faiths as she upheld their quintessential rootedness in Divine oneness: "The many in the One and the One in the many" (p. 109). It is reported that,

> In Shah-bagh [Bangladesh] there happened to be the grave of a Muslim *faqīr*. Once Ānandamayī Mā was seen performing *namāz* (Muslim prayer) at his grave. Spontaneously a prayer issued from Her lips which was identified by some bystanders as Arabic verses from the Qur'ān. During a *kīrtana*, Ānandamayī Mā noticed a Muslim watching Her from a distance. She moved towards him with a welcoming gesture, chanting: "*Allah, Allahu Akbar* (God is great)." On another occasion She walked up to some Muslim workmen and got them to chant in unison the praises of Allah. Gradually She acquired a number of devoted Muslim disciples.... As far as Mā is concerned, Hindus and Muslims or adherents of other

---

[2] Frithjof Schuon, "Vedānta," in *Spiritual Perspectives and Human Facts*, pp. 97–130.

religions ultimately are one: "*Kīrtana* and *namāz* are one and the same" (p. 23).

Ānandamayī Mā was recognized as a guide even by those who were not of her own faith tradition. On one occasion, a Muslim devotee is reported to have announced: "Although Mā was born in a Hindu family, She is also the Mā of the Muslims, She is our own Mā."[3]

While the Divine Mother realized that there was only the One, she also recognized that there were many paths to the One. It would be incorrect to assume therefore that individuals should practice no religion or that one can practice multiple religions simultaneously. On the contrary, she advocated that one should plumb the depths of their own given faith tradition rigorously: "Nevertheless, one should undoubtedly have firm faith in one's *Iṣṭa* [Beloved] and pursue one's chosen path with constancy and single-mindedness" (p. 130).

She intuitively understood that human diversity reflects a religious pluralism because the Absolute transcends both human and religious differences: "Just as individual human beings have been created with various tendencies, abilities, temperaments, so religious paths have come about in response to different religious needs" (p. 54). In fact, differences in human types require diverse spiritual practices: "Infinite are the *sādhanās*..." (p. 62). She taught that while there is one Reality, there are many paths to this Reality: "Essentially there is only He and He alone, although everyone has his own individual path that leads to Him. What is the right path for each depends on his personal predilection, based on the specific character of his inner qualifications" (p. 84). Stated differently, "As the path, He attracts each person to a particular

---

[3] Quoted in Bithika Mukerji, "Śrī Ānandamayī Mā: Divine Play of the Spiritual Journey," in *Hindu Spirituality: Vedas through Vedanta*, ed. Krishna Sivaraman (New York: Crossroad, 1989), p. 395.

line, in harmony with his inner dispositions and tendencies" (p. 130).

Hindu metaphysics distinguishes between *Nirguna Brahman*, pertaining to the Divine Essence, and *Saguna Brahman*, pertaining to the personal God to accommodate the differences in human types and their distinct ways of connecting with the transpersonal. The formless is approached through diverse forms:

> Whatever image arises in your mind, that you should contemplate; just observe in what shape God will manifest Himself to you. The same form does not suit every person. For some Rāma may be most helpful, for some Śiva, for others Pāravatī, and again for others the formless. He certainly is formless; but at the same time, watch in what particular form He may appear to you in order to show you the way (p. 89).

As the Divine has diverse forms, so does the spiritual master or *guru*, yet the One manifests itself in all *gurus*: "My *guru* exists in many forms as the *guru* of each and everyone, and everyone else's *guru* is in fact my *guru*" (p. 107). Each human type requires a unique religious form particular to the needs of the individual: "Where the Infinite is in question, the diversity of approaches is equally infinite, and likewise are the revelations along these paths, of endless variety. Is it not said: 'There are as many doctrines as there are sages'?" (p. 113). The reason why one religion does not work for all human beings is because: "The same method does not suit everyone" (p. 91). This again speaks to the existence of many messengers of God, but only one divine Reality.

Ānandamayī Mā viewed the Divine as both transcendent and immanent according to Hindu metaphysics:

> It is only because It shines ever within you that you can perceive the outer light. Whatever appears to you in the universe is due solely to that great light within you, and

only because the supreme knowledge of the essence of things lies hidden in the depths of your being is it possible for you to acquire knowledge of any kind (p. 87).

Similarly, "The Infinite is contained in the finite, and the finite in the Infinite; the Whole in the part and the part in the Whole" (p. 110).

While the external teacher or *guru* is needed for most individuals on the spiritual path, ultimately every truth that is confirmed by the outer *guru* is confirmed by the inner *guru*. "By virtue of the guru's power everything becomes possible; therefore seek a guru.... In very truth the guru dwells within, and unless you discover the inner guru, nothing can be achieved" (p. 88). The sacred symbolism of the human body itself reveals the indwelling Spirit: "If everything is the Lord and nothing but He, then one's body must also be He" (p. 118).

Ānandamayī Mā, responded in the following way when someone complained about her unwillingness to provide uniform answers to problems brought to her attention, recognizing that different perspectives might require different solutions:

> At least you have understood that there is a state where problems are no longer settled in any particular way... no solution is ever conclusive.... The resolution of a problem arrived at by the mind must of necessity be from a particular point of view; consequently, there will be room for contradiction, since your solution represents but one aspect (p. 51).

From the perspective of non-duality, all problems benefit from a vantage where the observer is no longer identified with the observed. Ānandamayī Mā applies an integral framework that recognizes both the relative and the Absolute to all situations: "What is emphasized from one point of view will be rejected from another. But where is the state in which difference and non-difference have ceased to exist?" (p. 117)

The human search for happiness outside the Divine is a futile endeavor as Ānandamayī Mā confirms, "Happiness that depends on anything, be it a person, money, comforts, and so forth cannot endure.... God alone can give lasting contentment" (p. 60). The Divine Mother's spiritual instruction always sought to guide the seeker or disciple beyond the ephemeral to the Eternal: "Look, what is there in this world? Absolutely nothing that is lasting; therefore direct your longing towards the Eternal" (p. 86).

She analogized that the whole of life was a pilgrimage and she noted as follows:

> There are two kinds of pilgrims on life's journey: the one, like a tourist, is keen on sightseeing, wandering from place to place, flitting from one experience to another for the fun of it. The other treads the path that is consistent with man's true being and leads to his real home, to Self-knowledge. Sorrow will of a certainty be encountered on the journey undertaken for the sake of sightseeing and enjoyment (p. 87).

To advance on the Path requires single-mindedness: "The true progress in one's spiritual experience depends on the sincerity and intensity of one's aspiration" (p. 127). Effort is essential: "On this pilgrimage one must never slacken: effort is what counts!" (p. 115) Yet, there are ordained aspects too, for Hindu spirituality also recognizes that "the moment of your birth has determined your nature, your desires and their fulfillment, your development, your spiritual search—everything" (p. 117). It is Divine grace that opens the spiritual path, "Everything is in God's hands, and you are His tool to be used by Him as He pleases" (p. 88).

Considering the diversity of human types, Ānandamayī Mā advocated the Invocation of the Divine Name or *japa-yoga* as a quintessential method for spiritual realization in the *Kali-Yuga* or "Dark Age". The book cites several passages in which she advocates this spiritual method: "God Himself in the role of the spiritual preceptor (*guru*) discloses His name to the pilgrim wandering in search of a guide" (p. 15); "Make an effort to let your mind be filled with God's name at all times. Be it at home or anywhere else, remember that nothing exists outside God" (p. 133); "Your medicine is the repetition of the Divine Name" (p. 135). When a grieving mother came to Ānandamayī Mā to find solace for the loss of her daughter, this is what is reported to have transpired:

> "Mā, I had forgotten about the loss of my daughter while you were here. Now that you are going away, I shall be submerged in sorrow as before."
>
> Mātājī (laying her hands upon the lady's heart): "No, it will not overwhelm you again if you think of God and repeat His Holy Name constantly" (p. 133).

The power of the Divine Name rests on the indivisibility between the Name and the Named, which is itself, the One: "the name and the One... are indivisible" (p. 109).[4] In repeating the Divine Name the seeker is able to remember God in all of his or her activities: "In every action remember Him" (p. 86). The spiritual aspirant is instructed to fix their attention single-mindedly on the Divine: "constant remembrance of the One" (p. 101); similarly, she stated "The wise ever live in remembrance of God" (p. 132). Not to remember the Divine is to err: "Forgetfulness of God is the greatest sin; His constant remembrance is the greatest virtue" (p. 132). The Divine Mother emphasized that there are many possibilities for ordinary householders to engage in spiritual practice in their day-to-day lives: renunciation, such as practiced by the homeless wanderers (*saṁnyāsis*), was only for those truly

---

[4] "God and His name are identical" (Śrī Rāmakrishna, "The Master with the Brāhmo Devotees," in *The Gospel of Ramakrishna*, p. 222). "There is but one Reality, which embraces all these attributions and relations called the Divine Names" (Ibn al-ʿArabī, *The Bezels of Wisdom* [New York: Paulist Press, 1980], p. 68).

prepared to undertake this unique way of approaching the Divine, and therefore she advised against it.

By turning the seeker's consciousness from the ephemeral to the Eternal, and loosening the attachment to the world in preparation for death, Ānandamayī Mā's method was to focus the seeker on the Eternal: "The pilgrim on the path of immortality never contemplates death. By meditation on the Immortal the fear of death recedes far away—remember this! In the measure that your contemplation of the One becomes uninterrupted, you will advance towards full, unbroken realization" (p. 61). By focusing on the deathless nature of one's identity *in divinis*, both birth and death take on a new meaning: "Who goes away—who else is it that arrives? What is the distinction between life and death? One who passes away, in fact, merges into the One who is ever-existent" (p. 43).

When illusory identity with the human body is seen for what it is and abandoned, then "death will die" (p. 92). At that point, one can authentically respond to the invitation: "Become drinkers of nectar, all of you—drinkers of the wine of immortality. Tread the path of immortality, where no death exists and no disease" (p. 79). In this context we are reminded of the well-known quote from Hindu metaphysics, "This great, unborn Self [*Ātman*], undecaying, undying, immortal, fearless, is indeed *Brahman* [Absolute]" (Brihadāranyaka Upanishad 4.4.25). One's transpersonal identity in the Divine is beyond birth and death: "Nor I, nor thou, nor any one of these, ever was not, nor ever will not be" (Bhagavad Gītā 2:12). On the topic of reincarnation, Ānandamayī Mā confirms: "there is no such thing as rebirth" (p. 124). We recall here Shankara's statement, "In truth, there is no other transmigrant but the Lord",[5] which categorically denies the possibility of individual human reincarnation.

---

[5] Śrī Śaṅkarācārya, quoted in Ananda K. Coomaraswamy, *The Bugbear of Literacy*, p. 120.

Ānandamayī Mā taught that there is a profound meaning in suffering. While it is often assumed that one suffers because the Divine has somehow forgotten the individual, this is not actually the case. Within the Divine Play of manifestation, known as *līlā*, it is the misperception of duality as the only reality which unavoidably leads to the notion of a separateness making suffering unavoidable: "The sense of separateness is the root cause of misery, because it is founded on error, on the conception of duality" (p. 87). Suffering, as many other sages have stated, can be transformative and can bring the human closer to the Divine: "Suffering should therefore be welcomed" (p. 69).

The empirical ego perceives separateness, and it thereby suffers. It is by spiritual practice and by turning one's heart and mind to the Divine that one can undo the knots of this mistaken identity: "what is called *granthi*—the knots constituting the I-ness. By meditation, *japa*, and other spiritual practices, which vary according to each one's individual line of approach, these knots become loosened, discrimination is developed, and one comes to discern the true nature of the world of sense perception" (pp. 97–98). The Divine Play (*līlā*) creates an impression of separateness but the seeker learns that Unity hides behind the veil of duality: "Who is it that loves and who that suffers? He alone stages a play with Himself.... The individual suffers because he perceives duality.... Find the One everywhere and in everything and there will be an end to pain and suffering" (p. 71).

Ānandamayī Mā affirms the transcendent unity of all phenomena: "there is the One and nothing but the One" (p. 99), though "[t]he assumption of duality is also within Oneness" (p. 117). There is nothing apart from Oneness, which is Absolute. Hindu metaphysics makes an important distinction between unqualified (*Nirguna*) *Brahman* and the qualified (*Saguna*) *Brahman*: "He is all in all, He alone is—the

One with form and without form" (p. 115). In its Advaitic form, it recognizes that "*Brahman* is One without a second" (p. 99).

Ultimate reality transcends linguistic limitations and the rational mind's definitions and conceptualization; it is beyond all such categorization, a view implied by the Upanishadic phrase *neti neti* (not this, not that). The Divine both can and cannot be discussed through the use of words. The cataphatic theology, also known as affirmative theology (*via affirmativa*), pertains to what can be spoken about the Divine or God. By contrast, the apophatic theology, also known as negative theology (*via negativa*), pertains to what cannot be spoken about the Divine Essence or Godhead. *Nirguna Brahman* or without qualities is synonymous with apophatic theology and *Saguna Brahman* or with qualities is synonymous with cataphatic theology.[6]

Because Ānandamayī Mā continually emphasized Divine immanence, rather than Divine transcendence, seekers may lose sight of the fact that transcendence precedes immanence and that there would be no immanence without transcendence,

---

[6] An example of how the religion of the First Peoples converges with Hinduism, the two poles of the Primordial Tradition or the *sanātana dharma* (eternal religion), is made here by Joseph Epes Brown: "*Wakan-Tanka* as Grandfather is the Great Spirit independent of manifestation, unqualified, unlimited, identical to the Christian Godhead, or to the Hindu *Brahma-Nirguna*. *Wakan-Tanka* as Father is the Great Spirit considered in relation to His manifestation, either as Creator, Preserver, or Destroyer, identical to the Christian God, or to the Hindu *Brahma-Saguna*." (Joseph Epes Brown, *The Sacred Pipe: Black Elk's Account of the Seven Rites of the Oglala Sioux* [Norman, OK: University of Oklahoma Press, 1989], p. 5). Within Islamic metaphysics, there is an analogous distinction made by the terms *tanzih* (declaring incomparability) and *tashbih* (affirming similarity). This is reflected in the Qur'ānic verses: "Nothing is like Him" (42:11) or "Utterly remote is God, in His limitless glory, from anything to which men may ascribe a share in His divinity!" (59:23), in juxtaposition with, "Wherever you turn, there is the face of God" (2:115) or "We are nearer to him than the jugular vein" (50:16). And yet both transcendence and immanence are necessary: "Naught is like unto Him, yet He is the Hearer, the Seer" (42:11).

yet both perspectives are needed to be balanced in an integral spiritual framework. Just as the Divine Mother emphasized our essential transpersonal identity in the Absolute, she also instructed seekers to see that they were inseparable from the One. This is consistent with the *Mahāvākyas* (great sayings) of Advaita Vedānta, such as *Aham Brahmāsmi* (I am Brahman) or *Tat tvam asi* (That art thou). Ānandamayī Mā declares: "What is there to be attained? We *are* THAT—eternal Truth. Because we imagine that it has to be experienced, realized, it remains apart from us" (p. 121). Within Sufism there is an analogous declaration, *Lā anā wa lā Anta: Huwa* (Neither I nor Thou but He). Ānandamayī Mā explains "Your true nature is to yearn for the revelation of what you are" (p. 114), which is to say, "To realize God means to realize one's self" (p. 62). Within Islamic spirituality, we recall the prophetic dictum: "Whoever knows himself, knows his Lord" and analogously in the Gospels, "The kingdom of God is within you" (Luke 17:21). The same fundamental message is affirmed in her teachings that the Divine seeks the Divine, and is itself the Divine: "The One who is the Eternal, the *Ātman* (true Self), He Himself is the traveler on the path of Immortality. He is all in all, He alone is" (p. 53). Ultimately, there is nothing that is not itself the Absolute:

> Thou art Mother, Thou art Father,
> Thou art Friend and Thou art Master,
> Truly, Thou art all in all.
> Every name is Thy Name,
> Every quality Thy Quality,
> Every form Thy Form indeed (p. 84).

When all things are seen through metaphysical transparency, the other and otherness are akin to a mirage that disappears when seen for what it truly is: "None will seem alien, all will be your very own Self [*Ātman*]" (p. 67). Shankara expresses this in a different manner, "Only the Self knows the Self". Likewise, in viewing reality through immanence, the transpersonal Self (*Ātman*), human beings can navigate the labyrinth of *samsāra*: "You see 'the many'; how will you go beyond this multiplicity? By finding your Self in the many" (p. 123).

Even though the Divine Mother was unequivocally non-dual in her perspective, caste restrictions were nonetheless enforced in her *āśrams*. She viewed herself to be beyond caste and held a similar outlook as Shankara, who stated, "No birth, no death, no caste have I" (p. 75). This position is likely due to the fact that perfected beings are beyond the limitations of caste, just as renunciants or homeless wanderers (*saṁnyāsis*), who renounce the world to live spiritual lives, are said to have no caste.

Perfection is in the "eternal now", which contains the whole of time, past, future and present: "In that supreme moment all moments are contained" (p. 91). All time from the metaphysical point of view is contained in the—"eternal now"—the past and the future are ultimately viewed as illusory. "In reality there is nothing but the one moment all along" (p. 117). While chronological time in a sense defines existence in the phenomenal world, there is a reality where time in its normal connotations disappears: "within all these countless moments lies the one single moment" (p. 117).

The Divine Mother also illuminates the true teachings of yoga. Yoga practices and fads are popular in the contemporary West, yet they are a truncated interpretation of what yoga truly is. Yoga has become another commodity for mass consumption. It has become desacralized, cut off from the Eternal. According to Ānandamayī Mā:

> If one practices *hathayoga* merely as a physical exercise, the mind will not be transformed in the very least.... Sustained effort ends in effortless being; in other words, what has been attained by constant practice is finally transcended. Then comes spontaneity. Not until this happens can the utility of *hathayoga* be understood. When the physical fitness resulting from *hathayoga* is used as an aid to spiritual

endeavor, it is not wasted. Otherwise it is not *yoga*, but *bhoga* (enjoyment).... Unless *hathayoga* aims at the Eternal, it is nothing more than gymnastics (p. 100).

The benefits of yoga, divorced from its spiritual roots, can only be a pale reflection of what yoga offers in its traditional context. As the Divine Mother cautions, such practices can even be harmful: "*Hathayoga* can be harmful only if pure spiritual aspiration is lacking" (p. 101).

The Divine Mother also warns that glimpses into the nature of reality should not be taken as *moksha* or *samādhi* (liberation). In this spiritually confused era of the *Kali-Yuga*, there are many so-called *gurus* and spiritual seekers alike mistaking one of the lesser peaks of the mountain for its summit.[7] A glimpse of the Absolute is not the same as the realization of the Absolute. Ānandamayī Mā teaches,

> You should understand that if a veil of ignorance has been burnt or dissolved, as it were, the seeker will, for a certain period of time, have unobstructed vision. Afterwards it becomes blurred again. All the same—what will be the result of such a glimpse? Ignorance will have become less dense, and true knowledge gained greater prominence; in other words, by the momentary lifting of the veil, the individual's bonds will have been loosened. In this condition there is a semblance of the attainment of real knowledge; in fact, it is also a state of achievement, although quite different from the state of final Self-realization. By the power of the *guru*, the veil has here been suddenly dissolved or consumed. But there is a realization, after which the possibility of its being obscured again by a reappearance of the veil of ignorance, simply cannot occur; this is true and final Self-realization (p. 110).

---

[7] We are reminded of Zen Buddhism and what is known as *kenshō*, an initial insight or awakening, but not necessarily realization itself or Buddhahood. What may appear as an insight into the nature of Reality can be confused with Realization itself, and serious seekers must be ever vigilant.

While sometimes questioned on her position on being of service to humanity or helping the world, Ānandamayī Mā did not emphasize a division between spiritual practice (*sādhanā*) and being of service to humanity. In this way she upheld the commandment "Thou shalt love thy neighbour as thyself" (Mark 12:31). The metaphysics of service, for her, involved a non-dual perspective:

> Widening your shriveled heart, make the interests of others your own and serve them as much as you can by sympathy, kindness, presents and so forth. So long as one enjoys the things of this world and has needs and wants, it is necessary to minister to the needs of one's fellowmen. Otherwise one cannot be called a human being. Whenever you have the opportunity, give to the poor, feed the hungry, nurse the sick.... Do service as a religious duty and you will come to know by direct perception that the person served, the one who serves, and the act of service are separate only in appearance (p. 67).

She emphasized taking time to pause and to contemplate during the busy-ness of day-to-day life, and to ask the following question: "Will this action lead me towards God-realization or not?" (p. 79)

When speaking to a group of children Ānandamayī Mā gave the following instruction:

> I shall tell you only five things to remember. One, always speak the truth; two, obey your parents and teachers; three, study as much as is expected of you; four, pray to God every morning that He should make you a good boy or girl, and if during the day you have done something untoward, then at night when going to bed, tell Him you are sorry and you will not let it happen again; five, if the above four are done, then you may be a little naughty if you like! (The children laugh with Mā and repeat the five-point program to learn it by heart) (p. 133)

The Divine Mother constantly reminded seekers that the Divine was inseparable from their own essence and beckoned the seeker to remove the veil of duality to perceive the true Self (*Ātman*) directly. She instructed:

> Give yourself up to the wave, and you will be absorbed by the current; having dived into the sea, you do not return anymore. The Eternal Himself is the wave that floods the shore, so that you may be carried away. Those who can surrender themselves to this aim will be accepted by Him. But if your attention remains directed towards the shore, you cannot proceed—after bathing you will return home. If your aim is the Supreme, the Ultimate, you will be led on by the movement of your true nature. There are waves that carry away, and waves that pull back. Those who can give themselves up, will be taken by Him. In the guise of the wave He holds out His hand and calls you come, Come, COME! (p. 102)

Due to the rise of secularism in our age, more and more people are questioning their faith and are labeled as either believers or nonbelievers, yet this is to forget, as Ānandamayī Mā reminds us, that such distinctions are inadequate: "It cannot be said that no one has faith. Everyone surely believes in something or other" (p. 87). It is often overlooked that belief in the existence of a purely materialistic worldview devoid of the sacred, is still a belief, but rather an often-unchecked and rampant belief. The Divine Mother diagnosed the current crisis facing the contemporary world as "over-secularization" (p. ix).

Considering the ongoing discrimination and countless atrocious acts of violence committed against women in the present-day, it is our hope that living embodiments of Divine Motherhood, such as Śrī Ānandamayī Mā, will provide integral ways of viewing and relating to the sacredness of the feminine. Rāmakrishna taught: "He who has realized God... perceives clearly that women are but so many aspects of the

Divine Mother. He worships them all as the Mother Herself."[8] Far from a call to romanticize the Divine Feminine, what is needed is the recognition of the transpersonal essence that disguises itself in all human beings and all life forms for that matter. Śrī Ānandamayī Mā is a remarkable testimony to the fact that with the Divine all things are possible. Her example and teachings show us that to actualize what we were born to be requires that we live in accord with one of the divinely revealed religions of the world. It is difficult to walk away from reading this work and viewing its illustrations without experiencing the sense of having been touched in a deep way by Śrī Ānandamayī Mā. One is left with the sense of having had *darshan* (sacred viewing) or taken part in *satsang* (association with truth), as if one has vicariously received her blessing. The contents of this volume are the crystallization of pure metaphysics; nonetheless the responsibility to absorb its message rests with the reader. The question arises: *Now that you have read it, what will you do with the message contained within its pages?* The Divine Mother urged the diverse seekers who approached her to realize that they were fundamentally inseparable from that which they were seeking and that each human being was called to action: "Man's calling is to aspire to the realization of Truth" (p. 79). The timeless call for the awakening of intelligence to the Spirit commences with the acknowledgment that one's own identity from the perspective of duality (*dvaita*) is essentially distinct from the Divine, and yet from the perspective of non-duality (*advaita*), it is fundamentally inseparable from the Divine Essence. The melding of life in a consciousness

---

[8] Śrī Rāmakrishna,"The Master and Vijay Goswami," in *The Gospel of Ramakrishna*, p. 168. "I clearly perceived that the Divine Mother Herself had become everything" (Śrī Rāmakrishna, "With the Devotees at Dakshineswar (II)," *ibid.*, p. 346). "I worshipped all women as representatives of the Divine Mother. I realized the Mother of the universe in every woman's form" (Śrī Rāmakrishna, "Divinity Everywhere," *ibid.*, p. 92).

of transcendence and immanence is essential for any serious seeker for, as Ānandamayī Mā affirms, "the ocean is contained in the drop, and the drop in the ocean" (p. 109).

5

*Eastern Light in Western Eyes: A Portrait of the Practice of Devotion**

> What Hinduism [*sanātana dharma*] offers... is the path of *bhakti* or *devotion*. The love of God. The experience of the love of God, the experience of *loving God*, is a spiritual absolute, an ultimate: there is nothing beyond it: it is supreme, because it is the Oneness: God is Love, and in our love for God, in that experience, we disappear into that Oneness, that infinite Bliss, *ananda*, which is the Reality.
>
> Marty Glass[1]

Eastern Light in Western Eyes by Marty Glass offers the contemporary Western reader a unique and insightful portrayal of the Hindu tradition—also known as the *sanātana dharma*—the primordial and eternal religion. Noteworthy exponents of the perennialist school have observed that it is through Vedānta in its non-dual (*advaita*) expression that the most direct formulation of the essential heart of all the world's religions becomes explicit. The author develops this work as if he had one foot firmly centered in Hinduism (*sanātana dharma*) and another

---

* Marty Glass, *Eastern Light in Western Eyes: A Portrait of the Practice of Devotion*. Sophia Perennis, 2003, 288pp.

[1] *Ibid.*, p. 8.

traversing all the spiritual traditions, articulating each in their doctrinal purity while remaining faithful to his own tradition.

> Where I may have fallen short of the mark, I hope the Truth of the Hindu tradition, *sanatana dharma*—and indeed of the Primordial and Universal tradition, Lex Aeterna, Hagia Sophia, Sophia Perennis et Universalis, the Perennial Philosophy—shines through anyway: for It is the Light of the World (p. 47).

This work is informed by three decades of the author's practicing the Hindu *dharma*, spending extensive periods in spiritual practice (*sādhanā*) in an old chicken coop that he transformed into a meditation chamber or what the author refers to as "Marty's Cell". In conjunction with the author's *modus operandi*, this book affirms that the practice of remembering the Divine is in THIS-HERE-NOW, in this very moment, and is not limited to the set times devoted to meditation or spiritual practice. It is from this perspective that the author writes this book, keen to assist others in discovering their own spiritual practice in the midst of their busy day-to-day lives, and buckling down to fearless practice.

When opening *Eastern Light in Western Eyes* one finds the memorable lines from the *Bhagavad Gītā* (XVIII.55.66), which set the devotional and didactic tone of this work:

> To love is to know Me,
> My innermost nature,
> The Truth that I am:
> Through this knowledge he enters
> At once to my Being...
> Abandoning all dharmas.
> Take refuge in me alone.

Readers will find many relevant aspects of the spiritual path discussed in Marty Glass's detailed Introduction of some forty-seven pages. The author summarizes the intricacies of

Shankara's metaphysics contained at the heart of the *sanātana dharma*:

> The essence of the Upanishadic message, or *sanatana dharma*, Eternal Truth, is summarized *Brahman satyam, jagan mithya: Ayam Atma Brahman*. Brahman is real, the world is not: this Self is Brahman. Which means that only the Absolute or Brahman, the impersonal Ground of all Being, is truly Real, all else being an *appearance*, called *maya*, superimposed upon that Reality, and the innermost Self of each of us, called the Atman, is identical with that Absolute: *Aham brahmasmi*, I am Brahman. Atman and Brahman are One (p. 9).

In order to provide the seeker with a solid context from which to recognize the intrinsic decline of the current era's spiritual standing and what this implies for the seeker, Glass identifies three crucial points that could be translated or interpreted through the traditional language of any spiritual path:

1. We live in the Kali-Yuga, the end of the cosmic cycle.

2. The Path indicated for the Kali-Yuga is *bhakti*.

3. The specific practice for the Kali-Yuga is Invocation of a Holy Name or, in Hindu terminology, *mantra-japa*: repetition of a Holy Name or *mantra* (p. 29).

Readers interested in the subject of the *Kali-Yuga* may be interested in the following other titles by the same author: *Yuga: An Anatomy of our Fate* (2004) and *The Sandstone Papers: On the Crisis of Contemporary Life* (2005).

Throughout this book, seekers will find valuable pointers, commentaries, reflections and most of all remembrances for embarking and traveling the spiritual path. Examples of these are: "RELIGION is direct experience of the Divine Reality, direct experience of the Truth" (p. 3). "Two great Paths, or *margas*, are recognized by the religion of India: *Bhakti*, or the Path of Love, and *jñāna*, the Path of Knowledge. Both lead to the same indescribable Realization, and each is present in the other" (p. 11). "The Advaitic or 'non-dual' position perhaps enjoys the greater prestige, but it does not deny, nor does it seek to, the authenticity of theistic experience" (p. 12). "The pain of our lives is the burden of selfhood" (p. 210). "Paradoxically enough, we have to pray for the ability to pray" (p. 214). "All human love is a quest for God, no matter how grotesquely or pathetically misdirected. All those people out there, chasing rainbows—they're really chasing Him. They just don't know it" (p. 217).

Other perennial exegeses by the author are found in the following selections yet are in no way limited to these alone: "On the road to yourSelf" emphasizes what will be discovered *en route* to the intrinsic condition of what it means to be truly human:

> In prayer and meditation everything accidental about us— the details of an individual life, everything that makes us appear particular and unique, our 'personality', the person our friends believe they know so well—gradually fades away and we emerge as what we truly and always really are: a human soul here in the universe and present before God. We become essential, generic, universal, representative, archetypal (p. 61).

The author continues underscoring the shortcomings of modern psychology or what is termed *psychologism* (the reduction of reality to psychological criteria), lacking any foundation in the transpersonal dimension, which is imperative for the development of the integral human condition. Reductionistic methods that exclude the transpersonal dimension are inept in discovering who and what the true Self is:

> To present ourselves before Him in sincerity means to discard every layer of our social selves, our 'worldly' selves, to remove the masks we wear in social situations and even, although to a lesser extent, when we are alone. Undiluted

honesty. It is definitely not the ego, the psychological self which 'pours its heart out' to a therapist, and for two big reasons. First, because the ego is precisely the 'lower self,' composed of fears and desires, which divine wisdom unanimously declares we are not; second, because this self is always defined by the past, by time—it's actually what we call our 'biography'—and is therefore a mental construct, whereas presentation before God always happens now, in immediacy, in a pure Present sometimes called 'the Eternal Now' (p. 62).

"Do we get what we deserve? Do we deserve what we get? What *do* we get? Who *are* we?" explores the not so obvious limitations of individual intention and effort and why the outcomes always fall short of the mark; thus exposing the utter dependence of the human individual upon what is supra-individual, what is beyond him or herself:

> It is axiomatic that Grace... cannot be coerced. There is nothing we can do, no effort or attainment on our part, no sacrifice, austerity or traditional practice—no 'worthiness', in other words—that can guarantee or determine a divine response. 'I can of mine own self do nothing' (St. John of the Cross); 'The Vision of God is possible only through His Grace' (Ananda Moyi; p. 90).

In "A Sequence on Identity", the author enters further into the crucial topic of human identity and the spiritual process of transmuting the empirical ego or personality based on separateness into the Supreme Identity. He speaks to both the transcendent and immanent as is known in the *sanātana dharma*: "the Vedantic doctrine, the doctrine of Atman [the Self] and Brahman [the Absolute], is the doctrine of identity *par excellence*, Self-Realization can be experienced as the realization or fulfillment of the Vedic Truth within us" (p. 127).

"Ask the Teacher" offers vital observations for those who are thinking about entering into a formal guru-disciple relationship and how this key relationship can be looked at in the broader context of the current era or the *Kali-Yuga*. The reader is reminded that "These are militantly secular times.... The traditional guru relationship is not available to the overwhelming majority of householders" (pp. 136–137).

In "A Sequence on the Heart", the author also explores the unanimous and traditional symbol of the heart and its function on the spiritual path.

> When we experience God as more dear to us, more loved by us, than anything or anyone else, we spontaneously equate Him with "my very heart." We think those words: "my very heart." It's intuitively evident to us that a love so complete, so absolute and so unqualified can only originate in a prior unity, in Oneness, in an identity of the lover with the Beloved that has always been the case only we didn't know it, and that Oneness is directly experienced in devotional meditation (p. 203).

This work also takes on challenging and unpopular topics of the spiritual path in "Getting up early enough to meditate, and similar challenges" that are often overlooked, but essential. The author reminds the seeker that "We do not enter a spiritual Path in the pursuit of happiness, to relax, to 'center' ourselves or to relieve stress, nor for any other airhead 'New Age' goal. We enter a spiritual Path because we were made for the Truth. The Path is not therapy and it is not easy" (p. 46).

For the author, in the truest sense of the *Advaitic* message, he cannot be other than that who is the source of the timeless and unanswerable question "Who am I?": "None of what I am writing here is literally true," the author continues, "but this is a figure of speech, a verbal convenience, a concession to the illusion of separate existence. Actually, It is everything and It is everywhere, and so am I. *Tat tvam asi*: That art Thou" (pp. 205–206).

In the section titled "I suggest this parry for that thrust," Marty Glass articulates an important truth about the spiritual path that is universal: "We surrender. Not because we have no other choice, but because we realize that 'I am Thine' was the truth all along anyway, and now we are confessing it, acknowledging it, accepting it. Embracing it" (p. 210).

In "Many people don't realize how important these two words are," the author discusses both Mercy and Grace in the context of duality and non-duality, giving the reader a primary orientation to the deeper meaning of these two concepts:

> And finally, Grace, as well as Mercy, is an illusion, for our status as recipients depends upon our erroneous conviction that we are separate beings. Grace, in other words, is a relationship within *maya*, the universal illusion or relative world or world-appearance.... The highest Truth is always non-dualism, the end of the Path is always non-dualism, absolute Identity: there is nothing but the Self, the One without a Second. Grace and Mercy only exist 'from our side', and our side, and we ourselves, are a dream (p. 222).

"Who put the serpent in Paradise? And *why*?" presents insightful perspectives on why evil exists in the world without introducing a protagonist-versus-antagonist polarity, for the providence of *Māyā* is much too multifaceted for such interpretations.

> Evil cannot and should not be argued away, nor a benevolent Providence demonstrated, by tormented redefinitions.... At the same time the existence of God requires no 'proof'—being evident to the human Intellect, which is in itself proof, as is Existence, and given in direct experience to those who sincerely seek Him—and is in no way contradicted or compromised by fatal household accidents, earthquakes, cancer, squalor, war or crimes against humanity (p. 242).

"I have great news: I lost my life!"—one cannot fail to sense the ironic and yet challengingly playful humor behind the author's title selections and general writing style, and the previous title does a superb job of demonstrating this point.

The notion of the "I" or "me" at the center of human existence needs to be cast off to travel the spiritual path as any assertion of separation—the author illustrates—is erroneous and therefore fictitious. "The original, central and fundamental 'point' in the path of devotion might be epitomized like this: *I have no 'life'. I am no one. Thou art all....* We have to get this notion of 'my life' out of our heads. There's no such thing. This is the very heart, the very core of the Teaching" (p. 247).

The author continues by encapsulating the core of Advaita Vedānta:

1. All consciousness, all awareness, is God;

2. There is only one Self in the universe;

3. That Self *is* the universe;

4. It is Infinity and Eternity, beyond all manifestation, in which universes appear and disappear forever like the myriad instantaneous jewels of light that scintillate on the surface of the ocean at sundown;

5. "I am the Self-Awareness of the universe that is the universe";

6. Tat tvam asi: That art Thou! (pp. 247–248)

Readers will take notice of the fact that the late doyen of the world's religions, Huston Smith, prepared the following endorsement for this work and has endorsed most of Marty Glass's books:

> ... Reliable from beginning to end, it is distinctive among the innumerable renditions of the Vedanta in two ways. First, because its author is an accomplished wordsmith, he makes the Vedanta's profundities—which delve as deep as those of any philosophical theology—read like an open book; and second, because he has worked for thirty years

to shape his life by those profundities, his vivid accounts of what he experienced along the way make his words jump off the page into the reader's heart. The book is inspiring. (from the back cover of the book)

We could not agree more with Professor Huston Smith's discerning observations regarding Marty Glass's book. May this book be of service to all seekers that yearn to discover the underlying spiritual significance of what it means to be integrally human. It is through devotion to spiritual practice and the active participation in a revealed tradition that the author shares not only his discerning theoretical orientation but also the depth of his wisdom, which is analogously waiting within each reader, for there is *the One-and-Only Reality*, even if it is currently unknown or unacknowledged.

Part II

The Taoist Tradition

6

*An Illustrated Introduction to Taoism: The Wisdom of the Sages**

> Tao is primordial; it is Absolute. In its descent it begets one. When one is begotten, Tao becomes relative and two comes into existence. When two things are compared there is their opposite and three is begotten.
>
> Yen Fu[1]

Of all of the world's religions, or more specifically the three religions of the Chinese civilization, Taoism is least known. While Buddhism and Confucianism are commonly known, why is it that Taoism, one of the great religious and philosophical movements in Chinese thought, remains relatively unknown? One reason might be that Taoism belongs to pure metaphysics, as Chuang Tzu alludes to in the following, "It cannot be conveyed either by words or by silence. In that state which is neither speech nor silence its transcendental nature may be apprehended" (p. 5). While each religion has an outer (exoteric or formal) and inner (esoteric

---

* Jean C. Cooper, *An Illustrated Introduction to Taoism: The Wisdom of the Sages*. Edited by Joseph A. Fitzgerald, Foreword by William Stoddart. Bloomington: World Wisdom, 2010, 160pp.

[1] Quoted in J.C. Cooper, *Yin & Yang: The Taoist Harmony of Opposites* (Wellingborough, UK: Aquarian Press, 1981), p. 71.

or mystical) dimension, it is said that "Taoism is a purely metaphysical and mystical religion. Other religions have their mystical aspects; Taoism *is* mysticism" (p. 5). Even though this work articulates the spiritual landscape of Taoism, its author also makes "points of contact with the perennial philosophy in other major religions... illustrating how, in many essential ways, they speak with one voice."[2]

The author of this book, Jean Campbell Cooper (1905–1999), was born in Zhifu (Yantai), in Northern China, where she spent her formative years in the Taoist, Buddhist and Confucian cultures of China. Cooper wrote and lectured extensively on themes of philosophy, comparative religion, and symbolism. She was a regular contributor to the journal *Studies in Comparative Religion*. The contents of the book under review incorporate sections from three of J.C. Cooper's works which continue to be among the most reliable introductions to Taoism. The three works are: *Taoism: The Way of the Mystic* (1972); *Yin & Yang: The Taoist Harmony of Opposites* (1981); and *Chinese Alchemy: The Taoist Quest for Immortality* (1984). This edited edition of selected chapters from Cooper's writings on Taoism contains 118 stunning color illustrations and includes an index.

Cooper recalls her upbringing within Taoist, Buddhist and Confucian culture in China:

> I was born in China and spent my early formative years there, my father having been in the consular service and later a director of one of the missions then operating in the county, so I was brought up by Christian parents and Taoist-Buddhist amahs [nurses], seeing more of the latter than the former. Thus, if one follows the Jesuit adage "give me a child for the first seven years," it is easy to

---

[2] *Ibid*, p. 11. "There are basic similarities in the perennial philosophy of all religions and, of necessity, they interact with one another, but similarities are not to be confused with identity; outwardly they are not one, they are many; it is the Power within them that is One," *ibid*, p. 90.

see why those years were more influenced by Eastern than Western thought and attitudes. I also grew up with the vivid contrasts between the imported Western opulence and the squalor of the city back streets, and, against these, the breathtaking and magical beauty of the mountain county where I was sent to boarding school at an early age. Overall, too, I learned the charm of the Chinese character, with its balance between Confucian social decorum and Taoist gamin individuality, as well as the beauty of the arts and crafts with which one was surrounded (p. vii).

Whereas Buddhism originated in India, both Taoism and Confucianism derive from the primordial hyperborean shamanism attributed to the legendary first Chinese emperor Fu-Hsi (2852–2738). It was Fu-Hsi who authored the *I Ching* or "Book of Changes". Lao Tzu and Confucius were in fact contemporaries. When the two masters met, Confucius is reported to have said to Lao Tzu: "The highest rung on my ladder corresponds to the lowest rung on your ladder" (p. x), thus highlighting that Confucianism is the exoteric or outer dimension and Taoism is the esoteric or inner dimension. The two founders of these doctrines have been recorded to have had the following encounter:

> 'Hast thou discovered Tao?' asked Lao Tzu. 'I have sought it twenty-seven years,' replied [Confucius] 'and I have not yet found it.' Whereupon Lao Tzu gave his visitor these few precepts. 'The sage loves obscurity; he does not throw himself at every comer; he studies times and circumstances. If the moment is propitious, he speaks; otherwise, he keeps silent. Whoever possesses a treasure does not display it before the whole world; in the same way, one who is truly a sage does not unveil his wisdom to the whole world. That is all I have to say to you; make what profit you can out of it!' On returning from this interview [Confucius] said, 'I have seen Lao Tzu; he is like the dragon. As for the dragon,

I know not how it can be borne by winds and clouds and raise itself to Heaven."[3]

The word *Tao* is often translated as "Way" and, as a doctrine, existed prior to Lao Tzu, the reputed founder of Taoism. For Lao Tzu the Tao or "Way" was associated with pure metaphysics:

> The transcendental First Cause, the Primordial Unity, the ineffable, the timeless, all-pervading principle of the universe, giving rise to it yet undiminished by it; supporting and controlling it; that which preceded the creation of Heaven and Earth. It is called the Absolute, the Ultimate Reality, the Nameless, the Portal of all Mystery, the Cosmic Order. Some liken it to the *Atman* of Hinduism, the "Suchness" of Buddhism, the *Eyn Sof* of Kabbalah, or the Monad of the Greeks, that which has neither qualities nor attributes (p. 6).

Any concept attributed to the Tao is ultimately misleading, as famously stated in the *Tao Te Ching*: "The Tao that can be expressed is not the eternal Tao, the Name that can be defined is not the unchanging Name" (p. 6). We find an almost parallel assertion by Meister Eckhart in the Christian tradition: "God is nameless, because no one can say anything or understand anything about him."[4] Chuang Tzu too affirmed: "Only the limited can be understood and be expressed."[5] (p. 7).

Consequently, as the *Tao Te Ching* states, there is no Creator in Taoism, all forms being latent in the Tao or "Way":

> There was something formless yet complete,
> That existed before Heaven and Earth;

---

[3] Quoted in René Guénon, "Taoism and Confucianism," in *Insights into Islamic Esoterism and Taoism* (Hillsdale, NY: Sophia Perennis, 2001), p. 56.

[4] Meister Eckhart, *The Essential Sermons, Commentaries, Treatises, and Defense*, (Ramsey, NJ: Paulist Press, 1981), p. 206.

[5] Quoted in René Guénon, *The Symbolism of the Cross* (Hillsdale, NY: Sophia Perennis, 2001), p. 120.

> Without sound, without substance.
> Dependent on nothing, unchanging,
> All-pervading, unfailing (p. 9).

As Chuang Tzu affirms, "Tao is without beginning, without end" (p. 9).

Sin, as is conceived in the Abrahamic monotheisms of Judaism, Christianity and Islam, is understood in Taoism in non-theistic terms such as lack of "harmony" or "balance". "Taoism has no doctrine of sin. Ethics should be incidental to spiritual values, and, indeed, there is no ideograph in Chinese which conveys the Western conception of sin and a sense of guilt" (p. 14). Instead, "Sin is, for the Taoist, rather a violation of the harmony of the universe than any personal infringement of a divine command and as such it creates disharmony and, therefore, disquiet in the individual and particular and thence in society in general" (p. 14). It is due to the human individual's deluded mind in failing to perceive the nature of reality clearly for what it is, and it is ignorance therefore that causes disharmony. "Ignorance is at the root of man's moral malaise; it is his lack of knowledge and understanding of his true nature and its identity with the Tao" (p. 16). To live in accordance with the *Tao* or "Way" is to be aligned with the harmony of the universe, and thereby beyond good and evil. So Chuang Tzu has noted, "The Sage has no deficiency in his character and therefore needs no morality" (p. 13). The Sage possesses an intrinsic morality based on attunement to the *Tao* or "Way": "He who knows the Tao is sure to understand how to regulate his conduct in all varying circumstances" (p. 13).

The two complementary poles of manifestation are known in Taoism as *yin-yang*:

> The *yin-yang* diagram shows the two great forces of the universe, the dark and light, negative and positive, female and male, to be held in complete balance and equality of power; together they control everything in the realm of manifestation. There is a point, or embryo,

of black in the white and white in the black. This is not fortuitous, but essential to the symbolism, since there is no being which does not contain within itself the germ of its opposite. There is no male wholly without feminine characteristics and no female without its masculine attributes, otherwise the dualities would forever remain in watertight compartments and the whole power of interaction be lost (p. 19).

The primordial unity precedes the dualism of the phenomenal world and not the other way around: "Every manifested being participates in the two principles [and this is expressed by the presence of the two terms *yang* and *yin*], but in different proportions and always with one or the other predominating; the perfectly balanced union of the two terms can be realized only in the 'primordial state'" (pp. 25–26).[6] When balance is disrupted physically, mentally or spiritually, the human being suffers as Chuang Tzu writes: "If the equilibrium of the positive and negative is disturbed... man himself suffers physically thereby" (p. 31).

The *yin-yang* are also expressed by two lines, *yin* depicted as a broken line and *yang* depicted as an unbroken line, which produce the Four Designs and ultimately give rise to the Eight Trigrams or the *Pa Kua*.

It is through the One that the many arise and through the One that they return. In the *yin-yang* interaction the manifest world appears. Chuang Tzu expands upon this:

> In the light of the Tao the affirmative and negative are one; the objective becomes one with the subjective.... When

---

[6] *Ibid*, p. 137.

subjective and objective are both without their correlates, that is the very axis of Tao, and when the axis passes through the center at which all infinites converge, positive and negative alike blend into an infinite One (p. 37).

Our attention to the underlying unity within the visible forms is taught by Lao Tzu: "To see all things in the yet undifferentiated, primordial unity" (p. 37).

Wu wei or "non-action" is not the end of all action, but rather the cessation of activity driven by the empirical ego. This is to say, "It is rather the end of action induced by desires and attachment to the realm of the illusions of the senses" (p. 53). Chuang Tzu elaborates on the principle of *wu wei* or "non-action":

> The sovereigns of old, abstaining from any action of their own, allowed Heaven to govern through them.... At the summit of the universe the Principle exerts its influence over Heaven and Earth, which transmit that influence to all beings and, having become in the world of men good government, it causes talents and abilities to flourish. Inversely, all prosperity comes from good government whose efficacy derives from the Principle through the intermediary of Heaven and Earth. This is why, the sovereigns of old desiring nothing, the world was filled with abundance; they did not act, and all things changed according to the norm; they remained sunk in their meditation, and the people behaved with the most perfect order. This is what the ancient saying sums up thus: For him who unites himself to Unity, all things prosper; to him who has no desire of his own, even the genii are obedient.[7]

Expounding on this theme, Kuo Hsiang writes: "Non-action does not mean doing nothing. Let everything do what it really does, and then its nature will be satisfied" (p. 53). Within

---

[7] Chuang Tzu, quoted *ibid.*, p. 116.

Hinduism, the *Bhagavad-Gītā* declares a similar teaching: "Let not the fruits of action be thy motive; neither let there be any attachment to inaction" (p. 53).

Taoism teaches that our true nature or primordial state is always present and that we are never without it. Wang Pi writes, "Everything has its own nature. It can be developed according to its nature, but not shaped or forced against it" (p. 57). From another perspective, Chuang Tzu avows, "Identify yourself with the Infinite. Make excursion into the Void. Exercise fully what you have received from nature, but gain nothing besides. In one word, be empty" (p. 80).

What in Taoism is called the Great Triad consists of Heaven-Man-Earth. "Heaven represents the Spirit or Essence, Earth the Substance and Man the synthesis of both and mediator between them, himself partaking of the dual nature of Heaven and Earth" (p. 67). The Perfect Man is thus the fulfillment of human nature as reflected in all of the *yin-yang* possibilities. The *Chung Yung*, from *The Book of Rites*, comments, "Heaven, Earth and Man are the basis of all creation. Heaven produces them, Earth nourishes them and Man completes them" (p. 67).

Chuang Tzu reminds inhabitants of the phenomenal world of its illusory and dream-like quality in his famous allegory: "Once upon a time Chuang Tzu dreamed that he was a butterfly, a butterfly flying about and enjoying itself. It did not know it was Chuang Tzu. Suddenly he awoke and veritably was Chuang Tzu again. We do not know whether it was Chuang Tzu dreaming that he was a butterfly, or whether it was a butterfly dreaming it was Chuang Tzu" (p. 113). Due to this predicament, one needs to observe with all clarity the fleeting appearances of the phenomenal world in order to see the One underlying them: "The mind of the perfect man is like a mirror. It does not move with things, nor does it anticipate them. It responds to things, but does not retain them. Therefore the Sage is able to deal successfully with things, but is not affected" (p. 119).

The spiritual crisis confronting the contemporary West became clearly manifest in the twentieth century, especially during the post-World War II era and the counter-culture of the 1960s, when the West's spiritual heritage was being ignored, if not discarded, by the ascendancy of a materialistic ethos. It was in this social ambiance that the traditions of the East—Hinduism, Taoism and Buddhism—were introduced to the West. One of the central shortcomings of the West's encounter with the East was the lack of accurate and reliable information on the Eastern teachings. It is in this context that J.C. Cooper's work is significant, for it provides a dependable introduction to Taoism, one of the three great religions of China. In a world where so much disharmony and disequilibrium dominate, there is much need for the return to the primordial unity where harmony and equilibrium can be found as "the Sages of old" have instructed and demonstrated. We conclude with the words of Chuang Tzu: "Knowledge of the Great Unity—this alone is perfection" (p. 61).

Part III

The First Peoples Religion and their Shamanic Traditions

7

*The Spiritual Legacy of the American Indian: Commemorative Edition with Letters**

The Spiritual Legacy of the American Indian contains an impressive collection of Joseph Epes Brown's classic essays in Native American studies, written over the first thirty-seven years of his academic career. The book, originally published in 1982 by Crossroad Publishing, has been out of print for some years. This commemorative edition contains an informative preface by the editors—Brown's wife, his eldest daughter, and ethnographer Michael Oren Fitzgerald, who was for three semesters his teaching assistant—as well as an introduction by the distinguished Swedish scholar Åke Hultkrantz (1920–2006). Also included within this commemorative edition is a section of previously unpublished letters by Brown, including personal correspondence he authored while he was conducting research and living with Black Elk, or *Hehaka Sapa* (1863–1950), the renowned twentieth-century Oglala Lakota spiritual leader.

According to Black Elk, it was a "godsend" that Brown arrived on the scene to participate in the renewal of the primordial spiritual traditions of the American Indians. Joseph

---

* Joseph Epes Brown, *The Spiritual Legacy of the American Indian: Commemorative Edition with Letters While Living with Black Elk*, Introduction by Åke Hultkrantz, edited by Marina Brown Weatherly, Elenita Brown, and Michael Oren Fitzgerald. Bloomington: World Wisdom, 2007, 168pp.

Epes Brown (1920–2000) was a professional anthropologist, who was adopted by Black Elk as a son and was given the Lakota name *Chanumpa Yuha Mani*, or "He Who Walks with the Sacred Pipe." It is rare to find an academic author whose work encompasses the fullness of a culture and its traditions as does that of Joseph Epes Brown.

Brown's works in the area of Native American studies have provided a remarkable service in advancing the understanding of pre-reservation American Indian life. He was instrumental in championing the viewpoint that "Native American traditions... are legitimate expressions of the *philosophia perennis*." In his original preface to this book, Brown states that "religion", in the primordial American Indian traditions, is not perceived as a separate activity divorced from everyday life, but is a central dimension contextualizing all of life and every moment of human existence:

> It has now become abundantly clear that it is a fundamental and universal characteristic of Native American cultures, as indeed of all primal... cultures, that "religion"—there is no equivalent word for this in any American Indian language—is not a separate category of activity or experience that is divorced from cultural or society. Rather, religion is pervasively present and is in complex interrelationships with all aspects of the peoples' life-ways (p. xiii).

Brown explains that, in primordial Native American cultures, it is the Great Spirit that brings true equilibrium and integration to both the "inner" and "outer" dimensions of the human individual. To forget one's spiritual center is to be less than human and it is a great error according to every sapiential tradition worthy of name. The early peoples also understood that although the Great Spirit was transcendent, it was immanent in the heart of man too, as this quote from Black Elk illustrates: "At the center of the Universe dwells *Wakan-Tanka* [the Great Spirit], and... this center is really everywhere, it is within each of us" (p. 29).

Nature was not just the natural environment *per se*; it was perceived as sacred and could be regarded as the "metaphysics of nature"—the inner precinct or temple of the early peoples, as Black Elk explains:

> We regard all created beings as sacred and important, for everything has a *wochangi*, or influence, which can be given to us, through which we may gain a little more understanding if we are attentive. We should understand well that all things are the works of the Great Spirit. We should know that He is within all things; the trees, the grasses, the rivers, the mountains and all the four-legged animals, and the winged peoples; and even more important, we should understand that He is also above all these things and peoples (p. 28).

At one point, Brown compares the ritual smoking of the sacred pipe to the Holy Communion of Christians. He explains, "These pipes represent the human being in his totality, or the universe of which humankind is a reflection. The bowl is the heart, or sacred center, and each section of the pipe is usually identified with some part of the human being" (p. 33).

That passage reflects one of Brown's central premises: "If we can understand... the truths the Indians find in their relationships to nature, and the profound values reflected by their many rites and symbols, then *we* may become enriched, our understanding will deepen, and we shall be able to give to the American Indian heritage its rightful place among the great spiritual traditions of humankind" (p. 34).

Brown identifies three central stages in spiritual development that are also found in some form or another in the world's religions: purification, perfection or expansion, and union— "each in turn is realized and then integrated within the next stage, so that ultimately they become one in the individual who attains the ultimate goal" (p. 34). In primordial traditions, he explains, life is renewed and the sacredness of existence is perpetuated through ceremonial sacrifice, and "where there is no longer affirmation or means for sacrifice, for 'making sacred,' where the individual loses the sense of Center, the very energy of the world, it is believed, will run out" (p. 77).

The previously unpublished letters of Joseph Epes Brown contained in this book are an invaluable resource, complementing his other works, especially his classic text *The Sacred Pipe: Black Elk's Account of the Seven Rites of the Oglala Sioux* (1953). These letters are particularly significant in that they provide new information regarding Black Elk's relationship to the Catholic Church and Lakota spirituality, and they disclose intimate details of Brown's participation in the work of restoring American Indian traditions.

Brown's letters indicate that the imminent crisis currently confronting the world was clearly foreseen by American Indian spiritual people. In one letter, he relates how Black Elk confided to him: "We have reached the end of a cycle; and leading into the beginning of the next new cycle there is a very narrow bridge... a great disaster is impending which shall bring this cycle to a close." (pp. 105–106)

Nonetheless, Black Elk's perennial wisdom posits that there is an alternative to the present disintegration of the modern and postmodern world, and that is to bring back the "Eye of the Heart" (*Chante Ishta*). Black Elk explains it in this way:

> I am blind and do not see the things of this world; but when the Light comes from Above, it enlightens my Heart and I can see, for the Eye of my Heart sees everything; and through this vision I can help my people. The heart is a sanctuary at the Center of which there is a little space, wherein *Wakan-Tanka* [the Great Spirit] dwells, and this is the Eye. This is the Eye of *Wakan-Tanka* [the Great Spirit] by which He sees all things, and through which we see Him.... In order to know the Center of the Heart in which is the Mind of *Wakan-Tanka* [the Great Spirit], you must

be pure and good, and live in the manner that *Wakan-Tanka* [the Great Spirit] has taught us. The man who is thus pure contains the Universe within the Pocket of his Heart (*Chante oqnaka*)" (p. 106).

Readers should benefit immensely from Brown's extensive knowledge of the first inhabitants of this continent. It is rare to find scholars who simultaneously exhibit both spiritual insight and profound empathy for the American Indian traditions, as Joseph Epes Brown does. We trust that this book will assist in the ongoing renewal of traditional American Indian spirituality—and also enrich studies in the *philosophia perennis*, "that perennial and timeless wisdom valid 'now and forever.'"

8

*Black Elk, Lakota Visionary: The Oglala Holy Man and Sioux Tradition**

> We Indians know the One true God, and we pray to Him continually.
>
> Black Elk[1]

Millions have been inspired around the world by the life and spiritual legacy of the Lakota holy man, Hehaka Sapa, more commonly known as Black Elk (1863–1950). It is in large part through John G. Neihardt's book *Black Elk Speaks*, first published in 1932, that Black Elk became widely known and revered. Even though numerous books have been written about the Lakota *wicasa wakan* or holy man, Harry Oldmeadow's book is indispensable as it not only corrects the historical record through drawing upon recently discovered sources, but situates Black Elk within a universal context that extends across the world's religions. This engaging account by Oldmeadow explores the fascinating life of Black Elk, his visions, his relationship with Catholicism, and his diligent efforts to revive the First Peoples religion.

---

* Harry Oldmeadow, *Black Elk, Lakota Visionary: The Oglala Holy Man and Sioux Tradition*. Foreword by Charles Trimble. Bloomington: World Wisdom, 2018, 256pp.

[1] "Foreword," to Joseph Epes Brown, *The Sacred Pipe: Black Elk's Account of the Seven Rites of the Oglala Sioux*, p. xx.

This book contrasts the misguided notions of "the vanishing Indian" and that the First Peoples are relics of history to be viewed solely in museums or in the anthropology aisles of the library as reminders of a distant and romanticized past. In fact the opposite is true. The First Peoples are still here and, although not generally known, there is a growing revival of the American Indian religion. It is without a doubt that the trauma of colonialism, racism, and forced assimilation has caused irreversible damage to the First Peoples, and it is with great sensitivity and respect that we recall anew the important reminder of Joseph Epes Brown (1920–2000), a renowned scholar of Native American traditions and world religions: "We are still very far from being aware of the dimensions and ramifications and our ethnocentric illusions. Nevertheless, by the very nature of things we are now forced to undergo a process of intense self-examination; to engage in a serious re-evaluation of the premises and orientations of our society" (p. 12). Oldmeadow suggests that a key obstacle with understanding the American Indian or any First Peoples religion is that "The extirpation of indigenous cultures is, *essentially*, not a clash of 'races' or even 'civilizations' but of Tradition and modernity."

Oldmeadow presents his three convictions for preparing this book on Black Elk:

> First, the spiritual heritage of the Plains Indians deserves a more honored and more fully understood place among the world's great religious traditions; second, Black Elk's account of his early life, his Great Vision, and the principal rituals of the Lakota comprise an eloquent expression of the heritage and one of the most radiant spiritual testimonies of our time; third, the Lakota visionary and his tradition offer the contemporary world profound lessons of the most urgent importance (p. xiii).

Oldmeadow clarifies from the onset that this book is not intended to be "a full-dress biography, nor a history, nor a systematic account of Lakota religious life" (p. xvi). The book consists of seven chapters and of three appendices that contain excerpts and selections from letters which help further situate Black Elk's life and important mission.

Oldmeadow proposes that any research conducted on Black Elk requires the following three books: *Black Elk Speaks* (1932) by John G. Neihardt; *The Sacred Pipe* (1953) by Joseph Epes Brown; and *The Sixth Grandfather* (1984) by Raymond DeMallie. He additionally examines the controversies that surrounded Black Elk and his collaborators, Neihardt (1881–1973) and Brown. While Neihardt's book provides a fascinating narrative on Black Elk and his remarkable visions, Brown's provides a more articulate presentation of traditional Lakota metaphysics, cosmology, and ritual life. DeMallie's book brings to light for the first time the transcripts from Neihardt's interviews with Black Elk obtained in 1931 and 1944 that formed the basis for *Black Elk Speaks* and *When the Tree Flowered* (1951). As well-intentioned as Neihardt was, DeMallie's book presents how Neihardt introduced and omitted information that was not as Black Elk shared with him. Yet it is safe to say that without Neihardt's book, non-Native peoples would know much less about the pre-reservation days and the sacred traditions of the Lakota.

Black Elk's conversion to Catholicism was surrounded by controversy and often misunderstood. Oldmeadow points out that there are three distinct schools of thought pertaining to Black Elk's relationship to the Christian tradition: "(a) no more than an expedient stratagem and that he remained true to the ancestral ways; (b) deep and sincere, entailing a repudiation of his old beliefs; or that (c) he somehow blended and reconciled Lakota tradition and Christianity" (p. 46).

Brown corresponded with anthropologist and one-time student Michael Steltenkamp about Black Elk's involvement with the Christian tradition: "I have felt it improper that this phase of [Black Elk's] life was never presented either by Neihardt or indeed by myself. I suppose somehow it was thought this Christian participation compromised his 'Indianness,' but I do not see it this way and think it time that the record was set straight." Some have suggested that Brown had deliberately structured his book by drawing a parallel between the seven Lakota rites and the seven sacraments of the Catholic Church, but this assertion according to Oldmeadow appears to be little more than a coincidence.

Brown provides a cogent account of Black Elk's "conversion" phenomenon through a lens that both situates the uniqueness and embraces all the sapiential traditions of the world:

> Throughout virtually all indigenous American Indian traditions, a pervasive theme has been that all forms and forces of all orders of the immediately experienced natural environment may communicate to human beings the totality of that which is to be known of the sacred mysteries of creation, and thus of the sacred essence of being and beings.... Such conditioning to openness of mind and being towards manifestations of the sacred makes it understandable that for these peoples religious matters of whatever origin are not open to either question or argument. When, therefore, the Christian message came to the peoples through dedicated missionaries who led exemplary and sacrificial lives, the people easily understood the truths of message and example due to the profundity of their own beliefs; it was not difficult for them to adapt new expressions of values into the sacred fabric of their own culture. The historical phenomenon is thus not conversion as understood in an exclusivistic manner by the bearers of Christianity, but rather a continuation of the people's ancient and traditional facility for what may be termed non-exclusive cumulative adhesion. If this process of polysynthesis can be accomplished with neither confusion nor dissonance, it is ultimately due to the ability of American Indian peoples to penetrate and comprehend

the central and most profound nature of all experience and reality (p. 110).

While it is true that Black Elk does at times make exclusivist claims suggesting that Catholicism replaced the old beliefs and practices of the Lakota traditions, these statements need to take into consideration the Jesuit disapproval of the book *Black Elk Speaks* and how this condemnation impacted Black Elk. American anthropologist Raymond DeMallie explains:

> [The publication of *Black Elk Speaks*] put Black Elk in an awkward position in relation to the Catholic Church. His reputation on the reservation was built as a Catholic catechist, not as a native religious leader. The Jesuit priests at Holy Rosary Mission were shocked and horrified at the suggestion that one of their most valued catechists still harbored beliefs in the old Indian religion. For them to accept *Black Elk Speaks* at face value necessarily called into question the genuineness of their success in converting the Lakotas to Catholicism. Rather than accepting the book as a true representation of Black Elk, they blamed Neihardt for telling only part of Black Elk's story. The priests objected most strongly to the epilogue portraying Black Elk as a believing, practicing "pagan" praying to the six grandfathers when he knew well that the Christian God was the only source of salvation. Ben Black Elk told the missionaries, no doubt truthfully, that he and his father had not realized that Neihardt intended to include the final prayer on Harney Peak in the book. Although the old man was embarrassed in front of the priests... he never denied the sincerity of his final appeal to the six grandfathers (pp. 102–103).

Brown's arrival, anticipated by the holy man himself, is a continuation of where Neihardt's work left off, yet Brown's work is centered on establishing a resurgence of Lakota spirituality. Michael Oren Fitzgerald notes the relevance of Brown's letters that have recently been made available:

> [They] provide a final chapter to Black Elk's life because of their sharp contrast to the despair in Black Elk's closing words in *Black Elk Speaks*, "you see me now a pitiful old man who has done nothing, for the nation's hoop is broken and scattered. There is no center any longer, and the sacred tree is dead." These words were spoken at a time when most American Indian traditional ceremonies were still outlawed.... Joseph Brown's arrival in 1947 was a catalyst that provided Black Elk the practical support to work toward perpetuating ancestral spiritual traditions, both through the recording of his account of the seven sacred rites of the Lakota and through Black Elk's efforts to reestablish an "Order of the Pipe" for his tribe (p. 112).

We are informed by Black Elk's daughter, Lucy Looks Twice, that during his last days, far from rejecting the traditional Lakota spirituality, Black Elk had emphasized that "The only thing I [Black Elk] really believe in is the pipe religion" (p. 99). Brown recounts that "Black Elk says he is sorry that his present action towards reviving Lakota spiritual traditions shall anger the priests, but that their anger is proof of their ignorance; and in any case *Wakan-Tanka* [the Great Spirit] is happy; for he knows that it is His Will that Black Elk does this work" (p. 112).

A missing link that is little known is Black Elk's association with Frithjof Schuon (1907–1998), foremost spokesman for the perennial philosophy, and how this relationship aided in the larger context of the Lakota holy man's mission. It was Schuon who, after reading the book *Black Elk Speaks*, felt that Black Elk had more to reveal about his religion, and asked his collaborators if there was someone who could try to find Black Elk. This proposition was discussed with Brown, who agreed to it and was able to find Black Elk in South Dakota in

September 1947; again, Brown's arrival was anticipated by the holy man himself.

Brown lived with Black Elk and his family for extended times over a two-year period. During this time, Schuon corresponded not only with Brown but also with Black Elk himself. We are told that the reason that Black Elk chose Brown to record the sacred rites of the Lakota was because he was sent by a "holy man from the East." Lucy Looks Twice (1907–1978), recalled to Brown about the Lakota holy man's final weeks, as Brown informs readers:

> Every afternoon at about the same time he would go into something of a trance as if he were talking with some unseen person. Once he scolded his daughter-in-law for entering the house at that time, for he said that she had made the man leave. When they asked him who it was who came to talk with him (more precisely this person came to pray for Black Elk, saying that he knew he was soon to die, and he wished to help him in his suffering), he said it was "a holy man from Europe." His relatives were frightened by these experiences, and Mrs. Looks Twice noticing a large wooden rosary which always hung over his bed—a Moroccan one that I had given him because of his fondness for beads, and for the *barakah*—took this away from him, and according to her after this he did not talk anymore with the "strange man." At Black Elk's death, possibly thinking that it had not been right to do this, she saw that this rosary was buried in the coffin with him (p. 116).

Schuon had written an introduction to the first French edition of *The Sacred Pipe*, and when parts of this introduction were read to Black Elk by Brown, he is reported to have been "extremely pleased." Additionally, it is not generally known that Black Elk was also in correspondence with Schuon's brother, Erich Schuon, who was a Trappist monk known as Father Gall (1906–1991). Black Elk adopted Father Gall as his son, whom he named Lakota Ishnala or "Lone Sioux" and

"[Black Elk] said that he had told you that you shall always be a Lakota, for when you die, your body, which is of earth, shall remain with the white man, but your soul shall return to us" (p. 98). Frithjof Schuon was adopted into both the Lakota and the Crow tribes.

The late doyen of the world's religions, Huston Smith (1919–2016), situates the First Peoples religion as one of the religions of the world: "The Native American religion embodies the *Sophia Perennis* [or perennial philosophy] in its own distinctive idiom" (p. 96). It is in this universal and metaphysical light of the perennial philosophy that the First Peoples religion needs to be situated, as Brown writes:

> It has long been necessary to situate correctly the so-called primitive religions in the context of the world's historical religions, and in so doing to recognize that in spite of many elements unfamiliar to the outsider, Native American traditions, at least where there has not been excessive compromise to the modern world, are in no sense inferior, but indeed are legitimate expressions of the *philosophia perennis*.[2]

In the great vision, Black Elk is taken to the center of the earth, where he sees the "whole hoop of the world" where all people and sentient beings are interconnected and all is rendered sacred in the Great Spirit or *Wakan-Tanka*:

> And while I stood there I saw more than I can tell and I understood more than I saw; for I was seeing in a sacred manner the shapes of all things in the spirit, and the shape of all shapes as they must live together like one being. And I saw that the sacred hoop of my people was one of many hoops that made one circle, wide as daylight and as starlight, and in the center grew one mighty flowering tree to shelter all the children of one mother and one father. And I saw that it was holy (pp. 36–37).

---

[2] Joseph Epes Brown, *The Spiritual Legacy of the American Indian*, p. 82.

The Great Spirit, as Black Elk informs us, is both transcendent and immanent:

> We should understand that all things are the work of the Great Spirit. We should know that He is *within all things*; the trees, the grasses, the rivers, the mountains, all the four-legged animals and the winged peoples; and even more important we should understand that *He is also above all these things and peoples* (p. 19).

According to Lakota metaphysics, transcendence becomes immanent at the center of the human being, allowing the Great Spirit to dwell within. As described by Oldmeadow, "The Great Spirit as Creator orders the cosmos through the seven directions (the four cardinal points, zenith, nadir, and the center where they all meet)" (p. 19).

The Lakota holy man discusses his motivation underlying the book *The Sacred Pipe*, which could also be said to indirectly refer to the book *Black Elk Speaks*:

> I [Black Elk] have wished to make this book through no other desire than to help my people in understanding the greatness and truth of our own tradition, and also help in bringing peace upon the earth, not only among men, but within men and between the whole of creation (p. 143).

One of the most celebrated and honored Lakota Sun Dance chiefs of the twentieth century, Fools Crow (1890–1989), describes Black Elk's role in preserving the First Peoples religion:

> My uncle, the renowned Black Elk, has earned a place above all of the other Teton holy men. We all hold him the highest. I have never heard a bad word about him, and he never said a bad word about anyone. All he wanted to do was love and serve his fellow man.... In the Indian custom, he was also a father to me. I stayed with him quite often, and sometimes for long periods of time. We also made a few trips together, and over the years talked about many

things. I learned a great deal about *Wakan Tanka*, prophecy, and medicine from him (pp. 45–46).

While many books have been written about the Lakota *wicasa wakan*, none have arguably explored the entirety of Black Elk's life and the centrality of his universal vision as this book by Harry Oldmeadow. We are confident that this work will assist with correcting the historical record and will draw more interest in the life and legacy of Black Elk. This book depicts how the spiritual legacy of Black Elk is instrumental in representing the ancestral traditions in the pre-reservation era, their destruction, and subsequently a powerful revival that continues into the present-day. It is in this light that Black Elk, the Lakota holy man, needs to be regarded. Through the timeless wisdom of the First Peoples religion, a corresponding universal metaphysics can be found that is at the heart of all religious and spiritual traditions of the world. It is through the Lakota saying imprinted in the hearts and minds of the people that we can identify the sacred unity within the created order: *Mitakuye oyasin*—"All my relatives" or "We are all related."

Part IV

The Buddhist Tradition

9

*Uncompromising Truth for a Compromised World: Tibetan Buddhism and Today's World**

> The Truth of Selflessness... emerges as the real remedy for all the crises of our time.
>
> Samdhong Rinpoche[1]

This book is an uncommon compilation of extraordinarily relevant themes regarding the current state of the contemporary world, presented in question and answer format to the Venerable Professor Samdhong Rinpoche. The themes explored within the text are rarely accessible to audiences outside the Tibetan community or those not practicing *Vajrayāna* (the "Diamond Vehicle") Buddhism, let alone from someone who holds a unique position of both spiritual authority and temporal power within an orthodox Tibetan Buddhist orientation, as does Samdhong Rinpoche. Another informing aspect of this book is its lack of interest in superfluous details pertaining to biographical information, which is so often overdone in today's world. The editor, Donovan Roebert, notes that

---

* Samdhong Rinpoche, *Uncompromising Truth for a Compromised World: Tibetan Buddhism and Today's World*, edited by Donovan Roebert, Foreword by H.H. the 14th Dalai Lama (World Wisdom, 2006, 264 pp.).

[1] *Ibid.*, p. 53.

"[Samdhong Rinpoche] conveyed to me his belief that it is the truth itself, and not the individual who speaks it" (p. xiv) that holds ultimate importance.

With this said, Samdhong Rinpoche was born on November 5, 1939 with the Tibetan name Lobsang Tenzin, in Nagduk village of Kham, in Eastern Tibet, before the Chinese invasion took place. He was recognized at the age of five to be the reincarnation of the Fourth Samdhong Rinpoche and was elected to be the *Kalon Tripa* or Prime Minister of the Tibetan Government-in-Exile. Following the invasion of Tibet in 1959 by the communist-inspired Chinese Army, Samdhong Rinpoche escaped into exile due to the impending threat on his life, and has since resided in India where the seat of the Tibetan Government-in-Exile resides. His Holiness Tenzin Gyatso, the 14th Dalai Lama, has contributed an insightful Foreword to this book, conveying his confidence and blessing in Samdhong Rinpoche to speak on behalf of the Tibetan people and the Tibetan Buddhist tradition.

The book is divided into the following six parts:

PART I: "THE LONG ROAD TO NOW". The editor summarizes this chapter in the following manner: "I wanted Rinpoche's views on how we have arrived at our present state. I wanted to address subjects concerning the central aspects of human history" (p. 5). Thus this chapter covers a copious spectrum of topics that will draw the interest of readers such as: Origins, Biological Evolution, Societies, Culture, Governance, Economics, Industry and Commerce, Law, Philosophy, Religion, Morality, Spirituality, Science, Art, Complexity and Escapism, Civilization and Decline and the Future in Prospect. The following paragraphs give paraphrased questions from the various sections, and then a few short representative samples of the Rinpoche's responses:

Origins: How did the physical world come into existence according to Buddhist cosmology? "In Buddhist doctrine mind has existed from beginningless time, whereas matter has a finite beginning. This also means that matter can come to an end but mind cannot; mind will always exist.... This is somewhat different from the majority of religions in our world, which believe in some form of Creator, either personal or impersonal, say, a creative force. Only the Buddhists believe in a collective karmic force rather than in some absolute Creator principle. But in my view these things only represent a difference in language, a different way of saying the same thing" (p. 8).

Biological Evolution: Does Buddhism accept evolutionary theory? "Evolution is basically a Western viewpoint" (p. 31).

Societies: What is the Buddhist point of view on the individual and his or her role in society? "What can any individual do to make the world a more compassionate place? Firstly, we must consider others as more important than ourselves! I think that is basic Truth" (p. 15).

Culture: What is the Buddhist idea of culture and how are issues of "cultural diversity" and "multiculturalism" viewed? "... Any confluence of culture should not become combined with domination or influence over each other: cultures should meet but cultures should remain within their own identity or within their own nature.... So first we should know what culture is, and secondly we should know how to converge these different cultures, and thirdly how to keep these different cultures from dominating each other, yet sharing the goodness" (p. 17).

Governance: What is the Buddhist theory of government? "I have always believed in Thoreau's saying that 'that government is best which governs the least'" (p. 19).

Economics: Are globalization ("free-market" capitalism) and spiritual life compatible?

"... So-called free trade and globalization of material things is not good for the well-being of humanity.... Globalization is very dangerous for human inner spiritual growth, human intelligence, and diversity of cultures. Cultures are being completely destroyed by the process of globalization" (p. 22).

Industry and Commerce: What was life like in earlier times before the industrial revolution and modernity? "Before the industrial revolution humanity was never deprived of their needs; all of them lived with their needs being provided by nature and by themselves, and it was good" (p. 24).

Law: What are the pitfalls of the majority rule? "The greatest demerit of today's social and democratic systems is that the representation of people is a one-way traffic, and the ideas and the rights of the minority are always superseded by the majority" (p. 28).

Philosophy: What is real knowledge? "The real knowledge of the thing is not subject to development; it is fully there from the time of its revelation and it might be transmitted down to a certain point in the lineage, then it begins to deteriorate" (p. 32).

Religion: What constitutes an authentic spiritual tradition? "But coming to the tradition of spirituality and the tradition of *Dharma*, these are again not an evolution. They are revelations of teachings coming from a Higher One. Therefore I always carefully define the word 'tradition.' An authentic tradition must have three attributes or qualities. First, it is taught or revealed by an authentic source or, we can loosely say, by a divine source. Second, it must be transmitted by means of an unbroken lineage from person to person. And third, it must be verifiable through common sense and self-knowledge. So if these three factors are present, then it is an authentic tradition. Otherwise a long perpetuated custom need not necessarily be a tradition" (p. 36).

Morality: What is ethical conduct from a Buddhist perspective? "... The seed of virtuous conduct (*Shila*) is required for one's own development and also for the establishment of social harmony" (p. 39).

Spirituality: Have spiritual traditions evolved through

time? "Spirituality is not evolved through the social and biological evolution of humankind. Spirituality is always there.... There is no evolution of spirituality" (p. 41).

Science: What is the Buddhist perspective on science? "... Scientists can learn a great deal from spirituality. Mainly they can learn that they should know the limitations of the ordinary mind.... The ordinary mind cannot attain to Absolute Truth" (p. 44).

Art: How has sacred art in the Buddhist tradition developed? "Buddhist religious art has not undergone processes of evolution.... For example, the mandala, the very complicated mandala, both mandala painting and the construction of the most complex kind: neither are the result of the gradual evolution of art.... These were revealed by the Enlightened One: how to make it, how to measure it, and how to color it; all this was revealed at the moment of beginning and has its own significance" (p. 47).

Complexity and Escapism: Can one escape worldly problems by engaging in spiritual life or spiritual practices? "There can be no spiritual practice which is motivated by the desire to escape from complexity.... In fact we have never tried to identify correctly the crisis of our time" (pp. 51–52).

Civilization and Decline: What is progress and what are the achievements of the West? "...What we have achieved is the amplification and enlargement of our vices" (p. 54).

The Future in Prospect: How will globalization affect the future of the world? "... We cannot accommodate a collective *Karma* to make everyone uniform. Diversity is a law of nature, and therefore diversity will always be there" (pp. 57–58).

PART II: THE MODERN INDIVIDUAL. This chapter examines how the human individual, by identifying with a false or fictitious "I," participates in the collective pathology or fragmentation that is rampant everywhere in the modern and post-modern world. Although Buddhism affirms the idea of *Anatman* (Sanskrit; *anatta* in Pali) or not-self versus the Hindu idea of *Atman* or self, both perspectives are metaphysically complementary (pertaining to the 'coincidence of opposites' or *coincidencia oppositorum*), not contraries, and are thus *de facto* still central to the perennial inquiry of 'who am I?' One of Samdhong Rinpoche's observations regarding the relationship between the two perspectives: "If we look more closely at the Indian tradition we find different schools of thought saying the same things in different language. The Vedic schools say that you cannot attain Enlightenment without recognizing the Atman (self) and the Buddhist schools say that you cannot attain Enlightenment without recognizing the Anatman (not-self)" (p. 69).

PART III: HUMANKIND IN SAMSARA, ON EARTH, AND IN THE UNIVERSE. This chapter covers subjects such as Environmental Destruction, Violence and War, America and the Superpower Principle, etc. The editor describes this section in this way: "I wanted Rinpoche to comment on some of the most pertinent collective ills that hold us back from achieving a present world order which might be more conformed to the truest yearnings of the whole of humanity" (p. 79). Some of Rinpoche's statements on this theme follow.

The Gap between Governments and the Governed: Are there blind-spots in democracy? "...Democracy for the most part is not real democracy. It is mostly hypocrisy. Democracy ordinarily assumes that, while the minority may have their say, the decisions are made by the majority according to the wisdom of the majority. But this is not what is actually happening today. In fact the will of a small minority leads the majority through domination over the will of the majority and by simply ignoring the majority" (p. 81).

Environmental Destruction: Is there something inherently destructive about the modern and post-modern outlook? Is there a correlation between the ecosystem and its effects upon mental health? What is the relationship between the inner and outer dimensions of the human individual? "The tendency of self-destruction and the tendency of suicide is, I think, inbuilt in postmodern civilization. And it is part of the ultra-modern or postmodern way of thinking.... Madness is the inability to discriminate between what is harmful and what is not. And I think that, in this regard, modern people have gone insane" (p. 86). Rinpoche continues:

> "One final thing I want to add here is that the outer environment is prevented from preservation due to the degradation of our inner environment. Unless we are able to improve our inner environment our efforts will not be very fruitful. Therefore, each individual should try to improve their inner environment and at the same time to act to preserve or improve the outer environment. Both should go hand in hand, otherwise we are only improving our outer environment, and this will carry us only so far" (p. 88).

PART IV: TIBET—THE MODERN WORLD'S HIDDEN TRAGEDY. In this section the reader can learn in more detail about the atrocities that have taken place and continue to be inflicted upon the Tibetan people under Chinese occupation and how these atrocities were and are still being ignored by the majority of the international community. Rinpoche states: "... The Tibetan race, has as its responsibility to preserve, promote, and disseminate a certain spiritual heritage, and this has been the case for the last 1500 years at least. Its particular responsibility or job has been to preserve a Buddhist-related spiritual heritage and Buddhist culture, for their own people and for the neighboring peoples: Mongolia, Manchuria, China, India. These neighbors were being benefited by the Tibetan people, and the Tibetan people were not meant to build up economic power or military power or political power. Their main responsibility was to the Buddhist spiritual and cultural heritage" (p. 138).

PART V: SATYAGRAHA AND AHIMSA (TRUTH-INSISTENCE AND NON-HARMFULNESS). It is here where one can learn more about Samdhong Rinpoche's efforts to promote a non-violent approach as did Mahatma Gandhi for the Indian people. Samdhong Rinpoche has taken a similar stand towards the cruelty and violence that the Tibetan people continue to experience in present-day Tibet. Samdhong Rinpoche relates the principles of *Satyagraha* and *Ahimsa* in a universal context as they apply to the religions of the world:

> So I would say that *Satyagraha* is an inviolable principle of all religious traditions—as far as my knowledge goes—no spiritual teaching would say that you can or should compromise the Truth. It cannot be given up to the convenience of worldly life. No teacher of Truth would teach against this principle.... The explanation of Truth may differ from religion to religion, but the importance of Truth and of remaining with that Truth: in this regard all religions are the same. And particularly when coming to Buddhism, we have more to consider. Buddhist teaching is unlike most of the other religious traditions in that it speaks of two different truths: the Absolute Truth and the relative or conventional truth (p. 169).

PART VI: THE FOUNDATIONAL VIEW—BUDDHADHARMA. This last section provides more extensive and specific details about Buddhist teachings. These teachings are presented in a manner that is accurate, clear and concise, benefitting those readers who are non-Buddhist, or who know very little, to those who have a firm footing on the Buddhist path. Here is an example of one important clarification from Rinpoche: "Today when we talk about the Buddha's teaching of selflessness or the not-self or *Shunyata* [emptiness], people mostly cannot comprehend the real connotations of these teachings; and they always fall into the error of negating the relative self. When you speak of selflessness, they take it to mean that they are completely devoid of self, that self does not exist at all" (p. 202). He also addresses a point that is often taken out of context and confused in the West amongst spiritual seekers and which can lead to the distortion of the mystical and esoteric dimensions of spiritual traditions: "You cannot be deceived by your inner teacher.... [However, it should be understood that] for very beginners, I don't think that without external guidance or without the transmission of an outer teacher, you can simply rely on books or your 'inner teacher'" (p. 227).

These dialogues with Samdhong Rinpoche will provide substantial support to spiritual seekers as they challenge the very assumptions that are crucial to the current era. In fact he makes it clear that the crisis of the post-modern world is no longer isolated in the West alone; it has become a global issue of paramount concern to all peoples. Samdhong Rinpoche's message is one of a primordial tradition that has only become available to those outside the Tibetan community relatively recently and is, it goes without saying, a tremendous blessing to the world. Yet it should be remembered that the disarray of this traditional civilization, while making this enlightened wisdom accessible, came at a tremendous price for the Tibetan people and the world at large. Perhaps it is the same price that all individuals living in the present epoch pay continually—to live in a troubled and broken world.

10

*Honen the Buddhist Saint: Essential Writings and Official Biography**

> Only repeat the name of Amida [Amitābha] with all your heart. Whether walking or standing, sitting or lying, never cease the practice of it even for a moment. This is the very work which unfailingly issues in salvation, for it is in accordance with the Original Vow of that Buddha.
>
> Zendō (Shan-tao)[1]

This is a remarkably accessible edition of the original volume that was first translated in 1925 by Reverend Harper Havelock Coates and Reverend Ryugaku Ishizuka, entitled *Honen the Buddhist Saint: His Life and Teaching* (1925). The initial work was encyclopedic in scope, consisting of five volumes offering the most detailed study of Hōnen available in the English language. The drawback of this monumental work was its inaccessibility, as it was daunting for Buddhist practitioners and lay readers to approach. However, this new abridged edition makes Hōnen available to Buddhist practitioners and general seekers alike providing what is most noteworthy in the

---

* Edited by Joseph A. Fitzgerald, Introduction by Alfred Bloom, Foreword by Clark Strand, Translated by Reverend Harper Havelock Coates and Reverend Ryugaku Ishizuka. World Wisdom, 2006, 192pp.

[1] *Ibid.*, p. 20.

life of this great medieval Japanese monk and his teachings. The Introduction contains a comprehensive overview of Pure Land Buddhism written by Alfred Bloom, a foremost authority on Shin Buddhism, and there is also a Foreword by Clark Strand, a Buddhist teacher, practitioner, and writer.

Hōnen Shōnin (1133–1212; Buddhist name: Genkū) was a 12th century Buddhist priest and saint, revered as the founder of the Jōdo (Pure Land) school of Buddhism, and as the master of preeminent disciples such as Shinran (1173–1263). It is striking that although the practice of Pure Land Buddhism (Jōdo-shū) continues to increase, with an estimated twenty million living practitioners in Japan alone, the spiritual legacy of Hōnen has for the most part not been recognized in the West. Hōnen understood the challenges of the socio-religious upheavals of the era in which he lived, and this led him to emphasize the significance of a spiritual method that could accommodate the diverse types of human beings regardless of socio-economic status or even spiritual literacy. Hōnen devoted his life to teaching and practicing *Nembutsu*—the repetition of *Namu Amida Butsu*—"Hail to Amitābha Buddha" or "the Name of Amida Buddha," which he confirmed was a method available to all who practiced it with devotion and sincerity, especially for those living in an age marked by the "decline of the Dharma" (*mappō*):

> In the next place, if we look at it from the standpoint of difficulty and ease, the *Nembutsu* is easily practiced, while it is very hard to practice all the other disciplines. For the above reasons thus briefly stated, we may say that the *Nembutsu*, being so easily practiced, is of universal application.... If the Original Vow required the making of images and the building of pagodas, then the poor and destitute could have no hope of attaining it. But the fact is that the wealthy and noble are few in number, whereas the number of the poor and ignoble is extremely large. If the Original Vow required wisdom and great talent, there

would be no hope of that birth for the foolish and ignorant at all; but the wise are few in number, while the foolish are very many.... We conclude therefore, that Amida Nyorai, when He was a priest by the name of Hōzō [Dharmākara] ages ago, in His compassion for all sentient beings alike, and in His effort for the salvation of all, did not vow to require the making of images or the building of pagodas conditions for birth into the Pure Land, but only the one act of calling upon His sacred name (p. 66).

It needs to be remembered that Hōnen did not invent the spiritual method of *Nembutsu*. This method was known and practiced under different names and forms—it is ancient and primordial—providing an integral approach to the interfaith dialogue that the current world urgently needs. The spiritual method of *Nembutsu* taught by Hōnen is the quintessence of Hindu *japa-yoga*: "He who thinks of Me constantly" (*Bhagavad Gītā* 8:14); in the *Zohar* (*Book of Splendor*) of Jewish mysticism, "The Holy One speaks His Name"; in Christianity it is known as the "Jesus Prayer" or "Prayer of the Heart", exemplified by St. Paul's admonition "Pray without ceasing" (1 Thessalonians 5:17); in the *dhikr* of Sufism (*taṣawwuf*), or the mystical dimension of Islam "Remember Me and I will remember you" (Qur'ān 2:152). This also extends to the religions of the First Peoples and Shamanic traditions, for they "know the One true God [*Wankan-Tanka*, the Great Spirit] and... pray to Him continually,"[2] as Hehaka Sapa or Black Elk (1863–1950) confirmed. Hōnen reminds the modern world of a universal method by which the resuscitation of the central organ of all spiritual traditions, East and West, may be born anew and thus flourish once again.

---

[2] Black Elk, "Foreword," to Joseph Epes Brown, *The Sacred Pipe: Black Elk's Account of the Seven Rites of the Oglala Sioux*, p. xx.

Part V

The Jewish Tradition

11

*Universal Aspects of the Kabbalah and Judaism**

> And the whole earth was of one language, and of one speech.
>
> Genesis 11:1

For those who have yet to discover the work of Leo Schaya (1916–1986),[1] it will be of interest that he was born into a family with Hasidic roots and with rabbis in its ancestry, received a traditional Jewish upbringing, and remained attuned with the quintessence of the Jewish tradition until his death. Some readers may recall that he is the author of the much-acclaimed book *The Universal Meaning of the Kabbalah* (1958), and was for a time editor of the French journal *Études Traditionnelles* (*Traditional Studies*) and founding editor of *Connaissance des Religions* (*Knowledge of Religions*). This new volume, *Universal Aspects of the Kabbalah and Judaism*, which is only his second book to be published in English, is a collection of Schaya's writings on the central theme of the "universal aspects" revealed in Judaism yet present in all the great religious

---

* Schaya, Leo, *Universal Aspects of the Kabbalah and Judaism*. Roger Gaetani (ed.). Bloomington: World Wisdom, 200 pp.

[1] See Robert G. Margolis, "At 'The Meeting of the Two Seas': An Introduction to Leo Schaya and His Writings," *Annals of Japan Association for Middle East Studies*, No. 13 (1988), pp. 399–418.

traditions. This book also includes an informative Preface by the Editor Roger Gaetani, and a Foreword by Patrick Laude, a distinguished perennialist writer; both of these pieces contribute important analyses of Schaya's work.

According to Jewish mystical exegesis, the one "language" of the above epigraph from the Torah may be understood as a direct reference to the *unanimous tradition*,[2] found not only within the Abrahamic monotheisms—Judaism, Christianity and Islam—but in all sapiential traditions of the East and West. It is from this point of departure that one is able to comprehend certain contentions that exist between the religions in their outer forms. Each religion in its orthodoxy confirms its own validity, and logically so, because it is addressing its own community, and until recently did not need to validate the truth of other religions.

It is in the modern and postmodern world that an unprecedented phenomenon has taken place: diverse beliefs now find themselves living beside one another, unlike in any previous era, thus indicating the urgent need for a deeper religious pluralism with better delineated bridges between faiths. To understand the relationship between human diversity and religious pluralism, one can greatly benefit from the integral framework provided by the perennial philosophy in order to make the forms of religion intelligible to one's own faith tradition. It is not enough to know that people have different faiths; one must know why they differ and simultaneously what unifies them at their metaphysical roots. Through this framework, human diversity is reflected in religious pluralism, and it is in this dissociation from the sacred that we become estranged from our own natures as beings created "in God's image", and from our common spiritual heritage, as Schaya illustrates:

---

[2] See Ranjit Fernando (ed.), *The Unanimous Tradition: Essays on the Essential Unity of All Religions* (Colombo: Sri Lanka Institute of Traditional Studies, 1999).

Human unity, initially traditional, by raising such a revolt against the divine Unity, compelled the latter to break it into ethnic fragments, dispersed over the entire earth and henceforth opposed one to another: and this through a lack of understanding caused by the confusion, or more precisely by the differentiation of their 'language' or single tradition into several 'languages' or divergent traditions, but with a foundation that remains unanimous thanks to its divine essence (p. 10).

A considerable obstacle in understanding religion today is the rise of secularism, religious fundamentalism and New Age pseudo-religions that concurrently obscure and disfigure what religion means in its fullness. This is precisely why religion, whose inner dimensions are neglected, cannot reveal its corresponding transcendent and universal dimension. A unique and paramount feature of this work under review is its exploration of the Jewish tradition by way of its mystical roots, which simultaneously elucidates its common ground with other religions. Although the mainstream media mistakenly confounds the distinction between the Jewish tradition and the identity and activities of the secular and political State of Israel, this is erroneous, for Judaism is not Zionism. This false premise has had and continues to have horrific consequences, not only for the plight of the Palestinians but for Jews, Christians and Muslims everywhere. In realizing that each religion has its temporal manifestation, and has been disclosed to different human communities in accordance with their needs and capacities, we are better able to discern the pre-temporal source of the unanimous tradition from which they derive: "What is fundamentally true of Judaism is also true of all genuine religions and traditions: there is but one Absolute, one Real, one God, the basis of all the revelations and their formal antinomies, the basis of all apparent dualism" (p. 26). Schaya once responded to a seeker by way of alluding to the Unity found at the heart of all authentic religions: "We are unconditional devotees of the Absolute!" (*Nous sommes des inconditionnels de l'Absolu!*; p. xiii). For, according to Schaya, each revelation aspires "to spiritualize man and finally reintegrate him with the Divine Absolute" (p. 1).

At the cornerstone of Schaya's work, two distinct and yet complementary facets of religion are at the foreground of the entire work, namely the outer and inner dimensions, for both are essential in understanding each revelation in its own and shared context. It is through the exoteric (or the outer) dimension that the wayfarer can prepare for the esoteric (or the inner) dimension. Although all paths ultimately lead to the Divine, we cannot circumvent the religious forms to access their interior, as we must travel one of those paths that have been readied and time-honored through the saints and sages of a particular tradition. It is in this context that we can better understand the esoteric dimension within the Jewish tradition, specifically as it applies to the Kabbalah:

> The word *qibbel*, 'he received'—as in the term *qabbalah*—is derived from *qabbel*, which means 'to receive,' but also 'to welcome' and 'to accept,' and implies also the ideas of being 'face to face with' or 'in the presence of' (*haqbel, qabbal*); here, it indicates direct reception of divine revelation by the man who is ready to accept it, to welcome it, standing before the Revelation's very source, in His very Presence, which brings enlightenment and redemption (p. 48).

Although the mistaken belief is rampant that religion is man-made, there is in fact nothing within religion that can be deemed to be a product of the human mind, for this would disavow transcendence and its essential importance to spiritual realization. Even though religion has been negatively labeled "organized religion," and not without some cause due to the antagonism it has faced and continues to face in the contemporary world, we must turn our minds once again to the original function of religion itself. In order to understand what religion signifies beyond present-day biases, we must return to the etymological root of the English word "religion", from the Latin *religare*, meaning "to re-bind," or "to bind back," by implication to the Divine or the Supreme Identity. For this reason, the popular thesis asserting "Spiritual but not religious," which now has its own acronym "SBNR", is not only a sign of the times but an impossible feat, since the human individual cannot transcend him or herself without access to what is beyond the human state.

We cannot enact the Psalmist's injunction to "take off the veil from mine eyes..." (119:18) without first adhering to an authentic religious form. The veil exists for the protection of the seeker, and it cannot be lifted prematurely without grave consequences; this is articulated in various ways through the traditional exegeses. In the same way that we give common courtesy to a friend by entering the house through the front and not the back door, we must likewise embark on the spiritual path through one of the revealed traditions and not attempt to access its precinct without the consent and blessing of the religion. The relevance of the Kabbalah for the Jewish tradition is of utmost importance in this context, inasmuch as the exoteric and esoteric domains are inseparable from the revelation of the Torah which Moses received on Mount Sinai:

> Moses [and with him the whole of Israel] received (*qibbel* = *qabbalah*) the written [and spoken] Torah on the summit of Mount Sinai: he transmitted it [with all its basic interpretations, rules, and levels of sacred exegesis, both esoteric and exoteric] to Joshua; Joshua transmitted it to the Elders, the leaders to the Prophets, and the Prophets transmitted it to the men of the Great Synagogue (*Pirkei Avot* 1:1, p. 63).

Through the spiritual hermeneutics of the perennial philosophy, the exoteric and esoteric domains meet one another in the Jewish tradition, in what Schaya terms the "inward Sinai". In participating in these two domains, the traveler may acquire the direct perception that "God is hidden in everything He creates," and also that "The entire creation is an illusory projection of the transcendental aspects of God into the 'mirror' of His immanence" (p. 94). Through this framework the Divine forms become transparent and the Semitic monotheisms of Judaism, Christianity and Islam converge with the revelations of the East in the affirmation of the "One without second". The connection between the Torah and the Kabbalah is made in the following analogy contained in the *Zohar*, and in principle it is more broadly analogous to the underlying realities found in the various traditions:

> The foolish see only the clothing of a man; if it is beautiful, the wearer is also beautiful. But the clothing covers something even more precious, and that is the soul. The Torah also has a body, which is the commandments [objects of the *Halakhah*]... it also has raiment, and those are the narrations corresponding to the *Haggadah* which, from one point of view, is inferior to the *Halakhah*, and, from another, superior.... Finally the Torah has a soul which was penetrated by those who were present near Mount Sinai, that is the fundamental root of all things, the real Torah [the real, revealing, and redeeming Presence of God, which is realized directly by the Kabbalah] (3152a) (pp. 64–65).

In fact this symbolism could be extended to the meaning of the human body according to the Kabbalah: "God created the human body 'in His image,' the image of the infinite 'Body' of the ten *Sefirot*, so that man, realizing his 'deiformity' can return from his 'fall-point' to his supreme starting point" (p. 71).

Schaya demonstrates that the Jewish tradition may be viewed symbolically as, "man—personified in Moses—ascending towards God while raising the fallen world with him so as to unite everything with the One at the summit of the Mountain of Illumination" (p. 8). In contradistinction, the Christian tradition may be viewed as "God descend[ing] into the world, incarnate as man, to bear his sins, to atone for him, to be assimilated by him, until 'man becomes God'" (p. 8). For this reason Christianity was thus contrasted with Judaism in an astute statement made in the Middle Ages: "The teaching [or doctrine] of Moses conceals what the teaching of Christ reveals" (*Moysis doctrina velat quod Christi doctrina revelat*). In the final disclosure of the Abrahamic monotheisms, the Islamic tradition has been articulated as "man is obedient to the One until his extinction in Him who is 'God in Heaven and God on Earth'" (p. 8). Islam, Schaya informs readers, has a unique role as the last revelation in the current temporal cycle, "Islam... actualizes... the *religio perennis*" and moreover:

> Islam is the 'last point' of the present circle or cycle of revelations—sealed by the 'Seal of the Prophets,' Muhammad—the final point which rejoins the primordial Point, the One revealing Himself to the whole of Humanity. This is why the religion of Muhammad confirms all earlier true beliefs, of which it represents both the everlasting quintessence and the final synthesis (p. 155).

From this point of view one can better coutextualize Islam's criticism of Jews and Christians as it relates to their deviations from the pure monotheism of Abraham; however, Islam does not dispute the validity of these traditions as they are both revealed expressions of the One.

It is at the culmination of the temporal cycle known in Hinduism as the *Kali-Yuga*, a principle not uncommon throughout the religions of the world, that we observe the human collectivity situated furthest away from the Divine radiance: "The traditions declare that we are now in the last age" (p. 42).

Another universal facet, found not only in Judaism but in all of the sapiential traditions, is the spiritual method of invocation of the Divine Name as prescribed at the end of the temporal cycle: "The Divine Name must be kept holy continuously and, in principle, it unites man with God at all times. Every day of his life, man must invoke the Name which saves and delivers him, and which so fills him with the Divine

Presence that It abides, remains, and acts within him as a living temple" (p. 56). It may possibly be the loss of the invocation of the Name YHVH that brought about the many punishments and deprivations, not to mention the loss of immanent union with the Divine that befell the Israelites.

Schaya poses a question of utmost relevance which in these desacralized times compels the modern mind to step back away from itself so that it can envision a resacralized world, a world that would recover its center: "If all men were immersed in contemplation of the only Truth and only Reality, where would the problems of humanity be? And if all those who have become incapable of such contemplation were to pray, if they were to serve the contemplatives and follow their advice, where would their difficulties be?" (p. 178). Schaya, in accord with the religious and spiritual traditions, goes on to state, unequivocally, that "the true destiny of man is contemplation" (p. 178). In commencing all activity through the contemplation of these integral metaphysical principles, we can ourselves return to the source of all that is.

It is clear that we can no longer turn our backs on the urgent need for thoughtful rather than superficial religious pluralism. It is easy to see that the consequences of doing so are far too great and that the human collectivity is already bearing witness to horrific events done in the name of religion.

From the myriad writings to appear on the subject of the Kabbalah, Leo Schaya's are some of the most referenced. This is for a good reason, as they continuously plumb the rich well of the Torah, and particularly its mystical dimension, in order to illuminate the fullness of the Jewish tradition. It is through works such as these that we can comprehend what we all share in common, but also how best to view our differences—namely, through the principle of unity in diversity. Schaya has provided contemporaries with an unerring compass, one which, if heeded, may, through the application of universal metaphysical principles, guide us through many of the pressing dilemmas confronting the modern and postmodern world. It is in times like these that we are especially reminded of the adage of the Kabbalists, which is also true for the perennial philosophy, "it is better to divulge Wisdom than to forget it."[3] It is our hope that this new collection of Schaya's work will allow readers who are within the fold of Judaism, as well as those from other faiths, to perceive the reality of our common heritage in the One, and then to think and act accordingly as a consequence. "Lift up your eyes on high and behold who has created these [things]" (Isaiah 40:26).

---

[3] Quoted in Frithjof Schuon, *The Transfiguration of Man* (Bloomington: World Wisdom Books, 1995), p. 10.

Part VI

The Christian Tradition

12

*The Rationale Divinorum Officiorum: The Foundational Symbolism of the Early Church, its Structure, Decoration, Sacraments, and Vestments**

> The parables of knowledge are in the treasures of wisdom.
>
> Ecclesiasticus 1:25

The world has seemingly been turned on its head—for we live in a time of great parody and confusion with conflicting and deceptive voices, as alluded to by Biblical passages that tell of "[men] speaking perverse things" (Acts 20:30), "vain talkers and seducers" (Titus 1:10), "erring and driving into error" (2 Timothy 3:13), all trademarks of modernism. In 1907, Pope Pius X (1835–1914) astutely diagnosed modernism as "the synthesis of all heresies."[1] The French metaphysician René Guénon (1886–1951) exposed what he termed the "modern deviation" in an unparalleled fashion in 1927:

> There can be nothing but antagonism between the religious spirit, in the true sense of the word, and the modern mentality, and any compromise is bound to weaken the

---

* Guilielmus Durandus. Louisville, KY: Fons Vitae, 2007, 480pp.
[1] Pope Pius X, *Pascendi Dominici Gregis* (September 8, 1907).

former and favor the latter, whose hostility moreover will not be placated thereby, since it can only aim at the utter destruction of everything that reflects in mankind a reality higher than the human."[2]

Intellectual myopia is today a proliferating symptom due to the eclipse of the Sacred, and so how does the contemporary mind go about understanding a medieval liturgical treatise such as *The Rationale Divinorum Officiorum* at a time when the forces of a desacralized world appear to be gaining momentum?

To do so, one has to suspend, if not unlearn, all that one has allegedly learned about the Middle Ages. In this process, it will become apparent how profoundly biased the contemporary mind is regarding its history and how many misconceptions prevail in particular about the Middle Ages, portraying it in negative terms as a backward and dark age. In contrast, the post-medieval world is celebrated, with the Renaissance, the Scientific Revolution and the European Enlightenment, being glorified as the forerunners of the modern and post-modern world. These events ushered in the secular outlook that dominates today, which is essentially non-Christian, even though the contemporary West continues to be mistakenly characterized as "Christian". Rather than promoting coexistence and tolerance between religions, hard secularism is in effect an attack on all religions: "The modern West is said to be Christian, but this is untrue: the modern outlook is anti-Christian, because it is essentially anti-religious."[3] Consider for a moment if what we thought we knew about the past, such as the Middle Ages, consisted more of half-truths and inaccurate conclusions, and if the past was actually something quite different from what we have imagined it to be.

---

[2] René Guénon, *The Crisis of the Modern World*, p. 95.

[3] René Guénon, *ibid*, p. 95.

If we can be receptive to this suggestion of open-mindedness, works like *The Rationale Divinorum Officiorum* will provide many insights about the nature of reality as it was known in the pre-modern world. This work is also important beyond the scope of the Western Church or the Roman Catholic Church, as it captures a world infused with the Sacred, which has analogous expressions across the diverse cultures of the pre-modern or traditional world.[4] Let us not forget that it was in the Middle Ages of the Christian West that the Latin term *philosophia perennis* or perennial philosophy was likely coined by Agostino Steuco (1497–1548). The Middle Ages produced mystics of the highest caliber such as Meister Eckhart (1260–1328) and Julian of Norwich (1342–1416), and many saints such as Bernard of Clairvaux (1090–1153), Francis of Assisi (1181/1182–1226), Bonaventure (1221–1274), Hildegard of Bingen (1098–1179) and Catherine of Siena (1347–1380). The modern reader should consider a preliminary question: Why is it that the contemporary world has not in its own right produced such exemplars of the Christian tradition?

Even though *The Rationale Divinorum Officiorum* was written at a time when the sense of the Sacred pervaded the human collectivity, there nonetheless were signs that a spiritual decline was beginning to take root. This decline is documented in the Proeme to the treatise written in 1284 (slightly before the late medieval period):

> How sad, in these times there are many who seem to hardly have any understanding of things they daily engage in, pertaining to the practices of the Church or her divine worship. Nor do they know what they signify or why they were instituted. (p. xx)

This intellectual atrophy that marked the post-medieval era

---

[4] See Reza Shah-Kazemi, *Paths to Transcendence: According to Shankara, Ibn Arabi, and Meister Eckhart* (Bloomington: World Wisdom, 2006).

has now, in the contemporary world, become a new norm, yet it was not unforeseen, as illustrated by the following scriptural texts: "their eyes be darkened, that they may not see" (Romans 11:10); and, foretelling that even the clergy would be indistinguishable from the laity: "And there shall be, like people, like priest" (Hosea 4:9).

In January 1959 the Church's decline reached its nadir with Pope John XXIII (1881–1963) announcing the creation of the Second Vatican Council, marking in the eyes of faithful Catholics a turning point. The Vatican II that occurred between 1962 and 1965 was in fact one of the defining events of the latter half of the twentieth century as it clearly exposed the secularist objectives within the highest reaches of the Church's hierarchy, which was attempting to reconcile the Church with the modern world. Consequently, a mass exodus occurred, some estimating that fifty per cent of Catholics have fled the Church since Vatican II, including numerous clergy, and it is estimated that merely one in four Catholics now attends mass. After five decades, the legacy of Vatican II has demonstrated that it has been a disaster, marking not only a continued crisis within the Church but an assault on the Church's Magisterium. On the question of where contemporaries are to place their obedience if betrayed from within the Church, Saint Peter instructs: "We ought to obey God rather than men" (Acts 5:29).

Given the current crisis facing the Catholic Church, what *The Rationale Divinorum Officiorum* offers to both Catholics and non-Catholics is the spiritual meaning underlying the Western Church and its myriad rites, so that contemporaries can deepen their understanding of the Christian tradition: "Everything that pertains to divine worship, the practices and vestments used by the Church are full of divine meanings and mysteries" (p. xix). It is through the inner or mystical dimension of religion that the outer dimension can become more intelligible, as Hugo de Sancto Victore writes: "Behold ye these things mystically: for not one is there without meaning" (p. xxviii). Our return to God requires all of what we are, yet this is challenged by the weakening of the sense of the Sacred in today's world, which has been replaced by an unbalanced psyche that is always multitasking and paying attention to everything except the Presence before it: "For the mind that is divided in several trains of thought hath less power in each" (p. 124).

Durandus's monumental opus, now made available to English audiences translated from the original Latin text, is arguably the most important medieval treatise available on the symbolism and ritual of the Western Church. Gulielmus Durandus or William Durand (1230–1296) was a French canonist and liturgical writer, the pope's secretary, subdeacon, papal governor, and dean of Chartres. This volume contains translations from three of the eight books of the *Rationale* consisting of *Book I: The Symbolism of Churches and Church Ornaments* (translated by John Mason Neale and Benjamin Webb), *Book III: The Sacred Vestments* (translated by T.H. Passmore) and eight chapters from *Book IV: On the Mass* (translated by Rama P. Coomaraswamy).[5] This volume includes the Proem by Gulielmus Durandus (translated by Rama P. Coomaraswamy) and an elaborate introductory essay from the 1893 edition of Book I: *The Symbolism of Churches and Church Ornaments* entitled "Sacramentality: A Principle of Ecclesiastical Design." Also included in this volume are two chapters from *The Mystical Mirror of the Church* by Hugo de Sancto Victore (1096–1141). The book is beautifully illustrated allowing the reader to be visually guided through the sacred landscape of the Christian tradition. Doyen of the world's religions, Professor Huston Smith, regarded this treatise to be a "true treasure".

---

[5] Cf. also Rama P. Coomaraswamy, *The Destruction of the Christian Tradition* (Bloomington: World Wisdom, 2006), and other related titles by the same author.

Durandus explains from the outset what is signified by the term "church" which is worth recalling: "The word church hath two meanings: the one, a material building, wherein the divine offices are celebrated: the other, a spiritual fabric, which is the collection of the faithful" (p. 3). A corresponding relationship was known since ancient times between the human body and that of the Church: "For the temple of God is holy, which temple ye are" (1 Corinthians 3:17). It has been said that "Our altar is our heart: for the heart is in a man what the altar is in a temple" (pp. 97–98). Hugo de Sancto Victore speaks to this theme: "Whatever things be here done visibly, the same doth God work by His invisible power in the soul, which is the true Temple of God" (p. xxxv). Durandus additionally explains what is meant by the term "Catholic", which is also important to recall: "The Church is called Catholic, that is universal, because it hath been set up in, or spread over, all the world, because the whole multitude of the faithful ought to be in one congregation, or because in the Church is laid up the doctrine necessary for the instruction of all" (p. 3).

Of all of the sacraments within the Catholic Church, the most essential is that of the baptism: "The sacrament of necessity only is baptism, which when administered by anyone, so it be in the form of the Church, in greatest extremity profiteth unto salvation. And it is said to be 'of necessity,' because without it no one can be saved, if it be neglected through contempt" (p. 119). A corresponding passage is as follows: "One Lord, one faith, one baptism" (Ephesians 4:5).

The sacred function of the Mass is paramount within the Catholic Church: "Of all the mysteries (*sacramenta*) of the Church, all are in agreement that the most important is the Mass celebrated on the most holy altar" (p. 233). The sacred origins and symbolism of the Mass reveal themselves as a mystery because they are supra-human in origin and cannot be changed by man: "the Mass is called a mystery because it is beyond us, and a sacrifice because it is offered before everyone and for everyone" (p. 252). With Vatican II, the Tridentine Mass has been replaced with a "New Mass" or *Novus Ordo Missae* ("New Order of the Mass") introduced by Pope Paul VI (1897–1978) in 1969, which reformed the Catholic liturgy, making it invalid as a sacred rite and no longer Catholic in its truest sense. This dire situation was not unforeseen by the last traditional Pope, Pius XII (1876–1958), who is reported to have said, "The day was coming soon when the faithful would only be able to celebrate the holy sacrifice of the mass on the secret altar of the heart."[6] Whatever spiritual possibilities are available at a given time are not dependent on what man wills but on the Divine will: "He that openeth, and no man shutteth; and shutteth, and no man openeth" (Revelation 3:7).

We are grateful to the publishers, Fons Vitae, for having made this treatise available in these troubled times. It is our hope that in the near future all eight books of *The Rationale Divinorum Officiorum* will be translated in their entirety as it is an indispensable guide for anyone interested in the medieval roots out of which the Christian tradition has arisen. It is works like this that will increase spiritual literacy, which is precisely what is needed to challenge the attacks on religion such as those made by the post-Conciliar Church of Vatican II. We live in a time when not only is the Western Church in crisis, but many religions of the world are facing similar challenges given the rise of secularism, extremism and New Age parodies. In an inverted world, where all of the social structures are fast disintegrating before our eyes, the insightful and timeless words of the Gospel bring transparency to the errors of modernism and post-modernism, demonstrating the truth of the scripture, "if a house be divided against itself, that house cannot stand" (Mark 3:25). Faithful or traditional Catholics can take heed that they are never without divine Mercy, no

---

[6] William Stoddart, paraphrasing Pope Pius XII, in *Remembering in a World of Forgetting*, p. 30.

matter how bleak their circumstances may appear: "I am with you alway, even unto the end of the world" (Matthew 28:20). Additionally, there is the Catholic saying from the traditional Mass: *Pax Domini sit semper vobiscum* ("May the peace of the Lord always be with you").

13
*Meister Eckhart on Divine Knowledge**

> *Aliquid est in anima quod est increatum et increabile; si tota anima esset talis, esset increata et increabilis; et hoc est Intellectus.*
> (There is something in the soul which is uncreated and uncreatable; if the whole soul were such, it would be uncreated and uncreatable; and this is the Intellect.)
>
> Meister Eckhart[1]

This classic work of C.F. Kelley's,[2] now reissued, was one of the original comprehensive studies on Meister Eckhart available in the English language which shifted the very way he was understood. Oddly enough, this groundbreaking work has been out of print and difficult to obtain until this republication. The Preface of this original work summarizes its magnitude: "What is here presented to the reader supersedes all former interpretations of Eckhart's teaching. It refuses to ignore what he precisely and repeatedly says cannot be

---

* C.F. Kelley. Cobb, CA: DharmaCafé, 2009, 312pp.

[1] *In agro dominico*, a. 27, *LW* V, 607. Also, though less complete, in German in *DW* I, 220, Predigt 13, *Ein kraft ist in der sêle, von der ich mêr gesprochen hân, – und wære diu sêle alliu alsô, sô wære si ungeschaffen und ungeschepflich.* ("There is a power in the soul, of which I have often spoken; were the soul entire like it, it would be uncreated and uncreatable.")

[2] *Meister Eckhart on Divine Knowledge*, New Haven, CT: Yale University Press, 1977.

ignored, that is, his exposition of the doctrine of Divine Knowledge in terms of the highest and most essential of all possible considerations" (p. xxii).

Johannes Eckhart, known as Eckhart von Hochheim and widely referred to as Meister Eckhart (1260–1328), was born at Hochheim in Thringen, Germany. Meister Eckhart was a German Dominican who lived during the High and Late Middle Ages, an epoch that was pervaded with tradition and "unitive knowledge". Notable scholars have described the High and Late Middle Ages as the richest age of mystical literature unparalleled in the whole of Christianity—Western or Eastern. Eckhart was an exceptional student, one also gifted with an administrative ability. He received the degree of doctor of theology from the University of Paris in 1302, where he also held the position of professor until he was called back to Germany to teach and fulfill administrative duties.

One of the distinguishing marks of the Dominican Order, in the direct line of St. Thomas Aquinas (1225–1274), was its emphasis on "the primacy of the Intellect" which is also to say the primacy of the Godhead (*Deitas/Gottheit*) and the pure or transcendent Intellect (*Intellectus/Verstand*). The intellect should not be confused with reason (*ratio/Vernunft*) yet at the same time they should not be considered as separate faculties: "Reason can never comprehend God in the ocean of his unfathomableness" (p. 100), and yet "Divine Knowledge never contradicts reason" (p. 167). The ground (*Grund*) of Eckhart's exegesis contains a staunch expression of the negative theology (*via negativa*) or *apophatic* mysticism that was expounded by St. Thomas Aquinas and particularly by Dionysius the Pseudo-Areopagite. And yet Eckhart also affirms *cataphatic* mysticism and what appears to transcend both *apophatic* and *cataphatic* perspectives—the absolute or the unmanifest Godhead evades all approximations and determinations.

Carl Franklin Kelley (1914–2008) was both a Christian

scholar and a contemplative. He belonged to the Benedictine Order and was a member of Downside Abbey in England. Friends such as the Eckhartian scholar, Professor Josef Quint (1898–1976), the neo-Thomist Jacques Maritain (1882–1973), and the English writer Aldous Huxley (1894–1963)[3] encouraged Kelley to articulate the metaphysical doctrine of Divine Knowledge that was central to Eckhart's teaching. He spent nearly two decades in reflective consideration, profoundly studying and writing the work that later became known as *Meister Eckhart on Divine Knowledge*. Kelley contextualizes the significance of Eckhart's teachings on Divine Knowledge for the postmodern seeker in an era saturated with pseudo-spirituality and laden with erroneous thinking:

> Being wholly traditional in the truest sense, and therefore perennial, the doctrine he expounds will never cease to be contemporary and always accessible to those who, naturally unsatisfied with mere living, desire to know how to live, regardless of time or place (p. xxiv).

In Kelley's Preface to the original work, he explicitly states the challenges, if not the sheer "impossibility", of translating the true meaning of Eckhart's terminology from medieval Latin and German into contemporary English. This work is divided into a dyad: "Part I: Preparatory Considerations" contains the following chapters: 1. Difficulties and Misconceptions, and 2. The Reality of the Divine Self; and "Part II: The Doctrine", comprises: 1. God and the Human Self, 2. The Word, 3. Primal Distinction, 4. The Inversion, 5. The Veils of God, and 6. The Detachment.

In the first chapter, "Difficulties and Misconceptions", Kelley underscores the implicit and explicit obstacles of understanding Eckhart's teachings from perspectives rooted in modern and postmodern bias, "Surely the greatest obstacles

---

[3] Huxley was the author of the widely regarded anthology *The Perennial Philosophy* (1944).

originate not from Eckhart but from ourselves; or rather from our own mental attitudes, which are grounded in prejudices and limitations wholly foreign to him" (p. 24). Kelley describes the essence of the perennial, or what is primary at the beginning of any spiritual path: "A fundamental qualification laid down by Eckhart for the study of the doctrine is the capacity to discriminate between eternal [Absolute] and temporal [relative] realities" (p. 42). Eckhart *ipso facto* states, "nothing manifested contains its original unmanifested source" (p. 42), which can be summarized in the axial distinction between "that which is primary [unmanifest and absolute] and that which is secondary [manifest and relative or contingent]" (p. 42). To mistake the relative for the absolute is, Eckhart notes, "the root of all fallacy" (p. 42).

In "The Reality of the Divine Self" the reader will find that many of Meister Eckhart's injunctions reflect the quintessence of Christian gnosis found in other non-dual doctrines and in the esoteric aspects of the world's religions,[4] or even in the religion of the First Peoples and their Shamanic traditions—"I am a knower" (p. 56) or "My truest *I* is God" (p. 96). Kelley describes being and knowledge are one—"knower and known are one in knowledge" (p. 58). He distinguishes between the relative and the absolute in regards to the human individual, "Thus he is aware of two certitudes: 'he was born in time,' yet 'he who is now the supratemporal intellective act [or reality] is not born'" (p. 63). Eckhart writes, "[Metaphysically] prior to the existence of the individual self, that unrestricted Knower is and is his own infinite Selfhood, knowing himself by himself" (p. 64): the human individual is what he knows and can only know as much as he is; what is transcendent can only be known by what is itself transcendent. The human

---

[4] "One might add that of all the Christian gnostics, Meister Eckhart is the closest to Sri Shankaracharya." (Jean Biès, *Returning to the Essential: Selected Writings of Jean Biès*, trans. Deborah Weiss-Dutilh [Bloomington: World Wisdom, 2004], p. 222).

individual was itself *a priori* transcendent or, in the words of Eckhart, of an uncreated and uncreatable origin *in divinis*: "And inasmuch as that which is in God is not other than God, then in principle my truest *I* [or innermost Self] is God" (p. 68). The metaphysical nature of the Self is a prolongation of "the entire created order" which "is sacred" (p. 72)—in fact the cosmos is a veritable *theophany*.

In the chapter, "God and the Human Self", Kelly describes Eckhart's view on the mystery of human identity within the context of the transcendent personality: "God is the transcendent and timeless Principle of which all individual beings, including the human being, are only contingent images or reflections" (p. 88). And yet the all-possibility of the Godhead is never individualized *per se*: "The Godhead with whom all manifestation is identical in principle, is fundamentally nonmanifested.... God [*Deus ad extra*] and Godhead are distinct as earth and heaven" (p. 90). Eckhart's view of the transcendent personality is aligned with the non-dual doctrine of Shankara's *neti-neti* or "neither this nor not": referring to the all-possibility of the Godhead, Eckhart states, "After all, God is neither this nor that.... There in the Principle all grass-blades, wood, and stone, all things are identical. This is the highest of all considerations, and I have fooled myself with lesser considerations" (p. 92). The negative theology (*via negativa*) or *apophatic* mysticism of Eckhart shines forth in his statement "He is the Principle without principle" (p. 93). And yet Eckhart simultaneously affirms a positive theology (*via affirmativa*) or *cataphatic* mysticism, "God is all-possibility and all-inclusive" (p. 101). The reader finds that any attempt to ascribe attributes to the Godhead falls short of the mark: "Every determination [of the Godhead] is a restriction, a negation" (p. 109); and again, "I know God, yet I do not know him" (p. 110). Thus a "negation of a negation is transcendently acknowledged as God's affirmation of himself" (p. 112).

The chapter "The Word" is demanding, as it approaches

the ineffable mystery of the Logos as the disclosure of Divine Knowledge to itself *via* the human individual. It is the Word as Revelation that leads the spiritual seeker outside the pale of mental activity to what is true and transcendent—*In principio erat Verbum*—"In the beginning was the Word" (John 1:1) and "all things were made [by the Word]" (John 1:3). Eckhart explains, "The nature of a word is to reveal what is hidden" (p. 131). The Christian doctrine of *creatio ex nihilo* is metaphysically connected to the Principle or the Word which never enters into the manifest order—for the Principle is prior to all manifestation—"All things come from God. He is in all things, yet pre-eminently all things are in him" (p. 141).

The chapter "The Primal Distinction" embodies the essence of the doctrine of non-dualism found throughout Eckhart's writings. Kelley notes: "the doctrine that Eckhart, following Aquinas, expounds is fundamentally the perennial 'doctrine of nonduality'" (p. 148). This perennial doctrine of non-dualism pervades Eckhart's teachings: "God speaks the One, but we understand two" (p. 147); and "God cannot be disturbed by any distinction or multiplicity." Again, "In truest reality there is no duality" (p. 149). With this said, the reader should bear in mind that "Although God is nondual and uncompounded in his limitless being, he is nevertheless God the Father, God the Son, and God the Holy Spirit, and these are not three Gods, but one God" (p. 116). Kelley reminds readers that those who have failed to perceive Thomist non-dualism are those who have not understood essence (*essentia*) and isness (*esse*)—"isness in itself alone directs the issuing forth of the possibilities of essence, it is the principle of all that is" (p. 159). Isness is prior to essence whereas essence is the supporting principle of all manifestation and even derives its name from *isness*—"essence by itself can never be an efficacious cause" (p. 151). Eckhart elaborates, "For it is in accordance with the reality of the intellectually higher (which is isness) to influence essence, just as it is natural for the lower (which is essence) to receive such influence" (p. 152). Isness never enters into the manifest order and is therefore outside the domain of dialectic as such—"Divine Knowledge in itself is neither a 'what' nor an 'is'" (p. 154).

The chapter "The Inversion" reflects on the affirmation made in the first chapter of Genesis identifying the universal and perennial source of Divine Knowledge: "all truth, by whomsoever it be spoken [or known], is from God" (p. 165). Eckhart illuminates a metaphysical, but nonetheless traditional outlook that could be applied to interfaith dialogue: "It is impossible ever to have two things completely equal in the universe or to have two things the same in every respect. For then they would no longer be two, nor would they stand in relation to one another.... We always find and confront diversity, difference in structure and the like, apart from the realm of Divine Knowledge" (p. 179). Diversity or multiplicity *de facto* only exists in the Godhead's transcendent unity for it must not be forgotten that it is in the One, the Godhead, that multiplicity originates. Eckhart repeatedly uses the negation of the negation (*negatio negationis*) when referring to the unmanifest Godhead, "Since every affirmation is a limitation and hence a negation, then the negation of an affirmation is a negation of a negation and as such divine, infinite affirmation" (p. 187).

In "The Veils of God" Meister Eckhart confirms, "there are as many ways of understanding as there are human knowers" (p. 190), and yet he declares "*there* is the True Man; in that Man all men are one Man" (p. 204). Even the veil of truth, he insists, must be cast off for the seeker to be reabsorbed into the unmanifest Principle. The Godhead is the Absolute Subject where "Opposites must be transcended" (p. 208). It is the Godhead alone that is "the Knower, Known, and Knowledge" (p. 212). Eckhart allows readers to comprehend original sin from a non-dual orientation: "prior to original sin there was original wholeness" (p. 214). Eckhart outlines the quintessence of all metaphysical doctrines—assuming all veils of the divine have been discarded: one "knows God through God" (p. 214), which is a common principle shared by Shankara, "only the Self [*Ātmā*] knows the Self [*Ātmā*]."[5] The chapter concludes that Divine Knowledge is integral to the human individual, who then no longer experiences the state of separateness abiding in the essence of the *Imago Dei*—Image of God:

> When I stood in the Principle, the ground of Godhead, no one asked me where I was going or what I was doing: there was no one to ask me.... When I go back into the Principle, the ground of Godhead, no one will ask me whence I came or whither I went. There no one misses me, there God-as-other [or God veiled in manifestation] passes away (p. 214).

The chapter "The Detachment" can perhaps be summarized in the following sentence "Man must accept the *given* before he can realize the *gift*." Eckhart refers to the process of detachment as the "divine journey", "the return of the Word to the Father" (p. 217). This "return" pertains to the relative or contingent order and not to that of the absolute or unmanifest order, for the Word "never goes anywhere" (p. 218). Kelley reminds the reader that of all of Eckhart's writings and teachings there is no theme more predominant than the doctrine of detachment and yet the zenith of this doctrine is summarized in the poverty of spirit or spiritual poverty—"A poor man is he who wants nothing, knows nothing, has nothing" (p. 222). Eckhart draws from the writings of St. Thomas Aquinas on this subject: "if a man has become detached from himself and all things, then God necessarily fills him" (p. 227). It is the "infallible necessity" that guides the human individual toward detachment and thus the unmanifest Godhead: "It is in spiritual poverty, detachment, simplicity, that the oneness between man and God is found. And this oneness is through grace, for it is grace that draws man away from earthly things [or struc-

---

[5] Shankara, quoted in Reza Shah-Kazemi, *Paths to Transcendence*, p. 207.

tural manifestation] and rids him of all things conditioned by mutability and corruptibility" (p. 227). The paradox of Eckhart's instruction is that the soul seeking transcendence or union must cease seeking itself—"the seeker must recede into Intellect which does not seek" and "The more one seeks God the less one finds God" (p. 236).

The republication of this formerly hard-to-find metaphysical beacon is of immeasurable value for contemporary seekers and scholars alike. Many books have attempted to excise Eckhart and even the function of mysticism from Western Christendom altogether, as if Meister Eckhart and mysticism in general could be divorced from the Church, its sacraments and rites. This notion, according to Kelley's work, is a grave misapprehension of the Christian tradition.[6] For those living in an era intoxicated by extreme materialism, progressivism and secularism, it is challenging to understand Eckhart's stance on the significance of the Church. "The Body of Christ"—the presence of Christ in this world and its magnitude in the transmission of "the spirit of Christ"—functions as a "second birth" for the devout practitioner. Eckhart was a mystic *par excellence* and yet he was indisputably traditional and orthodox in his outlook. Some have committed a grave error by attempting to reduce Eckhart's metaphysics to a psychological analysis and interpretation.[7] Given the spiritual entropy of the times, the following quote from Eckhart provides a paramount directive for those seeking esoteric or mystical truth when spiritual

---

[6] With this said it is important for readers to know that since the post-Vatican II revisions, the Roman Catholic tradition has faced an extreme crisis. For an excellent detailed analysis of what lead to this eclipse in the Western Church see: Rama P. Coomaraswamy, *The Destruction of the Christian Tradition*.

[7] "Meister Eckhart's view, therefore, is purely psychological" (C. G. Jung, "The Type Problem in Poetry," in *Psychological Types* [Princeton University Press, 1976], p. 248). It is not therefore surprising that Jung affirms: "the concept [of the] 'transcendent' is relative" (*Letters, Vol. 2: 1951–1961* [Princeton University Press, 1975], p. 378).

parodies are to be found everywhere; the inner dimension is inaccessible without the exoteric or outer dimension: "If thou wouldst reach the kernel, thou must break the shell."[8] This book is an essential resource to the research and reconciliation of the legacy of this paragon of Western Christendom. Readers will find the work to be an indispensable expression of the *philosophia perennis* or perennial philosophy[9]—found in all times and in all places. We will conclude this review with the edifying words of this great master—"Love is simply the will reintegrated into principal Truth" (p. 243).

---

[8] Meister Eckhart, quoted in Frithjof Schuon, "Preface," to *Sufism: Veil and Quintessence* (Bloomington: World Wisdom Books, 1981), p. 3.

[9] Readers interested in the topic of the perennial philosophy and the Christian tradition, see Mateus Soares de Azevedo (ed.), *Ye Shall Know the Truth: Christianity and the Perennial Philosophy* (Bloomington: World Wisdom, 2005).

14

*Christianity and the Doctrine of Non-Dualism**

> As for ourself, we will say unequivocally that after more than forty years of intellectual reflection on this doctrine [of non-dualism or *advaita-vāda*], having allowed it to impregnate us more and more profoundly, we have found nothing that has seemed incompatible with our full and complete faith in the Christian Revelation.
>
> A Monk of the West[1]

This semi-anonymous work was written under the pen name of "A Monk of the West" who has been identified as Alphonse Levée, a French Cistercian monk who, at the young age of twenty, found a copy of fellow countryman René Guénon's *Orient et Occident* (*East and West*) in a second-hand book stall while he was posted in Asia. This event had a tremendous impact that endured for the rest of his life and was instrumental in his decision to take up the monastic vocation. It was in the discovery of this work by Guénon that A Monk of the West found an integral metaphysical doctrine that was universal in its principles, known in the West as the *philosophia perennis*—perennial philosophy. The metaphysical doctrine

---

* Translated by Alvin Moore, Jr. and Marie M. Hansen (Sophia Perennis, 2004), 148 pp.
[1] *Ibid.*, p. 136.

of non-dualism (*advaita-vāda*), more commonly known as *Advaita Vedānta*, is not exclusive to Hinduism, but is also present in Buddhism, Taoism, Judaism, Christianity and Islam. It is in this universal light that *Christianity and the Doctrine of Non-Dualism* is articulated.

Though this book on "Christian Vedānta" is modest in its length, it is dense in its scope and reflection. The book begins with a thorough and insightful Preface by the late perennialist Alvin Moore, Jr. (1923–2005). The work consists of eight chapters and a Foreword: "Philosophical Monism and Non-Dualism", "I am Brahma", "In All Things Like Unto Men", "Without Me You Can Do Nothing", "Who am I?", "I am not the Christ", "East and West" and the Conclusion.

In the first chapter the author makes important distinctions that are often confused in our times: non-dualism is neither pantheism nor monism—"*the soul is not the Self [Ātmā]*" (p. 20), or again "*the Self (Ātmā) is not the human soul (jivātmā)*" (p. 24).

In the following chapter the author makes it clear that the human individual as an empirical "ego" or "I" is not a finality unto itself. It is not until a "reintegration" with what is transpersonal or supra-individual that true identity can exist, for "*there is no true identity save in God, because God alone is Identity.*" The author continues to clarify this idea in chapter five—"Who AM I?"—when he quotes from a traditional Hindu aphorism, "the I is *māyā* and the not-I is *Brahman*" (p. 94). Without this total "dis-identification" or detachment from the "ego" or "I", writes the author in Chapter Six, it is impossible for the "reintegration" with the Self (*Ātmā*) to occur, let alone the identification with the Supreme Identity. In the same chapter the author clarifies the misunderstanding of reincarnation, "In reality, the reincarnationist illusion has its root in a confusion of the psychic and the spiritual" (p. 111). This perspective is in accordance with Śrī Śaṅkarācārya's (788–820) dictum, "In truth, there is no other transmigrant but the

Lord," [2] categorically denying the possibility of the human individual reincarnating per se.

In closing, we would like to note that there is great merit in this work as a support in allowing the doctrine of non-dualism to be expressed once again within the Christian tradition, as it once did in the West. The book could also broaden the current understanding of the Christian tradition, which has become more and more eclipsed in the present era due to modernity and postmodernity's indefinite trend toward so-called "progress" and secularization. Such a perspective is polarized either to discredit the Christian tradition altogether, believing that it has somehow failed the human collectivity at large, or to provoke fundamentalism asserting a pseudo-monopoly on truth itself—blinded by the assumption that the only authentic religion is Christianity, and *ipso facto*, negating the possibility of all other spiritual traditions as "paths that lead to the same summit".[3] Beyond such polarities, the reader will be pleased to find that this book fosters religious pluralism, tolerance and inquiry from a non-reductionistic point of view, simultaneously acknowledging the "transcendent unity of religions".[4]

---

[2] Śrī Śaṅkarācārya, quoted in A. K. Coomaraswamy, *The Bugbear of Literacy*, p. 120.

[3] See A. K. Coomaraswamy, *The Bugbear of Literacy*, pp. 50–67.

[4] See Frithjof Schuon, *The Transcendent Unity of Religions*, trans. Peter Townsend, London: Faber and Faber, 1953. Mentions of this title refer henceforth to this 1953 edition.

Part VII

The Islamic Tradition

15

*What Does Islam Mean in Today's World? Religion, Politics, Spirituality**

It is imperative to clarify from the outset that, while the book here under review specifically addresses the relevance of the Islamic tradition in the modern and postmodern world, it could nearly as well have been titled *What Does Religion Mean in Today's World?* The question of the relevance of Islam is one and the same as the broader question of the relevance of religion itself. It is not only Islam that is currently under siege, but a large-scale assault is being waged on all of the world's religions and their spiritualities. What is this destructive force that systematically seeks to eradicate what is most sublime in the human condition? This is precisely what this timely volume seeks to answer and explain, given the radical misperception that surrounds the phenomenon of so-called religious fundamentalism, whether in Islam or any other religion. Stoddart summarizes the theme of his book as follows:

> This book deals with the nature of religion—Islamic and other—and how, in the present age, it has become subject to massive betrayal and perversion. It also touches on how religion is falsified by being amalgamated with secular political programs, which are superficial and outward

---

* William Stoddart, with a Foreword by Harry Oldmeadow (Bloomington: World Wisdom, 2012) 128pp.

in the extreme, and which are either entirely devoid of principles, or alternatively, imbued with fundamentally false principles (p. xvi).

While these matters are complex and not easy to comprehend, Stoddart discusses them with amazing precision and simplicity, combining metaphysical insight with sensitivity to the diverse perspectives at hand. The foreword by Harry Oldmeadow aptly highlights the importance of this work, especially for those who sincerely long to see beyond the propaganda machine and its dissemination of half-truths and blatant lies regarding Islam. The book comprises eleven chapters of varying lengths, each encapsulating what is most essential in the theme discussed.

The volume begins with the vital subject of revolution and its follies, powerfully and lucidly exposing its theoretical underpinnings. Stoddart explores the *sequelae* to World War II, beginning with the Beat Generation and its relationship to the psychedelic and sexual revolutions, followed by the hippies and the counter-culture. Stoddart informs readers that, while there were some serious and well-intentioned individuals involved in these movements (many of whom turned to the wisdom of the East, in the shape of Taoism and Hinduism and especially Buddhism, for guidance), the overall effect of their efforts was negative, helping to fuel the New Age movement which developed—at several removes—out of the Theosophical Society (founded in 1875). More detrimental revolutions followed, such as the Second Vatican Council (1962–1965) and the Iranian revolution (beginning in 1979). Stoddart outlines the destructive influence which these developments variously exercised:

The Vatican II Council directly concerned only Catholicism, but its relativizing, de-spiritualizing, and de-sacralizing spirit gradually, but inexorably, spread to the principal Protestant denominations, and even influenced the attitudes of the congregations (but not the dogmas and sacraments) of some of the Eastern Churches. The Iranian revolution directly affected only Shi'i Islam, but an ideology similar to that of Khomeini was also present in a slightly earlier revolution in Libya, namely the overthrow of King Idris of the Sanussi by Mu'ammar Gadhafi, and the establishment of a so-called "Islamic republic". Soon thereafter, these hollow and evil ideas gradually spread throughout the Islamic world.

Other similar revolutions with a much earlier origin should not be overlooked, as they precipitated the crises of the modern and postmodern world: "the nineteenth and twentieth centuries saw the appearance of the nefarious quintet: Darwin, Marx, Freud, Jung, and Teilhard de Chardin" (p. 3). When the notion of revolution is juxtaposed with that of tradition, its corrosive effects become self-evident, and contradictory to what it means to be integrally human and to humanity's inherent connection to the sacred.

After providing an overview of how revolutions have affected both the West and the world at large, Stoddart plumbs deeply into the significance of Islam and presents it in a light that will be new to most Westerners. He indicates how, far from being fanatical, Islam shows a profound degree of tolerance and good will toward other religions: as the cardinal Qur'ānic principle states, *"There is no compulsion in religion"* (2:256). Islam is often accused of wanting to convert the whole world to Islam, yet the same could be said of the two other universal religions, Buddhism and Christianity. Stoddart addresses this important issue:

> It is frequently alleged that Islam wants to convert the whole world to Islam. The reader, who has got this far in my discourse, may be surprised when I unhesitatingly concur! For this is indeed the case, and I can say it without a qualm, because it is exactly the same with Christianity and Buddhism (p. 30).

Unlike Hinduism and Judaism (each one being "the religion of a people", and seeking no converts), Buddhism,

Christianity, and Islam are "universal religions" (each one seeking converts in all nations); it is thus quite inevitable that there be competition between them.

With this said, we can however also refer readers to the following Qur'ānic verse that evokes Islam's tolerance: "*O People of the Book! Ye have no faith until ye observe the Torah and the Gospel, and all that has been revealed unto you by your Lord*" (5:68). And what is the purpose of all of the diverse religions of the world, if they could have been one religion? The following celebrated verse addresses this question:

> Had God willed, He would have made you a single community, but He wanted to test you by that which He has given you. So compete with one another in good works. Every one of you will return to God and He will inform you about the things wherein you differ (Qur'ān 5:48).

Many examples could be cited in illustration of this attitude; the Qur'ān is full of them.

Stoddart refers to the unanimous sense of the sacred that pervaded pre-Renaissance (that is to say, medieval) Christianity, as it pervaded the religions of the East (such as Hinduism and Buddhism, and also the shamanistic traditions). In fact, all traditional societies and civilizations have a common core that is sacred, and that directs the course of all action. With the advent of the eighteenth-century "Enlightenment" and its legacy of modern science, the West began to lose its sacred character and thus its shared metaphysical reality. Stoddart's chapter "The Clash of Civilizations", taking its title from a phrase popularized by Samuel P. Huntington, debunks Huntington's position in less than two pages:

> Certainly, the terrorists come from Islamic countries, but they have broken injunction after injunction of the Qur'ān and of Mohammed. Their main achievement is to have created the "Islamophobia" that is today so prevalent in the

West; they are beyond doubt the worst enemies that Islam has ever had (p. 49).

An immensely useful chapter, that will benefit all, is "Religious and Ethnic Conflict in the Light of the Writings of the Traditionalist or Perennialist School". Stoddart states:

> The doctrine of the transcendent or esoteric unity of the religions represents not a syncretism, but synthesis. What does this mean? It means that we must *believe* in all orthodox, traditional religions, but we can practice only one. Consider the metaphor of climbing a mountain. Climbers can start from different positions at the foot of the mountain. From these positions, they must follow the particular path that will lead them to the top. We can and must believe in the efficacy of all the paths, but our legs are not long enough to enable us to put our feet on two paths at once! Nevertheless, the other paths can sometimes be of help to us. For example, if we notice that someone on a neighbouring path has a particularly skillful way of circumventing a boulder, it may be that we can use the same skill to negotiate such boulders as may lie ahead of us on our own path. The paths as such, however, meet only at the summit. The religions are one only in God (p. 68).

A much needed understanding that goes beyond simplistic interfaith dialogue is laid out: "We must be capable of the cardinally important intuition that *every religion*—be it Christianity, Hinduism, Buddhism, or Islam—*comes from God and every religion leads back to God*" (p. 70). Likewise, we must remember that "each religion has within it a verse corresponding to 'No man cometh to the Father but by Me'" (John 14:6), otherwise it would not be a religion, but no more than a man-made philosophy or ideology incapable of saving anyone. In fact, if this one principle were fully comprehended, it could likely put a halt to the needless bloodshed and warfare that are committed in the name of religion, as each faith tradition would be understood to be an affirmation of its singular authenticity on the exoteric level while affirming its universal Truth on the esoteric level, which is no less authentic.

The concluding chapter, "A Message of Hope", perfectly describes the inner disposition that is a remedy for the prevailing postmodern relativism and nihilism. Stoddart quotes the preeminent perennialist author Titus Burckhardt, who writes:

> Since nearly all traditional forms of life are now destroyed, it is seldom vouchsafed to man to engage in a wholly useful and meaningful activity. But every loss spells gain: the disappearance of traditional forms calls for a trial and a discernment; and the confusion in the surrounding world is a summons to turn, by-passing all accidents, to the essential (p. 86).

Dismal as the prospects for integral interfaith dialogue and mutual understanding may be when viewed through the lens of the mass media syndicates, this volume by William Stoddart, who has been an ardent student of these matters for most of his life, functions as a beacon in the face of the contemporary disarray. Stoddart leads his reader through the book's complex and multifaceted themes with a penetrating discernment rooted in the timeless truths of the perennial philosophy. This book is a "must-read" for anyone interested either in Islam or in religion in general. The book ends with the consoling Biblical verse which speaks to the heart of all plenary traditions: *Magna est veritas et praevalebit*—"Truth is great and it shall prevail" (1 Esdras 4:41).

16

*Know Yourself: An Explanation of the Oneness of Being**

When propositioned with the question "If you were stranded on a deserted island and could only have one book with you, which would it be?" it is books like *Know Yourself* which come to mind. Why? The short answer is that it is a crystallization of transcendent wisdom that speaks across the religions and directs the reader to their innermost center. The book is proof that it is the Divine alone that makes the Divine known to the human individual and not the human *per se* who can deign to know the Divine. It is not the human individual as a separate ego identity that comes to know the Divine, but the Divine in the human individual that comes to know Itself. From the purely human perspective, Divine's grace and intercession are required.

The interesting way in which this work was introduced to the contemporary West is outlined in the introduction to the book under review. The first English translation was undertaken by Thomas Hunter Weir (1865–1928) and published in 1901 by the *Journal of the Royal Asiatic Society* under the heading "Translation of an Arabic Manuscript in the Hunterian Collection, Glasgow University". In 1976 it appeared under the title "*Whoso Knoweth Himself...*" from the

---

* Ibn ʿArabī/Balyānī, translated from Arabic by Cecilia Twinch (Cheltenham, UK: Beshara Publications), 2014, 80pp.

Treatise on Being (*Risalat al-wujudiyyah*), and it was reissued in 1988 under the same title. *Know Yourself* is a new translation completed by using several Arabic manuscripts from libraries in the United Kingdom, Turkey and Syria. Cecilia Twinch, Senior Research Fellow of the Muhyiddin Ibn 'Arabi Society and translator of this volume explains why this revised translation is significant, "*Know Yourself* is intended to be as accessible as possible to people with no knowledge of Arabic and who do not necessarily have much knowledge of the cultural context of the book" (p. 3).

Another curious phenomenon concerning this work is that while it is often attributed to Ibn 'Arabī and was undoubtedly created under his spiritual influence, it was likely penned by Awḥad al-Dīn Balyānī (d. 686/1288). Balyānī, a Persian Sufi master from Shiraz, was thought to have been a student of the Andalusian poet Shushtarī (1212–1269), who in turn was an exemplary student of the Sufi philosopher Ibn Sab'īn (1217–1268), a close contemporary of Ibn 'Arabī (1165–1240), the Spanish-born mystic known as "the greatest master" (*al-Shaykh al-akbar*). In fact, both Ibn Sab'īn and Ibn 'Arabī were from Murcia. The magnitude of Ibn 'Arabī's influence within the Islamic world is immense; he has produced what some estimate to be three hundred books, yet only ninety-three or so survive today. Professor Seyyed Hossein Nasr (b. 1933), pre-eminent Islamic philosopher and renowned scholar of comparative religion, speaks about Ibn 'Arabī's influence: "It would not be an exaggeration to say that Ibn 'Arabī is the most influential intellectual figure in the Islamic world during the past seven centuries, if the whole world is considered."[1]

The mystery that surrounds the authorship of this book has captivated Western *intelligentsia* and scholars alike:

Abdul Hadi—otherwise known as the Swedish painter

---

[1] S. H. Nasr, *Islamic Philosophy from Its Origin to the Present: Philosophy in the Land of Prophecy* (Albany, NY: State University of New York, 2006), p. 135.

and author Ivan Aguéli (1869–1917), who initiated the well-known French scholar René Guénon (1886–1951) into Sufism[2] and founded the secret Sufi society Al-Akbariyya in Paris in 1911—published an Italian version of the treatise in 1907, followed by a French translation which appeared in the journal *La Gnose* in Cairo in 1911. In the introduction to the French version, Abdul Hadi wrote that he was three-quarters of the way through his translation when he heard that the work had already been translated into English: 'I don't know where, or when, or by whom.' Although he notes that many manuscripts were attributed to Balyani or Balabani and other variations on the name, as well as to Suyuti, he was inwardly convinced that its author was Ibn 'Arabi (p. 70).

Professor Michel Chodkiewicz (b. 1929), formerly the Director of Studies at the École des Hautes Études en Sciences Sociales in Paris, states that this book has been misattributed to Ibn 'Arabī and that it was his disciple, Balyānī, who wrote it, a view espoused also by Professor James Morris (b. 1949).

Martin Lings (1909–2005), Keeper of Oriental Manuscripts in the British Museum and the British Library, wrote of the book's significance: "It is one of the most important of all Sufi treatises."[3] The reason for this remarkable appraisal is evident from the work itself.

Knowledge corresponds to multiple levels of Reality and not all knowledge corresponds to one and the same level. This is very important to understand. The two cardinal distinctions

---

[2] "Guénon was initiated [in 1912] by Aguéli into the Sufi *tarīqah*, by receiving the *barakah* or blessing at his hands" (Robin Waterfield, *René Guénon and the Future of the West: The Life and Writings of a 20th-Century Metaphysician* [Hillsdale, NY: Sophia Perennis, 2002], p. 29). It is worth mentioning that it was the Egyptian Sufi Shaykh 'Abd al-Raḥmān 'Ilaysh al-Kabīr (1840–1921), who initiated Aguéli into Sufism in 1902 through the Shadhiliyah-'Arabiyyah Tarīqah, and to whom Guénon dedicated his book *Le Symbolisme de la Croix* [*The Symbolism of the Cross*] (1931).

[3] M. Lings, *A Sufi Saint of the Twentieth Century*, p. 122.

are the relative and the Absolute. This includes all modes of knowledge, from the sensible perception of the contingent to the direct or non-dual perception. Without this recognition, books like this one that speaks to the highest levels of spiritual realization can cause confusion in the mind of the reader. A sublime example of this and of integral metaphysics found in the perennial philosophy is made in the following statement found in this text: "You yourself are the object of your quest" (p. 26). This may sound true for some, but what does this really mean? It is definitely not referring to "you" as you see yourself, but as a transpersonal identity. Statements like these are unintelligible to the empirical ego or rational mind and require a higher faculty of perception beyond the relative point of view, a cognitive vantage known within Sufism as the ʿaql or Intellect. It is this noetic faculty, sometimes known as the "eye of the heart", which is immanent in the human individual and can directly perceive Truth. The following from the opening page preceding the text articulates whom the book is intended for:

> We are speaking with those who have determination and energy in seeking knowledge of their self in order to know God, and who keep fresh in their heart the image of their seeking and longing for union with God, and not with those without aim or intention (p. v).

It hardly needs mentioning that the pitfalls surrounding the contemporary seeker are myriad given the secular ambiance and the many spiritual parodies appearing to be authentic vehicles for spiritual realization. Religions in the contemporary world have become challenged with many ill-fated factors that did not previously exist in the manner that they do today. This is why seekers and travelers of the Path need to be ever more discerning about these matters.

Each word in this exposition attributed to Ibn ʿArabī/Balyānī is concisely situated to provide the directness of the

Absolute. It is an unperishing elixir of other-worldly wisdom that seekers and travelers alike can be nourished by and, by grace, transfigured, bridging the transcendent and the immanent, rendering human identity in all of its complexity transparent and perceptibly Divine. "He is seen everywhere, according to the Qur'anic verse, *Wherever you turn, there is the face of God* [2:115]. Yet at the same time, God remains beyond our perception, *Eyes do not perceive Him* [6:103]. He is both transcendent and immanent, and He unites all opposites in Himself" (p. 64). Again from one perspective the Divine is wholly other ["There is nothing like Him" (42:11)] and from another perspective the Divine is intimately close ["We are nearer to him than the jugular vein" (50:16)]. In the Divine both can exist simultaneously without contradiction, as there are distinct levels of perception depending on the understanding of the human individual. According to Islam and its spiritual or Sufi psychology, the acme of human identity is none other than the Supreme Identity: "By the word 'self', the Prophet meant 'being'. The being of the one who reaches this spiritual level is no longer their being whether inwardly or outwardly, but it is the very being of God" (p. 45). Examples of transcendence and immanence, and of their identity, are found unanimously across the religions.

The primordial nature or *fitrah* that each human individual is born with is immutable despite the veils of forgetfulness that distort this integral identity. This primordial nature nonetheless is always present despite the human individual's experience in the world of duality. From this point of view we can understand the following statement: "There is no need for any change since that person was not the existence of their own essence but was simply ignorant of the knowledge of their self" (p. 32). In the end only the Divine can know the Divine; Shankara states a similar principle in a slightly different manner, "only the Self [*Ātmā*] knows the Self

[*Ātmā*]."[4] With the continual remembrance of the Divine, the human individual is aware of its innate primordial nature. The Qur'an makes this clear: "*Verily in the remembrance (al-dhikr) of God do hearts find rest!*" (12:28). With the gradual obscuring of the primordial nature, one loses one's way and cannot obtain salvation through any identity except one's innately endowed nature. In fact, to deny our primordial nature is, as Meister Eckhart expresses, paradoxically only to reaffirm the Divine as nothing exists outside the Divine: "The more he blasphemes, the more he praises God."[5] A non-dual understanding is elaborated here: "in reality there is neither union nor separation, distance or closeness, since union is only possible between two things and if there is only one there can be neither union nor separation" (p. 37). Again, the reason for this is that nothing exists outside the Divine Unity, affirmed in the Islamic tradition by the principle of *tawḥīd*. From the point of view of Sufi metaphysics, Ibn ʿArabī teaches the doctrine of *waḥdat al-wujūd*, the "Oneness of Being" or the "Unity of Existence". The interconnectedness of the whole of Reality is made evident in passages such as: "When this secret is revealed to you, you will know that you are not other than God but that you yourself are the object of your quest" (p. 26).

A final and important point covered in this work relates to the issue of religious pluralism and ecumenical dialogue, which is essential in today's world. Each human collectivity has its own messengers sent by the Divine, as articulated in the Qur'anic verse: "*For every community (umma) there is a Messenger*" (10:47). We need to go beyond approaches that solely advocate tolerance or coexistence among the world religions (though undoubtedly worthy goals), to a deeper

---

[4] Shankara, quoted in Reza Shah-Kazemi, *Paths to Transcendence*, p. 207.

[5] "Anyone who blasphemes God himself praises God" (Meister Eckhart, "B. The Bull 'In agro dominico' (March 27, 1329)", in *Meister Eckhart: The Essential Sermons, Commentaries, Treatises, and Defense* [New York: Paulist Press, 1981], p. 78).

appreciation of the inner unity underlying the diversity of the faith traditions. The esoteric or mystical dimension is underscored in the following: "No sent prophet, perfect saint or angel brought close knows Him. His prophet is He, His messenger is He, His message is He and His word is He. He sent Himself from Himself, through Himself to Himself. There is no intermediary or means other than Him. There is no difference between the sender, that which is sent and the one to whom it is sent" (p. 19).

Know Yourself deserves to be included in every spiritual seeker's and traveler's library, especially in a time when religion and spirituality have become so removed from the daily life of the human collectivity. Those interested in Sufi psychology, including perennial psychology, will also find this volume important. In our challenging age, having good books like this one becomes indispensable. It goes without saying that books alone cannot take the place of a formal spiritual affiliation nor can they be a substitute for spiritual guidance, as it is all-too-easy to lose one's way on the Path. Yet books may serve an important role in the spiritual life and can certainly be a tremendous support. This sublime and slender volume, while originating within the Islamic tradition and its inner dimension of Sufism, contains keys that are found universally across all of the sapiential traditions. In essence, it is a condensed version of the essential truths found within the perennial philosophy, the heart of all religions. We are grateful for this revised translation of this remarkable book attributed to Ibn 'Arabī/Balyānī, which has been made available once again to readers in the West.

17

*The Sufi Doctrine of Rumi**

> Hail, O Love that bringest us good gain—thou art the physician of all our ills.
>
> Rūmī[1]

The outpouring of interest in Rūmī (1207–1273) or, as he is known within the world of Islamic spirituality, Jalāl al-Dīn Muḥammad Rūmī, or simply Mawlānā, "our Master", in the contemporary West is an overwhelming confirmation of the timeless relevance of traditional wisdom that is neither of the East nor the West. He is the originator of the renowned "mystical dance" (*semā*), which later became known as the "dance of the whirling dervishes", still practiced by the Mevlevi or Mawlawiyya Sufi order founded by Rūmī's followers after his death. How is it that a poet from the thirteenth-century, born in Balkh (Khurasan or present-day Afghanistan), who lived most of his life and was buried in Konya (Turkey), has become a celebrated figure in America today? This is again evidence of his universal message that transcends religious and sectarian boundaries, national, cultural, and ethnic divisions and is not limited to time or place. With the rise of Islamophobia, including extremism and xenophobia in

---

* William C. Chittick, *The Sufi Doctrine of Rumi: Illustrated Edition*. Foreword by Seyyed Hossein Nasr (Bloomington: World Wisdom, 2005), 120pp.

[1] Quoted in p. 11.

all its forms, the message of the saints and sages such as Rūmī provide an antidote to the increasing ignorance, hatred and violence that are besieging the world today.

The Sufi Doctrine of Rumi is a revised edition of a work that was initially published in 1974 in Iran by the Aryamehr University in Tehran, to celebrate the seven-hundredth anniversary of Rūmī's death, when Professor Chittick was an assistant professor of Religious Studies at the university. This new edition is colorfully decorated with calligraphy and Persian and Turkish miniature paintings, which are truly stunning for the eye to gaze upon. Seyyed Hossein Nasr, one of the world's most respected writers and speakers on Islam and its mystical path, Sufism, was then the Chancellor of Aryamehr University. Nasr discusses the importance of this work for future Rūmī studies in his Foreword:

> This study of Dr. Chittick has the great merit... of approaching the subject [of Rūmī's metaphysical teachings] from a strictly traditional point of view untainted by the modernistic fallacies which have colored most of the other studies devoted so far to this subject in Western languages.... May the message of Rūmī serve as a beacon of light to dispel the shadows which prevent modern man from seeing even his own image in its true form and from knowing who he really is (p. viii).

Rūmī's major works are the *Dīwān-i Shams-i Tabrīzī* of some forty thousand verses, and the *Mathnawī*, containing some twenty-five thousand verses and often regarded as "the Quran in the Persian language". Although no work could fully encompass the totality of Rūmī's teachings, readers may ask, why yet another book? While numerous books are available, they often miss the mark and do not provide insight into the mystical symbolism of Rūmī's spiritual universe. Chittick speaks about his intentions behind preparing this work:

> Despite numerous studies of him [Rūmī], until now there

has been no clear summary in English of the main points of his doctrines and teachings.... For those who know [Rūmī] only through the popularizing translations [of his poetry], this little book may provide some insight into his universe of meaning. Unlike most Sufi poets, Rūmī explains the meaning of his imagery and symbolism. My task is simply to juxtapose various verses and prose passages to let him say what he wants to say (pp. xii, xiv, 1).

While Rūmī is well-known and celebrated in the present-day, what is lacking are authoritative works accessible for general readers that offer an introduction in clear and accessible language to his magical poetry. This book does just that as it provides an authoritative and accessible presentation of Rūmī's magisterial teachings and its fundamental themes vis-à-vis the Islamic tradition, which is central to his spiritual universe. The lack of knowledge pertaining to the Islamic tradition tends to obstruct Western readers from understanding the depth of Rūmī.

Sufism is regarded as the inner or esoteric dimension of Islam and is a spiritual path by which the human being can transcend his or her individual egoism to reach the Divine. Chittick explains the distinction and relationship between the inner and outer dimensions of religion:

> Exotericism by definition must be limited in some sense, for it addresses itself to a particular humanity and a particular psychological and mental condition—even though its means of addressing itself is to some degree universalized and expanded through time and space to encompass a large segment of the human race. Esotericism also addresses itself to particular psychological types, but it is open inwardly towards the Infinite in a much more direct manner than exotericism, since it is concerned primarily with overcoming all the limitations of the individual order (p. 13).

Chittick clarifies the role of the Prophet Muhammad

within Sufism as some have tried to separate Sufism from the Islamic tradition as if one could be a Sufi without being a Muslim:

> For the Sufis themselves one of the clearest proofs of the integrally Islamic nature of Sufism is that its practices are based on the model of the Prophet Muhammad. For Muslims it is self-evident that in Islam no one has been closer to God—or, if one prefers, no one has attained a more complete spiritual realization—than the Prophet himself, for by the very fact of his prophecy he is the Universal Man and the model for all sanctity in Islam. For the same reason he is the ideal whom all Sufis emulate and the founder of all that later became crystallized within the Sufi orders (p. 16).

Rūmī confirms that all Sufi orders link back like a chain (*silsilah*) to the Prophet and that without the Prophet Muhammad there would be no Sufism. This is expressed in his lyrical verse: "God's way is exceedingly fearful, blocked and full of snow. He [the Prophet] was the first to risk his life, driving his horse and pioneering the road. Whoever goes on this road, does so by his guidance and guarding. He discovered the road in the first place and set up waymarks everywhere" (p. 17).

To the surprise of many Rūmī admirers—who would never accuse him of being narrow-minded—rather than being against orthodox interpretations of religion, Rūmī speaks of orthodoxy as a spiritual necessity to the union with the Divine: "The (right) thought is that which opens a way: the (right) way is that on which a (spiritual) king advances" (p. 88). The following is another poetic articulation of Rūmī's perspective on orthodoxy: "Alter yourself, not the Traditions: abuse your (dull) brain, not the rose-garden (the true sense which you cannot apprehend)" (p. 89).

According to Rūmī, the true nature of the relationship between the Divine and the world of form requires a transcendent wisdom that is outside the reach of normal or rational knowledge:

> It... is neither inside of this world nor outside; neither beneath it nor above it; neither joined with it nor separate from it: it is devoid of quality and relation. At every moment thousands of signs and types are displayed by it (in this world). As manual skill to the form of the hand, or glances of the eye to the form of the eye, or eloquence of the tongue to the form of the tongue, such is the relation of that world to this (p. 31).

Although the Divine confirms the unity of all phenomena in the manifest world, when viewed through the lens of the relative or duality, all things appear as separate and disjointed from one another without a trace that they are essentially interconnected on a higher level. Likewise, knowledge cut off from its transcendent source characterizes the fallen consciousness of humanity. Chittick writes, "The fall of man is the result of the blinding of the 'eye of the heart' (*chashm-i dil* or *'ayn al-qalb*), which alone sees with the vision of gnosis." Due to the fallen consciousness which attaches itself to what is transitory, human beings do not see things as they are but rather in a distorted way: "Therefore union with this (world) is separation from that (world): the health of this body is the sickness of the spirit. Hard is the separation from this transitory abode: know, then, that the separation from that permanent abode is harder" (p. 83). According to Rūmī, the fallen consciousness of Adam is not limited to the Abrahamic monotheisms of Judaism, Christianity and Islam, but extends and includes the whole of humanity:

> Sick, surely, and ill-savored is the heart that knows not (cannot distinguish) the taste of this and that. When the heart becomes whole (is healed of pain and disease), it will recognize the flavor of falsehood and truth [since "God taught Adam the Names"]. When Adam's greed for

the wheat [the forbidden fruit] waxed great, it robbed Adam's heart of health.... Discernment flees from one that is drunken with vain desire (p. 57).

The loss of the sense of the sacred is itself the forgetting of the Divine. Rūmī asserts, "Forgetfulness (of God), O beloved, is the pillar (prop) of this world; (spiritual) intelligence is a bane to this world" (p. 60).

Sufism teaches that Universal or Perfect Man (*al-insān al-kāmil*) is the prototype of both the microcosm and the macrocosm, the human being and the cosmos. That is to say that Universal or Perfect Man is "the perfect human model who has attained all the possibilities inherent in the human state." For Universal or Perfect Man the misidentification with the empirical ego has relinquished itself, "the human ego with which most men identify themselves is no more than his outer shell" (p. 50). Chittick explains the need for consciousness to be in ceaseless contemplation of the Real in order to remedy the forgetfulness of the Divine: "the maintenance of the world depends on the balance between the contemplative who has realized the state of Universal Man, and fallen man, who lives in a state of forgetfulness" (p. 61). The theomorphic identity of all human beings is the Universal or Perfect Man, as Rūmī teaches:

> The owner of the Heart [Universal or Perfect Man] becomes a six-faced mirror: through him God looks upon (all) the six directions. Whosoever hath his dwelling place in (the world of) the six directions, God doth not look upon him except through the mediation of him (the owner of the Heart).... Without him God does not bestow bounty on any one (p. 62).

Rūmī reminds readers that the original function of every human being is to be the Universal or Perfect Man in order to act as a channel of grace in the world. In fact, not to do so, is to forfeit what it means to be human:

> There is one thing in this world which must never be forgotten. If you were to forget everything else, but did not forget that, then there would be no cause to worry; whereas if you performed and remembered and did not forget every single thing, but forgot that one thing, then you would have done nothing whatsoever (p. 63).

The saints and sages of the world's religions remind the human collectivity of their original or theomorphic nature and provide methods of realizing this transpersonal identity:

> In the composition of man all sciences were originally commingled, so that his spirit might show forth all hidden things, as limpid water shows forth all that is under it—pebbles, broken shards, and the like—and all that is above it, reflecting in the substance of the water. Such is its nature, without treatment or training. But when it was mingled with earth or other colors [when Adam fell], that property and that knowledge was parted from it and forgotten by it. Then God most High sent forth prophets and saints, like a great, limpid water such as delivers out of darkness and accidental coloration every mean and dark water that enters into it. Then it remembers; when the soul of man sees itself unsullied, it knows for sure that so it was in the beginning, pure, and it knows that those shadows and colors were mere accidents (pp. 64–65).

Identity itself belongs to the Divine and thus the mystery of human identity cannot be resolved without the inclusion of what transcends the empirical ego. Rūmī astutely writes: "The idol of your self is the mother of (all) idols…" (p. 82)

Whether the human being chooses to do good actions or evil ones, all creation confirms the existence of the Absolute. Rūmī writes, "…(both) infidelity and faith are bearing witness (to Him): both are bowing down in worship before His Lordliness" (p. 40). The secret of the Prophetic Tradition that affirms "Die before ye die" is a call for self-effacement before the Divine in order to be reabsorbed in the Divine. Rūmī states that ultimately death in this life is an alchemical process of spiritual transformation; it is a journey of homecoming and not of departure in order to return to the Supreme Identity:

> O you who possess sincerity, (if) you want that (Reality) unveiled, choose death and tear off the veil [of your self-existence]—
>
> Not such a death that you will go into the grave, (but) a death consisting of (spiritual) transformation (p. 72).

Rūmī casts light on the famous, yet no less controversial dictum by the great Sufi mystic al-Ḥallāj (858–922), which is an instruction on how to approach the Divine:

> Take the famous utterance "I am God." Some men reckon it a great pretension; but "I am God" is in fact a great humility. The man who says "I am the servant of God" asserts that two exist, one himself and the other God. But he who says "I am God" has naughted himself and cast himself to the winds. He says, "I am God": that is, "I am not, He is all, nothing has existence but God, I am pure nonentity, I am nothing." In this the humility is greater (p. 79).

The deepening of our understanding of the mystical dimension of the religions will aid in creating more spiritual literacy across the faith traditions and will simultaneously revive the meaning and significance of the outer or formalistic dimension of religion. For Rūmī and all saints and sages of the sapiential traditions are upholding the right understanding of their own faith traditions and how to approach them accordingly. The *shahādah* or the essential declaration of faith in Islam, *Lā ilāha illā Llāh*, "There is no god but God," when seen through the discerning and contemplative "eye of the heart" becomes a crystalline distillation of Rūmī's metaphysical teachings. Two main steps on the Path are contained in the *shahādah*, the first consisting of the "annihilation of self" (*fanā*) and the second the "subsistence in God" (*baqā*), for when the illusory nature of human identity dissociated from the Divine reality is seen for what it is and it becomes evident that the Divine is all that exists, concentration on the Real becomes possible. This formula may also be understood as "There is no self but the Self" or, correspondingly, "There is no reality but the Reality," being universal in principle and applicable to all faiths.

As the centuries pass, Rūmī continues to demonstrate his profound presence in the hearts and minds of those who are attracted to his message, which calls for nothing less than a re-sacralization of this world and union with the Divine. The importance of this book is that it guides readers through the fundamental themes of Rūmī's complex spiritual labyrinth, making his symbolic language intelligible to readers unfamiliar with his teachings or the mystical dimension of Islam. It is truly remarkable to find the timeless in time; and it is not only through Rūmī but all of the saints and sages of the world's faith traditions that such examples of pure metaphysics may be found, urging a resurgence of the sacred that is ever-present in this very moment. We conclude with two lines from Rūmī's *Dīwān* inviting all to take part in the pilgrimage of the Heart: "Make a journey out of self into [your real] self, O master, / For by such a journey earth becomes a quarry of gold" (p. 98).

18

A Spirit of Tolerance:
*The Inspiring Life of Tierno Bokar**

> The rainbow owes its beauty to the variety of its shades and colors. In the same way, we consider the voices of various believers that rise up from all parts of the earth as a symphony of praises addressing God.
>
> Tierno Bokar[1]

With the unremitting bombardment of news and media coverage depicting contemporary Africa in a state of total disarray—ridden with famine, disease, genocide, war—we are blessed for this profound testimonial of Amadou Hampaté Bâ's extraordinary Sufi master of Africa, Tierno Bokar (1875–1939). It is through the universal message of this Malian mystic that the world's spiritual traditions, not only Islam, can honor what has been regarded as the "religion of the heart", or the "transcendent unity of religions"[2]—fearlessly affirmed in *The Tarjumān al-ashwāq*[3] of Ibn 'Arabī (1165–1240), the

---

* Amadou Hampaté Bâ. Introduction by Louis Brenner, edited by Roger Gaetani, translated from French by Jane Casewit. Bloomington: World Wisdom, 2008, 236 pp.

[1] Quoted on p. 126.

[2] See Frithjof Schuon, *The Transcendent Unity of Religions*.

[3] Ibn 'Arabī, *The Tarjumān Al-Ashwāq*, trans. Reynold A. Nicholson (London: Theosophical Publishing House, 1978)

Spanish-born mystic known as "the greatest master" (*al-shaykh al-akbar*). Considerable interest regarding this great spiritual teacher of Mali is due to the acclaimed play *Tierno Bokar*, by renowned director Peter Brook, which was adapted for the stage from Bâ's book by Marie-Hélène Estienne. It is with the hopes of the editors and publisher that this volume will accompany other key contemporary works, such as that of Martin Lings' book on Shaykh Ahmad al-Alawī (1869–1934).[4]

During his youth, Amadou Hampaté Bâ (1900–1991) became a disciple of Tierno Bokar while attending a Qur'ānic school under Bokar's direction in Bandiagara, Mali. Bâ was to become a well-known Malian diplomat, writer and influential voice of Africa—providing information and insight into its history, religion, literature, culture and life. He is the author of the following celebrated quote: "In Africa, when an old person dies, it is as if a library has burned down" (p. xvii). Without Hampaté Bâ's efforts to put this testimony into writing, the modern world would perhaps know nothing of this great master, Tierno Bokar, since this work contains most of the only recorded words of this man of remarkable spiritual insight.

This new translation, *A Spirit of Tolerance: The Inspiring Life of Tierno Bokar*, is divided into a tripartite discourse—Part 1: *His Life*; Part 2: *His Words*; and Part 3: *His Teachings*. There are also two important appendices: Appendix I: *The Pearl of Perfection*[5] and Appendix II: *Sufism and Brotherhoods* (*Ṭuruq*) *in Islam*, offering a broad overview of the different Sufi orders, including relevant photographs depicting the ambiance of where Tierno Bokar lived, his disciples, the mosque of Bandiagara, his tomb, as well as illustrations of present-day Malian life. The book also contains significant biographical notes on the authors and those who helped prepare the book.

---

[4] *A Sufi Saint of the Twentieth Century: Shaikh Ahmad Al-Alawi, His Spiritual Heritage and Legacy* (Cambridge, UK: Islamic Texts Society, 1993).

[5] *Jawharat al-kamāl*, revealed by the Prophet Muhammad in a vision to Si Ahmad al-Tijani in 1781.

Louis Brenner, who provides the Introduction, is arguably the most knowledgeable scholar in the English speaking world on the writings of both Hampaté Bâ and the life and thought of Tierno Bokar.

PART ONE, "HIS LIFE": Tierno Bokar Salif Taal was known as "the sage of Bandiagara" in Mali, West Africa. From an early age his life was infused with the spirit. His maternal grandfather was Seydou Hann, a great Sufi mystic of the Qadiri order, and later the Tijāniyya. In addition, Tierno benefited from the innate wisdom of his other family members which provided a pivotal support to his traditional education. And yet his education took place in juxtaposition to a social milieu that was characterized by an atmosphere of turmoil: with the seething combination of compulsory modernizations and foreign occupation, tribal and sectarian differences were escalating. From an early age he learned to find peace within himself and to converse regularly with God. Bokar provides us with some advice offered by his mother to guide him in "the greater *jihād*":

> Write the Divine Name *Allāh* on a wall, next to your bed so that when you awaken the Name will be the first image that your eyes fix upon. When you get up, pronounce it with fervor from the depths of your soul, so that it is the first word to come out of your mouth and to enter your ears. At night when you go to bed, fix your eyes on the Name so that it is the last image contemplated before being taken off into the temporary death of sleep. If you persist, the light contained in the four letters will spread over you and a spark of the divine Essence will enflame your soul and illuminate it (p. 14).

By the age of fifteen, Bokar had virtually memorized the Qur'ān, the rituals and laws of Islam, and the lives of the saints such as al-Ghazālī (1058–1111), Ibn 'Arabī and Muhammad al-Dabbar, and yet his knowledge was in no way restricted to only this. Readers will be interested to note that "the *Meccan Revelations* [*al-Futūḥāt al-Makkīya*] of the great Andalusian spiritual master Ibn 'Arabī was his [Tierno Bokar's] favorite book" (p. 21).

Tierno Bokar was tremendously unassuming and did not wish to be addressed with any titles, even that of spiritual master or teacher—"We are all teachers and we are all students"—referring to his students as "brother" (p. xv). Tierno Bokar received initiation (*al-bay'a*) into the secrets of the Tijani Sufi order by Amadou Tafsir Bâ. At the age of twenty-six, Bokar's *shaykh* informed him, "I have nothing more to teach you" (p. 23). By the age of thirty-three, Tierno Bokar was the director of the Bandiagara *zāwiya*, which was called "the refuge of love and charity".

A central and unforgettable element of Tierno Bokar's life has to do with the disagreement that emerged in the Tijani order over certain ways of reciting a particular Tijani prayer, known as *The Pearl of Perfection*. There were those who practiced the "eleven beads" and those who practised the recitation of "twelve beads". The disagreement came about when the founder of the order, Ahmad al-Tijani, arrived late on one occasion:

> One day he was delayed, and the students started the *wazīfa* [a Tijani litany] without him. They had already finished the eleventh recitation of *The Pearl of Perfection* when the Shaykh was at last able to join them. Spontaneously, and so that the Shaykh could give them his benediction as was the custom, they repeated the prayer a twelfth time, after which the Shaykh blessed them (p. 44).

Without any observation, positive or negative, from the Shaykh, some of his disciples began to practise the "twelve beads", a practice that was later adopted by the Umarian branch of the Tijāniyya found in Mali and Niger.

Later in his life, having received a crucial letter from Alfa Hashimi Taal (brother of the king of Bandiagara), Bokar traveled to meet with Shaykh Sharif Hamallah, a clan rival, in order to better comprehend this dispute between the two practices. During his stay Bokar had a *metanoia*, or "change of mind", and asked to receive *tajdīd* (renewal of his *wird*) into the "eleven beads". On Bokar's return to Bandiagara, the news had spread quickly of the renewal of his *wird* into the "eleven beads" with Sharif Hamallah. It was from this point on that Tierno Bokar experienced extreme hardships: he was essentially ostracized by his clan and family and forbidden to teach or pray publicly. Tierno Bokar's school was destroyed and he and his two wives and children were placed under house arrest. He spent the remaining years of his life in sheer solitude and yet he never lost confidence in God's benediction nor did he cease to be a spiritual light to all those who dared to visit him under such adverse conditions.

PART TWO, "WORDS": Tierno Bokar taught in the traditional method that was known and used throughout Africa which was oral rather than written. Contrary to the modern bias against oral traditions, the "word" was perceived as being potentially sacred, originating from what was transcendent and divine, and was referred to as the "life-giving word". The author points out that, "In Islam, as in many other religious traditions, esoteric knowledge is taught by word of mouth" (p. 111).

In this section of the book, "the sage of Bandiagara", Tierno Bokar, expresses a universal truth regarding the ineffable nature of the Absolute or the Divine Reality which is beyond all conceptualization:[6]

---

[6] Given Tierno Bokar's unanimous recognition of both the inner (esoteric) and outer (exoteric) dimensions of the world's spiritual traditions, it is appropriate to point out that the terrestrial inability to project any certainty onto what is Absolute is known through the *via negativa* and apophatic theology, which is acknowledged in the testimonies of the perennial philosophy. This is reminiscent of the sacred formula of the (first) *shahādah*: *Lā ilāha illā 'Llāh* (There is no divinity but God), similarly the first aphorism

God is the bewilderment of human intelligence because on one hand, if you affirm His existence, you cannot, in any case, prove it materially or mathematically. On the other hand, if you deny His very existence, you deny your own existence, which is merely the effects of His existence. Of course, you do exist. And even if one cannot prove God materially, it is nonetheless necessary to remember that the non-visibility or non-tangibility of a thing is not absolute proof of its nonexistence.

Finally, God is the bewilderment of intelligence because everything that you conceive in your thought and give form to in your speech as being God ceases by this very fact to be God. It becomes no more than *your own way* of conceiving Him. He escapes all definition (p. 135).

Throughout this book readers will notice that Tierno Bokar continuously acknowledges and affirms the underlying significance of the world's religions:

With all my heart, I desire the coming of the era of reconciliation amongst all religions of the earth, the era in which these united religions will support each other to form a spiritual and moral canopy, the era in which they will be at

---

of the *Tao Te Ching*: "The Tao that can be named is not the Tao", *neti-neti* (not this, not that) of the Upanishads, or the Hindu doctrine of *saguna Brahman* (qualified) in contrast to *nirguna Brahman* (non-qualified), and the *negatio negationis* (negation of negation) or the distinction between God (*Gott*) and Godhead (*Gottheit*) central to Meister Eckhart's teachings. These distinctions of different orders of reality and their corresponding ineffability are also found in the First Peoples religions and their Shamanic traditions. For example, when referring to *Wakan-Tanka*, the "Great Spirit" or "Great Mysterious", the Lakota make the distinction between *Tunkashila* and *Ate*—"Grandfather" and "Father"—Godhead and God. "*Tunkashila*" refers to what transcends the created order which is Infinite and Unqualified and "*Ate*" refers to the created order of the phenomenal world. Yet both determinants underscore an essential underlying unity which is not confused in *Wakan-Tanka*—the "Great Spirit" or "Great Mysterious".

peace in God by resting upon three supports: Love, Charity, Brotherhood.

There is only one God, and there can be only one Way that leads towards Him, one Religion of which its various worldly manifestations are like branches spreading out from a single tree. This Religion can only be called Truth, and its dogmas can only be three: Love, Charity, Brotherhood (p. 159).

PART THREE, "HIS TEACHINGS": one of the principal methods of Tierno Bokar's instruction was to meet the seeker at his or her own level of receptivity which was in accordance with the Prophet's instruction: "Speak to people according to the level of their understanding" (p. 110). Tierno Bokar often made use of the potent symbol of the river that was widely used by the different Sufi *turuq* when describing stages of the spiritual path:

> There are three ways to know a river: First of all, there is the man who has heard the river spoken about and becomes capable by imitation and repetition to describe it without having seen it himself. This is the first degree of knowledge.
>
> Then there is the man who has undertaken the journey and who has arrived at the banks of the river. Seated on the banks of the river, he contemplates it with his own eyes and is a witness to its majesty. This is the second degree of knowledge.
>
> Finally, there is the man who throws himself into the river and becomes one with it. This is the supreme degree of Knowledge (p. 199).

This book stands out as a traditional testimony to the universal spiritual heritage of all people through the life of a twentieth-century African saint, Tierno Bokar. In addressing the diverse readership we hope that this testimony may be instrumental in leading more people, especially the younger generations, to reconnect to their own spiritual traditions.

"The sage of Bandiagara" provides this astute aphorism for the modern world: "Do not go seeking fortune by begging in far-off places, you who are seated upon a sack of gold. Make use of this fortune, make it grow by trading in it with others" (p. 155). Readers will find that Tierno Bokar, like his fellow Sufi companion Ibn ʿArabī, affirms the religion of the heart.

19

*Introduction to Sufi Doctrine**

> Whereas the ordinary way of believers [exoteric] is directed towards obtaining a state of blessedness after death, a state which may be attained through indirect and, as it were, symbolical participation in Divine Truths by carrying out prescribed works, Sufism contains its end or aim within itself in the sense that it can give access to direct knowledge of the eternal [esoteric].
>
> Titus Burckhardt[1]

This classic work by Titus Burckhardt, which first appeared in English in 1959 from the French *Du Soufisme*, has been republished and made available once again to interested readers. We can confidently say that this work is just as relevant today as it was then, and perhaps it is even more important today as the postmodern world continues to pull further away from its spiritual heritage. Burckhardt articulates with precision and intimacy the essence of traditional Sufism known as Islamic mysticism or *taṣawwuf*, in a manner that makes its doctrines and methods available to western audiences. Although its title describes this work as an "introduction" to Sufism, learned students of Sufism, Islam, comparative religion and Sufi psy-

---

* Titus Burckhardt. Translated by D.M. Matheson, Foreword by William C. Chittick. World Wisdom, 2008, 152 pp.

[1] *Introduction to Sufi Doctrine*, p. 3.

chology or spiritual psychology will gain much benefit from reading this work.

Titus Burckhardt (1908–1984) was one of the leading members of the perennialist or traditionalist school of comparative religion who had first-hand knowledge of Sufism. This qualified him to write about its doctrines and methods including authoritative translations of classic Sufi works such as those of Ibn ʿArabī. In the Foreword to this new edition William C. Chittick, leading translator and interpreter of classical Islamic philosophical and mystical texts and widely acknowledged for his works on Rūmī (1207–1273) and Ibn ʿArabī (1165–1240), describes the impact of Burckhardt's work on him as a young man: "The book meant a great deal to me when I first discovered it as an undergraduate forty years ago. I had been studying the Orientalist books on Sufism and after three months had pretty much convinced myself that I knew the topic rather well. This book stopped me in my tracks" (p. ix).

The work is divided into three parts. Part I deals with *The Nature of Sufism*. In the first chapter, *Al-Taṣawwuf*, Burckhardt clarifies much of the confusion around what Sufism is by contrasting it with what it is not. Fundamentally, in order to understand the doctrines of Sufism one needs to learn what esotericism is, which Burckhardt confirms: "There are doctrines which can be understood only from the 'inside' through a work of assimilation or penetration that is essentially intellectual and, for that very reason, goes beyond the limitations of discursive thought" (p. xiii). He also answers the question regarding what is the relation between Sufism and Islam.

> It may appear strange that Sufism should on the one hand be the 'spirit' or 'heart' of Islam (*rūḥ al-islām* or *qalb al-islām*) and on the other hand represent at the same time the outlook which is, in the Islamic world, the most free in relation to the mental framework of that world, though it is

important to note that this true and wholly inward freedom must not be confused with any movements of rebellion against the tradition: such movements are not intellectually free in relation to the forms which they deny because they fail to understand them (p. 4).

In the second chapter, *Sufism and Mysticism*, the author clarifies the misunderstandings around the term "mysticism" which has been grafted a meaning that has a strong tendency to be marked by "individualistic subjectivity" which Burckhardt declares not to be the same as *taṣawwuf* or Islamic mysticism. Yet the word "mysticism" as it applies to its original meaning shares a common significance with *taṣawwuf*. In chapter three, *Sufism and Pantheism*, Burckhardt declares that Sufism is not pantheism and reminds readers that pantheism is "an error explicitly rejected by every traditional doctrine" (p. 17). In chapter four, *Knowledge and Love*, Burckhardt illustrates the complementary relationship of both knowledge and love and how they are both essential to the Sufi path. "The language of love makes it possible to enunciate the most profoundly esoteric truths without coming into conflict with dogmatic theology. Finally, the intoxication of love symbolically corresponds to states of knowledge which go beyond discursive thought" (p. 21). Students of Sufi psychology will find chapter five, *The Branches of the Doctrine*, to be very instructive as it provides many psychological insights that pertain to what is authentically transpersonal. "The connection with the metaphysical order provides spiritual psychology with qualitative criteria such as are wholly lacking in profane psychology..." (pp. 26–27). In chapter six, *Sufi Interpretation of the Qur'ān*, Burckhardt reminds the reader that "Since Sufism represents the inner aspect of Islam, its doctrine is in substance an esoteric commentary on the Qur'ān" (p. 31).

In Part II, *The Doctrinal Foundations*, chapter seven, *The Aspects of Unity*, Burckhardt writes: "The Islamic doctrine is contained as a whole in the *Tawḥīd*, the 'affirmation of the Divine Unity'" (p. 43). It is through the doctrine of Unity that Burckhardt affirms the "transcendent unity of religions", acknowledging the commonality between the Sufi doctrine and the doctrine of non-duality found in Vedānta. In chapter eight, *Creation*, Burckhardt summarizes this chapter by quoting the *hadīth qudsī* "I was a hidden treasure; I wished to be known (or, to know) and I created the world," thus confirming that the creation of the world is a manifestation of the Divine to the Divine and not of the Divine to the empirical ego (p. 50). In chapter nine, *The Archetypes*, he clarifies that archetypes have a transpersonal origin *in divinis*, and that they have no correspondence with what modern psychology has termed "archetypes". In chapter twelve, *Universal Man*, Burckhardt describes the perennial doctrine of transcendence and immanence:

> It may thus be said that man, who is a microcosm, and the universe, which is a macrocosm, are like two mirrors each reflecting the other. On the one hand man only exists in relation to the macrocosm which determines him, and on the other hand man knows the macrocosm, and this means that all the possibilities which are unfolded in the world are principially contained in man's intellectual essence (p. 64).

In Part III, *Spiritual Realization*, chapter fourteen, *Three Aspects of the Way*, Burckhardt summarizes this chapter: "The Divine Reality is at the same time Knowledge and Being. He who seeks to approach that Reality must overcome not only ignorance and lack of awareness, but also the grip which purely theoretical learning and other 'unreal' things of the same kind exert on him" (p. 76). In chapter fifteen, *The Intellectual Faculties*, Burckhardt articulates the primacy of the intellect (*'aql*) which is not to be confused with modern and postmodern notions of the "intellect", "reason" or "mind": "Now this purely intellectual knowledge implies direct identification with its object and that is the decisive criterion which distinguishes intellectual 'vision' from rational working of the mind" (p. 84). Chapter sixteen, *Rites*, illuminates the human necessity and spiritual normativity of rites on the spiritual path. In chapter seventeen, *Meditation*, Burckhardt makes it clear that the proper abode of meditation is discernment between the real and the illusory. Chapter eighteen, *Contemplation, According to Muhyī-d-Dīn ibn 'Arabī* is summarized in the words of Ibn 'Arabī: "Thus God is the mirror in which you see yourself, as you are. His mirror in which He contemplates His Names. Now His Names are not other than Himself, so that the analogy of relations is an inversion" (p. 102).

This work is a quintessential resource for traditional Sufi studies, as it crystallizes the very substance and essence of the Sufi path, perhaps as astutely as any theoretical presentation could do outside formal participation in a *ṭarīqah* (path or way). The path symbolized by a radius traveling from the periphery of a circle to its center illustrates the unanimity of all spiritual paths affirming the Sufi saying: "The ways *(ṭuruq)* towards God are as numerous as the souls *[nafas]* of men" (p. 114). It is Sufis who realize themselves through knowledge, like Muhyī al-Dīn ibn 'Arabī, *al-Shaykh al-Akbar* (The Greatest Master), who exemplify the religion of the heart, which this work reflects unequivocally.

Part VIII

Other Themes in World Spirituality

20

*The Underlying Religion: An Introduction to the Perennial Philosophy**

> There is... one sole religion and one sole worship for all beings endowed with understanding, and this is presupposed through a variety of rites.
>
> Nicholas of Cusa[1]

When exploring the foundations of transpersonal psychology and even humanistic psychology (Maslow, 1968, 1994) it becomes evident that the perennial philosophy is central to their tenets, as is verified (Ferrer, 2000; 2002) and supported by key figures of the transpersonal field such as: Frances

---

* M. Lings and C. Minnaar (eds.). Bloomington: World Wisdom, 2007, 368pp.

[1] *Ibid.*, p. xii. Readers may be intrigued by the title of this volume, since the expression "perennial philosophy" is commonly attributed to Aldous Huxley. But he did not coin the phrase, in spite of the common misconception. Rather Huxley published under this title, in 1945, an anthology which was widely recognized, and from this time on he was associated with the perennial philosophy. What is not commonly known is that there is a group of writers and spiritual practitioners that have dedicated their lives to the exposition of the perennial philosophy—they are known as the 'perennialist' or 'traditionalist' school of comparative religion. Although not a "school" *per se*, it is sometimes referred to as such, which can lead to misunderstandings, for the truths articulated by the perennial philosophy are not the exclusive possession of any school or individual, nor can they be invented for that matter.

Vaughan (1982); Robert Hutchins (1987); Ken Wilber (1994); Kaisa Puhakka (2008); Bryan Wittine (1993); Stanislav Grof (1998); and Roger Walsh (1993).

Due to the pivotal function of the perennial philosophy within both transpersonal and humanistic psychology, this volume will be of paramount interest to researchers and practitioners, and it belongs in every library of transpersonal and humanistic psychology.

This recent anthology was compiled by Clinton Minnaar and the late Dr. Martin Lings (1909–2005), one of the leading perennialist authors of the twentieth century, who was the Keeper of Oriental Manuscripts and Printed Books at the British Museum.

This anthology is organized into seven themes, each theme having its corresponding essays:

I. "TRADITION AND MODERNITY", describes the hiatus that divides the sacred orientation of the traditional world from that of the secular and progress-driven modern and postmodern world.

> Nothing and nobody is any longer in the right place; men no longer recognize any effective authority in the spiritual order or any legitimate power in the temporal; the "profane" presume to discuss what is sacred, and to contest its character and even its existence; the inferior judges the superior, ignorance sets bounds to wisdom, error prevails over truth, the human supersedes the divine, earth overtops heaven, the individual sets the measure for all things and claims to dictate to the universe laws drawn entirely from his own relative and fallible reason. "Woe unto you, ye blind guides," the Gospel says; and indeed everywhere today one sees nothing but blind leaders of the blind, who, unless restrained by some timely check, will inevitably lead them into the abyss, there to perish with them (pp. 317–318).

II. "TRADITIONAL COSMOLOGY AND MODERN SCIENCE" underscores the implicit limitations of modern science, its failures and destructive tendencies for not receiving its directives from divine principles utilized since time immemorial in both East and West.

> At the heart of the traditional sciences of the cosmos, as well as traditional anthropology, psychology, and aesthetics stands the *scientia sacra* which contains the principles of these sciences while being primarily concerned with the knowledge of the Principle which is both sacred knowledge and knowledge of the sacred *par excellence*, since the Sacred as such is none other than the Principle (p. 117).

III. "METAPHYSICS" gives a clear exposition on what is and what is not integral metaphysics according to the perennial philosophy, which has nothing to do with New Age spirituality.

> In truth pure metaphysics is neither Eastern nor Western, but universal, being in essence above and beyond all forms and all contingencies. The exterior forms in which it is clothed only serve the necessities of exposition, so as to express whatever is expressible. These forms may be Eastern or Western; but under the appearance of diversity there is always and everywhere a selfsame basis, at least wherever true metaphysics exits, and this for the simple reason that truth is one (p. 95).

IV. "SYMBOLISM" locates symbols outside the pale of modern psychology, or outside that of the "unconscious" from which they are commonly thought to originate, rather than from their true origin *in divinis* as authentic "archetypes".

> The answer to the question 'What is Symbolism?', if deeply understood, has been known to change altogether a man's life; and it could indeed be said that most of the problems of the modern world result from ignorance of that answer. As to the past however, there is no traditional doctrine which does not teach that this world is the world of symbols,

inasmuch as it contains nothing which is not a symbol (Lings, 1991, p. vii).

V. "THE PERENNIAL PHILOSOPHY" provides a revision and an expansion, *mutatis mutandis*, of what has been commonly attributed, and often wrongly, to the perennial philosophy or the "transcendent unity of religions". It is through the perennial philosophy that true and authentic interfaith dialogue can proceed, for both differences and similarities are taken into account without compromising the integrity of each tradition. Ibn ʿArabī writes:

> My heart is capable of every form: it is a pasture for gazelles
>   and a convent for Christian Monks,
> And idol-temple and the pilgrim's Kaʿba [Mecca],
>   and the tables of the Torah and the book of the Qurʾān;
> I follow the religion of Love, whichever way his camels take;
>   my religion and my faith is the true religion (p. 224).[2]

VI. "BEAUTY" makes it clear that it is incumbent upon anyone on a spiritual path to live within a context of beauty for spiritual support, thus highlighting the inherent dangers and pitfalls of not having such an integral milieu.

---

[2] Ibn ʿArabī (1165–1240), also known as Shaykh al-Akbar (the Greatest Master), is an exponent *par excellence* of the perennial philosophy. In the quote above he introduced an Andalusian model of religion that allowed the three Abrahamic faiths—Judaism, Christianity and Islam—to live side by side in peace for many centuries. Not only were these diverse traditions living and fostering a spirit of "tolerance" toward the multiplicity of spiritual forms but they were each flourishing in an esoteric ecumenicism providing some of the most exalted examples of true and authentic mysticisms East or West that simultaneously embraced the 'transcendent unity of religions'. Some of these axial mystics are Moses Maimonides (1135–1204), St. John of the Cross (1542–1591), St. Teresa of Ávila (1515–1582), Ignatius of Loyola (1491–1556), Solomon ibn Gabirol (1021–1058), Ibn Rushd or Averroes (1126–1198) and it cannot be forgotten that the Zohar, first found in Spain during the 13th century, is considered one of the most important works on Kabbalah or Jewish mysticism.

"It is told that once Ananda, the beloved disciple of the Buddha, saluted his master and said: Half of the holy life, O master, is friendship with the beautiful, association with the beautiful, communion with the beautiful." "Say not so, Ananda, say not so!" the master replied. "It is not half the holy life; it is the whole of the holy life" (p. 249).

VII. "VIRTUE AND PRAYER" provides important notes on spiritual guidance, complementing the previous chapters dealing predominantly with that of traditional doctrine.

All great spiritual experiences agree in this: there is no common measure between the means put into operation and the result. "With men this is impossible, but with God all things are possible," says the Gospel. In fact, what separates man from divine Reality is but a thin partition: God is infinitely close to man, but man is infinitely far from God. This partition, for man, is a mountain; man stands in front of a mountain which he must remove with his own hands. He digs away the earth, but in vain, the mountain remains; man however goes on digging, in the name of God. And the mountain vanishes. It was never there (p. 308).

The Afterword entitled "The Revival of Interest in Tradition", written by the late perennialist Whitall N. Perry (1920–2005), provides a condensed overview of the formative figures of the perennialist or traditionalist school and their unique contributions.

21

*Pray Without Ceasing: The Way of the Invocation in World Religions**

> Pray without ceasing.
>
> I Thessalonians 5:17

If the presupposition held is that the human being exists in both the horizontal and vertical domains, that is, both in time and in the timeless, both in the physical and that of the metaphysical, it is easier to comprehend and consequently situate the significance of prayer as a quintessential bridge between these two distinct domains. Without prayer as a vital link to connect these two domains, they remain separate, opaque, and disconnected, as if impervious to one another without the aid of a higher reality. It can be argued that without prayer it is not possible to be truly what the human state is intended to be in its most complete sense. Yet to think and see from this point of view in an era so deprived of the sacred, one needs to be vigilant about the very presuppositions held about the nature of reality and about the course this paves for the wayfarer on the Path. We cannot overlook that the modern world and its prolongation, the postmodern world, are not neutral or value-free—that is, without their own theoretical tenets that are antagonistic to metaphysics and integral spirituality.

---

* Edited by Patrick Laude. Bloomington, World Wisdom, 2006, 240pp.

This anthology compiled by Patrick Laude provides extraordinary foundational texts on the experience of prayer, complemented by essays on the remembrance and realization of the Divine. According to the diverse saints and sages, to abide in the Divine Name is to abide in none other than the Divine Presence itself, meaning there is no distinction between the Name and the Named. The Name is none other than the transpersonal reality itself. Prayer allows for a direct relationship with the Divine, establishing a link between the human and the Divine. When surveying the diverse traditions and the mystical dimensions of the world's religions, it becomes apparent that prayer defines the centrality of the human condition and holds an eschatological relevance. This is because human beings cannot go beyond themselves by effort alone; they need an agency that transcends the empirical ego. Prayer provides an integral method of accessing the transpersonal dimension, a method known as *japa-yoga* in Hinduism, *nembutsu* in Buddhism, the Jesus Prayer in Christianity, and *dhikr* in Islam. In his insightful introduction to the book, Laude explains that "the invocation is not only a prayer of the human to the Divine, it is also a prayer of the Divine to itself through a human intermediary" (p. xiv). He adds, "The invocation realizes the *raison d'être* of all religious practices since the latter ultimately aim at recognizing, remembering, and assimilating the supreme Reality" (p. xvi). It has also been underscored that in order to make this pilgrimage to the One, spiritual guidance and an affiliation to a divine Revelation is needed for the methodic repetition or invocation of the Divine Name to be efficacious.

It is imperative to define our terms and recall that the etymological root of the English word "religion" is the Latin *religare*, meaning to "to re-bind" or "to bind back", by implication to the Divine or a transcendent Reality. The function of prayer is to do just this, to assist in the reintegration of the human with the Divine. In fact, each of the world's religions provides doctrines (theories) and methods (practices) on how to make the journey or return to the Spirit. Prayer, from this perspective, informs in its wholeness what human identity is *in divinis*.

Within the Hindu tradition (known as the *sanātana dharma* or "eternal religion"), the medieval poet and philosopher Tulsīdās frames the paramount nature that prayer holds in the final phase of the temporal cycle, and its essential connection to the invocation of the Divine Name: "In this *Kali* Age salvation is not gained by knowledge, *karma*, and worship. But only by taking shelter in the Name" (p. 10). Śrī Rāmakrishna makes a providential observation concerning the Divine Name and its identification with the transpersonal dimension: "God and His name are identical" (p. 69). Swami Ramdas confirms this same teaching, "God and His Name are not distinct from one another. The Name is God Himself" (p. 149). According to the *Bhagavad Gītā* it is sufficient at the moment of death to recall the Divine Name in order to abide in the divine Presence itself:

> And at the hour of death, he who dies
> Remembering Me,
> Having relinquished the body,
> Goes to My state of being.
> In this matter there is no doubt...

It is furthermore added,

> Therefore, at all times
> Meditate on Me (or: Remember Me [*mam anusmara*])
> With your mind and intellect
> Fixed on Me.
> In this way, you shall surely come
> To Me.... (p. 3)

Chaitanya, who revitalized the *bhakti* movement in India, emphasizes that the practice of the invocation of the Divine Name can be observed in all situations and at all moments of the day and is available to all seekers regardless of one's ethnic, racial, socio-economic, or religious identity:

> The names of the Lord are many, they are filled with power like Himself and He has laid down no laws regarding their repetition (they can be repeated anywhere and at all times by anybody of any caste, age, or denomination). Alas! such is His Grace, and yet we on our part have not yet developed full love and enthusiasm for the name of the Lord (p. 4).

Swami Ramdas tirelessly emphasized the universality of this spiritual practice that is available to all: "Whatever race, caste, creed, or color you may belong, take up the Name of God" (p. 150).

Renowned exponent of *Advaita Vedānta* or non-duality, Shankara recognizes the spiritual validity of *japa* when writing: "Remember, nothing can save thee at the last moment except the shelter of the Lord, so sing thou His sweet Name Govinda! Govinda!... (p. xiv). Indulge not in formal ceremonies. Dwell in the Atman. Cross the Ocean of transmigration singing the sweet name—Govinda! Govinda! Govinda!" Shankara elsewhere writes, "Control thy soul, restrain thy breathing, distinguish the transitory from the True, repeat the holy Name of God, and thus calm the agitated mind. To this universal rule apply thyself with all thy heart and all thy soul" (p. 69). When a devotee asked Ramana Maharshi the following question: "Can *advaita* be realized by *japa* of holy names; say Rāma, Krishna, etc.?" The Sage of Arunachala unequivocally affirmed, "Yes" (p. 156).

Kabīr, who was regarded as a saint by Hindus, Sikhs, and Muslims alike, stressed that: "The True Name is the only thing to repeat. It is the best gift to make" (p. 7). The highly esteemed *bhakti* poet Mīrābāī recalls discovering the Divine Name and its impact on her life: "I discovered the great secret in uttering the Name and adhering to this quintessence of *śāstras* (scriptures), I reached my Girdhar through prayers and tears" (p. 9).

Within the Buddhist tradition, Hōnen stresses the practice of *nembutsu* or the invocation of the name of Amida: "cease from all other religious practices, apply yourself to the Nembutsu alone." He recounts the Buddha Shakyamuni expressing, "Give yourself with undivided mind to the repetition of the name of the Buddha who is in Himself endless life" (p. 13). The chief disciple of Hōnen, Shinran, makes an important link between the invocation of the Divine Name and mindfulness practice: "Saying the Name is constant mindfulness" (*nen* 念, p. 25). Respected author on Tibetan Buddhism, Marco Pallis, points out that the six-syllable formula *Om mani padme Hum*, while facilitating complex mystical correspondences contains "the quintessence of the teaching of all the Buddhas" (p. 107).

Within the Jewish tradition, the Old Testament instructs: "I will praise Thy Name continuously and will extol it in all things" (Ecclesiastes 51). Rabbi Isaac of Akko discusses the mystery of the Divine Name and its connection between the finite and the Infinite as a means of transpersonal union within the Jewish tradition and its mystical dimension:

> Remember God and God's love constantly. Let your thought not be separated from God. I declare, both to individuals and to the masses: If you want to know the secret of binding your soul above and joining your thought to God—so that by means of such continuous contemplation you attain incessantly the world that is coming, and so that God be with you always, in this life and the next—then place in front of the eyes of your mind the letters of God's name, as if they were written in a book in Hebrew script. Visualize every letter extending to infinity. What I mean is: when you visualize the letters, focus on them with your mind's eye as you contemplate infinity. Both together: gazing and meditating (p. 33).

Maimonides explains that only those who received special

instruction were permitted to invoke the tetragrammaton YHVH:

> A priestly blessing has been prescribed for us, in which the name of the Eternal (YHVH) is pronounced as it is written (and not in the form of a substituted name) and that name is the "explicit name." It was not generally known how the name had to be pronounced, nor how it was proper to vocalize the separate letters, nor whether any of the letters which could be doubled should in fact be doubled. Men who had received special instruction transmitted this one to another (that is, the manner of pronouncing this name) and taught it to none but their chosen disciples... (pp. 87–88).

Within the Christian tradition, we recall the words: "Whosoever shall call on the name of the Lord shall be saved" (Acts 2:21). Saint Philotheos of Sinai discloses that remembrance itself is to be in the divine Presence: "The blessed remembrance of God—which is the very presence of Jesus" (p. 35). In the classic of Eastern Orthodox spirituality *The Way of a Pilgrim*, an anonymous seeker receives a powerful and memorable instruction from his spiritual father on how to practice the Jesus Prayer or the Prayer of the Heart:

> The continuous interior Prayer of Jesus is a constant uninterrupted calling upon the divine Name of Jesus with the lips, in the spirit, in the heart; while forming a mental picture of His constant presence, and imploring His grace, during every occupation, at all times, in all places, even during sleep. The appeal is couched in these terms, "Lord Jesus Christ, have mercy on me." One who accustoms himself to this appeal experiences as a result so deep a consolation and so great a need to offer the prayer always, that he can no longer live without it, and it will continue to voice itself within him of its own accord (p. 41).

The Islamic tradition highlights the paramount nature of

remembrance as instructed in the Qur'ān: "Remember Me, and I shall remember you" (2:152), "Your Lord hath said: Call upon Me and I will answer you" (40:60), and "To God belong the most beautiful Names, so call upon Him by them" (7:180). Within the mystical dimension of Islam, known as *taṣawwuf* or Sufism, Ibn 'Aṭā' Allāh al-Iskandarī asserts, "Invoking causes God's remembrance of the servant, which is the greatest honor and loftiest distinction" (p. 57). He continues, "Invoking removes hardness from the heart and engenders tenderness and mildness. Forgetfulness of the heart is a disease and an ailment, while remembrance is a cure for the invoker from every malady and symptom" (p 59). From a spiritual point of view, life and death take on a different meaning as indicated in the following: "The invoker is alive even if he be dead; while the forgetful man, even though he is alive, is actually to be counted among the dead" (p. 61). Shaykh Aḥmad al-'Alawī also emphasized the importance of the way of invocation as a means of fixing consciousness on the divine Reality: "Remembrance is the mightiest rule of the religion.... The law was not enjoined upon us, neither were the rites of worship ordained, but for the sake of establishing the remembrance of God" (p. 195). He also stressed that this remembrance "is not to be restricted to a certain time or place, but can be practiced at all times and in all places" (p. 203). Rūmī poetically speaks to the role of invocation of the Divine Name: "Do not apply musk to the body, rub it on the heart. / What is musk? The sacred name of Him who is full of Majesty" (p. 140).

Within the Shamanic or primordial religion of the First Peoples, as Patrick Laude points out:

> In shamanistic practices the world over, as in Africa or in Central Asia, invocations are numerous, pervading the whole of life: every qualitative action, in craft for instance, is introduced by a specific invocation that effects an "actualization" of the invisible entities, or an "animation"

of the "matter" of the activity. This animation by the word is expressed by a sense of the "power" (*nyame*) inherent in invocations.... The shamanistic path primarily invokes an increased receptivity to the presence of the Divine in Nature. In that sense pure receptivity is in itself a kind of invocation (p. xi).

Medicine man and Sun Dance Chief Thomas Yellowtail states the following about the practice of the invocation of the Divine Name: "Each day, whatever I am doing, I am always praying and thinking of God... all the time I am praying... continually praying to God, remembering the name of God" (p. 145).

It has been shown that spiritual aspirants are unable to directly contemplate the transpersonal domain. They therefore require symbols in order to access the transcendent, as Titus Burckhardt eloquently illustrates: "Man cannot concentrate directly on the Infinite, but by concentrating on the symbol of the Infinite, attains to the Infinite Itself" (p. 80). Frithjof Schuon summarizes the significance of the invocation of the Divine Name and its relationship to the Absolute:

> The sufficient reason for the invocation of the Name is the "remembering of God"; in the final analysis this is nothing other than consciousness of the Absolute. The Name actualizes this consciousness and, in the end, perpetuates it in the soul and fixes it in the heart, so that it penetrates the whole being and at the same time transmutes and absorbs it. Consciousness of the Absolute is the prerogative of human intelligence and also its aim (p. 71).

French philosopher Simone Weil also affirms the way of invocation as it applies across the diverse religions: "Every religious practice, every rite, all liturgy is a form of the recitation of the name of the Lord" (p. 206). Leo Schaya articulates the important function of the invocation of the Divine Name: "God, by invoking his creative and redemptive name, causes everything that exists to issue from him and to return into him; by invoking his name with him, every being is born from him, lives by him, and is united with him" (p. 100).

The editor of this volume deserves to be congratulated for this timely work, which is a true gem in that it not only highlights the unique and diverse religious and mystical perspectives, but elucidates their central spiritual method of prayer and the invocation of the Divine Name as it is found across all of the world's sapiential traditions. It is this practice of remembrance that facilitates the human beings journey or rather return to the Absolute. In a single volume the editor, Patrick Laude, has taken significant time and effort to compile many powerful illustrations of this central practice. This is an excellent reference book that will provide tremendous value for seekers and students of comparative religion, esoterism, or mysticism, interfaith dialogue, and cross-cultural studies as it demonstrates the common ground on which the transcendent unity of religions may be realized. Through the way of remembrance, the human being can realize the divine Unity that is both immanent and transcendent and that is a reflection of integral human identity *in divinis*. Many are the paths and ways to the One, yet through the universal spiritual practice of the invocation of the Divine Name this reality can be crystallized in the heart and mind of the wayfarer so that, as Antony the Great explains, there is no one praying, only the actualization of prayer itself: "The only real prayer is the one in which we are no longer aware that we are praying" (p. 161).

22

*The Essential René Guénon: Metaphysics, Tradition, and The Crisis of Modernity**

> It is truly strange that people ask for proof concerning the possibility of a kind of [transcendent] knowledge instead of searching for it and verifying it for themselves by understanding the work necessary to acquire it.
>
> René Guénon[1]

"The civilization of the modern West appears in history as a veritable anomaly" (p. 68)—written in 1924, this statement typifies the prophetic eschatology of the French metaphysician René Guénon (1886–1951). At last such a work as this one has come to pass in order to bring together the magisterial and erudite *oeuvre* of Guénon, the founder, along with Frithjof Schuon (1907–1998), of what has become known as the "Traditionalist" or "Perennialist" school of thought. Other notable luminaries of this school were Ananda K. Coomaraswamy (1877–1947) and Titus Burckhardt (1908–1984).

It may surprise readers unfamiliar with Guénon that he was referred to as the "Great Sufi" by a definitive sage of the

---

* Edited by John Herlihy, Introduction by Martin Lings. Bloomington: World Wisdom & Sophia Perennis, 2009, 328pp.

[1] *Ibid.*, p. 80.

twentieth century, Śrī Ramana Maharshi.² Coomaraswamy, the seminal art historian, pointed out that Guénon was not an "Orientalist" but what in India would be deemed as a "master." Schuon affirmed that Guénon was intrinsically pneumatic or a *jñānic* type, and stated that "On symbolism Guénon is unbeatable." Seyyed Hossein Nasr (b. 1933) wrote the following regarding Guénon's first book: "It was like a sudden burst of lightning, an abrupt intrusion into the modern world of a body of knowledge and a perspective utterly alien to the prevalent climate and world view and completely opposed to all that characterizes the modern mentality."³ The praise for Guénon is not limited to these statements, but is extended by decisive intellects and philosophers of the twentieth century.

Who René Guénon was as a person is a complex question that has puzzled the curious and frustrated the trivial, yet "individualist considerations" pertaining to his person, including biography, meant little or nothing to Guénon. A remarkable point to note is that Guénon did not put forward, or even attempt to create, a "new" or "novel" theory, nor was he interested in the "originality" of his ideas. His role and significance in the modern world was to illuminate wholeheartedly the universal metaphysics of the Primordial Tradition—known as the *philosophia perennis* or the perennial philosophy—"Truth is one, and it is the same for all who, by whatever way, come to know it" (p. 78). He was to re-establish its primacy for contemporaries who were authentically seeking this uncompromised truth that was "in conformity with the strictly traditional point of view" (p. 44), and known by many

---

[2] See Samuel Bendeck Sotillos, "René Guénon and Sri Ramana Maharshi: Two Remarkable Sages in Modern Times," Parts I–IV published in *The Mountain Path*, Vols. 51, Nos. 2, 3, 4, and Vol. 52, No. 1 (see Bibliography for full details).

[3] Seyyed Hossein Nasr, "The Rediscovery of the Sacred: The Revival of Tradition," in *Knowledge and the Sacred* (Albany, NY: State University of New York Press, 1989), p. 101.

different names. This may appear odd to those living in the present time, since, as he noted with mathematical precision in *The Reign of Quantity and the Signs of the Times*, it is novelty, not to mention monetary gain, which are central motivating factors to all current activity.

Contrary to the timeless and universal tradition, there is in the present *Weltanschauung* an endless talk of "change", as if present-day individuals had realized the inherent bankruptcy of the times—"disequilibrium cannot be a condition of real happiness" (p. 39). What kind of change is being suggested is not clear, yet change from the present conditions itself is surely beckoned. The "change," if we could so term it, was for Guénon not change in a future orientated "progress" but change for the realignment of the first principles underlying the traditional doctrines of the world's spiritualities. In this sense, the direction of change was not going forward or even backward but points to what is rooted in the immutable and eternal. Guénon suggested that if those in the current era could perceive the perilous end of "progress," it would unequivocally come to a halt: "If our contemporaries as a whole could see what it is that is guiding them and where they are really going, the modern world would at once cease to exist as such" (p. 46).

Some might question the relevance of such an obscure metaphysician in the context of today's world and suggest that establishing an "intellectual elite" to counteract the perilous crisis of a disintegrating era—"the growing disorder in all domains" (p. 43)—is a utopian ideal, indicating his extreme naïveté or blatant ignorance. Hitherto, the large-scale crisis that Guénon astutely perceived did not only come to light and continue to unfold, but has degenerated into further disarray since he first identified and diagnosed the "intellectual myopia" or "intellectual atrophy" of an age that was well into the *Kali-Yuga* or "Dark Age"—"what has no parallel is this gigantic collective hallucination by which a whole section of humanity has come to take the vainest fantasies for incontestable realities" (p. 71).

Along with a vital introduction by Martin Lings (1909–2005), who was a close associate of Guénon for many years while living in Egypt, there is also a key preface by John Herlihy, author of numerous books on traditional spirituality and the modern world. This work consists of four parts: "The Modern World", "The Metaphysical World", "The Hindu World", and "The Traditional World." This book also contains two helpful appendices to better acquaint those unfamiliar with Guénon. They include an overview of his life and also a concise list of both French and English publications.

A defining and axial feature of the traditionalist or perennialist critique of the modern and postmodern world is the conflation of the intellect or *intellectus* with reason or *ratio*. Rationalism in all its forms is essentially defined by a belief in the supremacy of reason, proclaimed as a veritable "dogma," and implying the denial of everything that is of a supra-individual order, notably of pure intellectual intuition; this carries with it logically the exclusion of all true metaphysical knowledge.

This reductionism has given rise to a whole host of other confusions and misunderstandings such as the inversion of the "Self" with "ego", or "Personality" with "individuality," which is properly assimilated to what has been termed the "multiple states of being":

> The human individual is both much more and much less than is generally supposed in the West: much more, by reason of his possibilities of indefinite extension beyond the corporeal modality, to which, in short, everything belongs that is commonly studied; but he is also much less, since far from constituting a complete self-sufficient being, he is but an outward manifestation, a fleeting appearance assumed by the true being, which in no way affects the essence of the latter in its immutability (p. 88).

In his monumental essay "Eastern Metaphysics" Guénon demonstrated that the integral metaphysics of the perennial philosophy was neither of the East nor of the West, but found unanimously at the heart of all sapiential traditions regardless of time or place:

> In truth, pure metaphysics being essentially above and beyond all form and all contingency is neither Eastern nor Western but universal. The exterior forms with which it is covered only serve the necessities of exposition, to express whatever is expressible. These forms may be Eastern or Western; but under the appearance of diversity there is always a basis of unity, at least, wherever true metaphysics exists, for the simple reason that truth is one (p. 77).

With regard to universal metaphysics Guénon makes it clear that: "Exoterism and esoterism must be regarded not as two distinct and more or less opposed doctrines, which would be quite an erroneous view, but as the two aspects of one and the same doctrine" (p. 166). This differs radically from New Age thought, which seeks to abolish transcendence in favor of immanence, and thereby loses any guarantee of truth and objectivity, that is to say the necessary "right-thinking" that is the first item on the noble Eightfold Path of Buddhism. The opposite error, the abolition of immanence in favor of transcendence, is that of "Deism", which renders impossible any contact between God and man. For Guénon, as for the perennial philosophy, it is necessary that one be practicing an orthodox spiritual form, and it is for this purpose that both the "outer" and "inner" dimensions of exoterism and esoterism are made available, for "the same teaching is not understood in an equal degree by all who receive it... there are therefore those who in a certain sense discern the esoterism, while others, whose intellectual horizon is narrower, are limited to the exoterism" (p. 167).

The Essential René Guénon brings together the broad and illuminating spectrum of Guénon's corpus in a single volume like no other anthology currently available, which could very well realign the collective nucleus of sapiential wisdom to truly and integrally shift the predominant paradigm. Paradoxically, the more the current dissolution of what appears as the "eleventh hour" gains sway, the evermore relevant and indispensable Guénon's work becomes. It is our hope that this recent anthology will provide an antidote to the "intellectual myopia" of the times, in order to reaffirm the *sophia perennis*—"multiple paths all leading to the same end" (p. 85). On a concluding note, although the present crisis is skillfully veiled and exclusively contextualized in economic terms, Guénon would indefatigably confirm that it is rather a prolongation of the very same *Kali-Yuga* accelerating in its steadfast progression: "it can be said in all truth that the 'end of a world' never is and never can be anything but the end of an illusion" (p. 67).

23

*Touchstones of the Spirit: Essays on Religion, Tradition and Modernity**

> A sense of the sacred is fundamental for every civilization because fundamental for man; the sacred—that which is immutable, inviolable and thus infinitely majestic—is in the very substance of our spirit and of our existence.
>
> Frithjof Schuon[1]

We live in a rather extraordinary time; we have access to the great wisdom traditions of the world, which has never before been possible. Now regardless of inner qualification or formal commitment to a traditional form, anyone can acquire texts that were previously inaccessible to outsiders, and it goes without saying that what is sacred was never taken frivolously. An important question, seldom posed, is: what is the cost of this accessibility? For example, as highly regarded as Tibetan Buddhism is today, rarely is it considered that in order for not only the modern West, but the world at large to have access to its spiritual heritage, Tibetan civilization was essentially decimated and is still today, some sixty years later, under occupation. The same could be said for all the traditional societies, especially those of the indigenous and shamanic

---

* Harry Oldmeadow. World Wisdom. 2012. 298 pp.
[1] *Understanding Islam*, p. 26.

societies. Many of their teachings would be inaccessible to outsiders if it were not for their elders deciding that it is better to share their wisdom in the face of genocide than to lose their wisdom forever. The crisis of our times is coupled with a perplexing phenomenon of extremes—on the one hand there is the mass disintegration of traditional societies and on the other hand there is the mass dissemination of its illumined wisdom. While there are tremendous spiritual benefits for those living in today's world, this remarkable opportunity comes with great responsibility. From the outset we are mindful of Professor Oldmeadow's striking assertion that sets the precedent for *Touchstones of the Spirit*: "Let us start with a recognition that there is indeed a fundamental crisis in the modern world and that its root causes are spiritual" (p. 106).

This work is divided into three parts: I. Echoes of Tradition, II. The Wastelands of Modernity, and III. East and West. Oldmeadow elaborates on these themes: "This compilation of essays is structured around three themes: the timeless messages of Tradition; the obscuration of this perennial wisdom in the modern world; and the spiritual intercourse between East and West which holds out some hope that we may yet recover something of what we have lost" (p. 212).

The first part contains an interesting collection of essays on a wide spectrum of subjects offering a unique look at the integral spirituality of the Australian Aborigines and its relationship to the other religious and wisdom traditions of the world. While it is quite fashionable to claim that all of the religions are one, Oldmeadow delves deeper into the inherent limitations of modern Western philosophy as well as comparative religion when they are not contextualized within the principial knowledge of the perennial philosophy. Although all religions are one in their essence, their forms are multiple. The explanation for the existence of multiple religions is precisely because they are all different—for this reason it has been said that the Divine never speaks the "same" language twice. The author takes the reader into the heart of Shankara's metaphysics in order to elaborate on Advaita Vedanta and the doctrine of *māyā*. He explores the profundity of the Bodhisattva ideal and expands upon Western interpretations. He also provides an original essay on the modern notion of biography with its many detrimental ramifications. The last piece in this section is devoted to a book by Joseph Epes Brown (1920–2000), a remarkable scholar of Native American traditions.

The second part of the book "Wastelands of Modernity" is superbly and profoundly encapsulated in the essay "The False Prophets of Modernity":

> Some of the symptoms: ecological catastrophe, a material sign of the rupture between Heaven and Earth; a rampant materialism and consumerism, signifying a surrender to the illusion that man can live by bread alone; the genocidal extirpation of traditional cultures by "modernization"; political barbarities on an almost unimaginable scale; social discord, endemic violence, and dislocations of unprecedented proportions; widespread alienation, ennui, and a sense of spiritual sterility amidst the frenetic confusion and din of modern life; a religious landscape dominated by internecine and inter-religious strife and by the emergence of xenophobic fundamentalisms in both East and West; the loss of any sense of the sacred, even among those who remain committed to religious forms, many of whom have retreated into a simplistic and credulous religious literalism or into a vacuous liberalism where "anything goes" (p. 107).

Another insightful essay contained in this section is "Frankenstein's Children: Science, Scientism, and Self-Destruction", which further elaborates on the inherent flaws of modern science as it attempts to make an absolute of itself and usurp all of Reality into its fold by impinging on sacred science: "By its very nature modern science is thus unable to apprehend or accommodate any realities of a supra-sensorial order. Science (a method of inquiry) becomes scientism (an ideology) when it refuses to acknowledge the limits of its own competence" (p. 130). There are many insights to ponder in the essay "Computers: An Academic Cargo Cult?", including an inquiry into the true meaning of intelligence and its relationship to what has been termed culturism. "The Past Disowned" explores the postmodern outlook and its hazardous implications for education. This section concludes with a review of Eckhart Tolle's *The Power of Now*, an overnight New Age best seller whose shortcomings Professor Oldmeadow exposes in the light of the *sophia perennis*.

Part three presents an overview of the work of two seminal representatives of the perennial philosophy, Ananda K. Coomaraswamy (1877–1947) and Frithjof Schuon (1907–1998). In the third part there is also an essay on Western scholarship and its attempts to articulate the wisdom of the East; another contains homage to the doyen of the study of the world's religions, Professor Huston Smith (1919–2016). Additionally, there is an essay offering a rare look at Swami Abhishiktananda (Henri Le Saux), a relatively unknown French Benedictine who immersed himself for numerous years in Advaita Vedanta and contributed to an integral understanding of the Hindu *dharma*. This section ends with an insightful essay on inter-religious understanding and lays out valuable pointers as to how to make it more complete.

Never before have there been so many counterfeit spiritualities, nor has spirituality previously been turned into a business as it has today, and in no other time have we witnessed the massive destruction of traditional societies, something which has become a global pandemic. Paradoxically there are more tangible points of contact with the sacred than ever before. How is one to make sense of this? According to the unanimous teaching of all the spiritual traditions of the world, we are living at the end of a temporal cycle. Professor Oldmeadow takes no prisoners in critiquing the errors of the modern and postmodern mindset, yet he also supplies the principles that permit us to move beyond the current impasse. For all those seeking to reclaim the sacred in the midst of the ambiguity and confusion of the present age, *Touchstones of the Spirit* offers an impressive spectrum of pointers to assist in this search.

24

*The Mystery of Individuality: Grandeur and Delusion of the Human Condition**

> You see yourself as the drop in the ocean, but you are also the ocean in the drop.
>
> Rūmī[1]

Seldom does one come across a book that so completely plumbs the depths and heights of the human condition as does this recent volume by Mark Perry (b. 1951), the son of American Perennialist author Whitall N. Perry (1920–2005).[2] In articulating what human individuality is in light of the universal spiritual heritage of all times and places, Perry

---

* Mark Perry, Foreword by William Stoddart. Bloomington: World Wisdom, 2012, 328pp.

[1] Quoted *ibid.*, p. 105.

[2] We do not mention Mark Perry's father arbitrarily, as many within the "fourth force" of modern psychology or transpersonal psychology are familiar with Whitall N. Perry's encyclopedic anthology *A Treasury of Traditional Wisdom*, recently reissued as: *The Spiritual Ascent: A Compendium of the World's Wisdom* (Louisville, KY: Fons Vitae, 2008), consisting of more than a thousand pages and praised as the "Summa of the Philosophia Perennis". It was Ananda K. Coomaraswamy (1877–1947), one of the great art historians of the twentieth century who suggested that it was time for someone well-versed in the world's religions to compile in a single volume the spiritual wisdom of the ages, which bore its fruit after a seventeen-year labor.

uncompromisingly exposes the contemporary wasteland in its various nuances and fearlessly enters into divisive and taboo topics.

This book reminds us that we are living in a time where the human microcosm is not only under attack from within modern science through *scientism* (the reduction of Reality to what can be exclusively verified through the five senses) and its derivative modern psychology or *psychologism* (the reduction of Reality to a psychological criterion), but also from the movements within contemporary spirituality that zealously seek to undermine the way that the plenary traditions were interpreted by the saints and sages of those traditions. What comes to mind are not only the common New Age parodies, but their less simplistic and more sophisticated forms that appear to be anything but New Age and are for this reason more dangerous. The following are examples of this more refined presentation of New Age thought: the alleged "integralization" of the World's Religions and the call for the "democratization" of enlightenment.

If we were not living in an inverted era known as the *Kali-Yuga* or "dark age" where everything is turned on its head, these fundamental errors would be clear as day and would not require further reflection, for they would be seen in their transparency as a Promethean attempt to relativize the Absolute, in order not only to make *gnosis* or transcendent knowledge available for mass consumption–which by its very nature it cannot be–but attempts once and for all to lower Spirit to the dictates of the terrestrial masses. The assumption that the plenary revelations need updating or that they can even be updated by conjectural whims is a negation of their supra-individual origin; that is to say that neither religion nor its inner corollary, spirituality, is man-made. On the contrary, it is the human individual that needs to adapt to the terms of the timeless truths of the sapiential traditions and not the other way around. To assume that the world's religions are not integral is a fundamental oversight of what religion is and it is a betrayal of the Spirit, since religion and spirituality are integral *in divinis*; if they were not so, they would be incapable of not only saving but also liberating souls throughout the ages. At the core of this outlook is none other than the old bugbear, *evolutionism* (the notion that the greater can derive from the lesser) coupled with *syncretism* (the indiscriminate mixing of heterogeneous ideas and forms in an attempt to fashion a synthesis).

Readers may be interested to know what others have said of this work. Doyen of the World's Religions, Professor Huston Smith (1919–2016), who is no stranger to those within psychology—especially transpersonal psychology and humanistic psychology—wrote a powerful and memorable endorsement for Perry's work: "Few writings in recent years have done as much to further—in ways that make life feel different—my understanding of the ultimate nature of things. Perry's thoughts are as advanced as one will find anywhere—this is clearly the higher mathematics of the human spirit."[3] A lesser known figure to those within transpersonal psychology, yet widely known as a representative of the perennial philosophy, William Stoddart (b. 1925) writes: "I know of no other author who expounds and reflects the specifically *spiritual* teachings of Frithjof Schuon [1907–1998] as intimately and authentically as does Mark Perry, who, all his life, had the advantage of being a close associate of Schuon" (p. x).

This book, consisting of twelve chapters, is an in-depth inquiry into the paradoxical nature of human individuality. While the term "individuality" is commonly used in our day-to-day lexicon, its deeper significance is not properly understood in its metaphysical, philosophical and spiritual context. On the one hand, the human individual is an autonomous entity

---

[3] See Huston Smith, "Preface," to Mark Perry, *On Awakening and Remembering: To Know is To Be* (Louisville, KY: Fons Vitae, 2000), pp. 11–14.

possessing its own existence separate from others and on the other hand the human individual is mysteriously connected to all humans, including the natural world, which is rooted in the supra-individual or Divine. Our apparent separateness as individuals is the quintessence of what is destined by the manifest world, yet it is the unmanifest that underscores and presupposes the manifest order—as everything originates in the One, so It returns to the One. The traditional or perennial method that Perry expounds takes into consideration the environmental factors that shape the human being and the temporal cycles that in turn shape the atmosphere in which the individual lives. Not to do so creates a detrimental disconnect between the human individual and the social milieu which skews all one's ability to understand these subtle and complex matters. Human individuality and all of its nuances become intelligible when viewed through the lens of spiritual anthropology and the guiding image of archetypal man and woman created in the image of God. "Although the subject matter of this book deals with man created in the image of God, we are not speaking in the name of a single religion, or of a single spiritual credo, but in that of the *philosophia spiritualis* which is timeless gnosis" (p. 13).

Although modern psychology has painstakingly attempted to establish what human individuality is, it has been unable to do so because of its own theoretical underpinnings which have cut it off from the Sacred. While behaviorism has precariously cast off both the Spirit and the soul from modern psychology, psychoanalysis has discarded Spirit and salvaged in its place the human psyche; humanistic psychology has endeavored to reclaim what is human after its disfigurement, while transpersonal psychology likewise acknowledged the key role of the human being, and emphasized the primacy of Spirit. Yet as long as transpersonal and humanistic psychology accept the principal errors of behaviorism and psychoanalysis, of which they are a logical derivative, they are enabling theoretical positions that fundamentally contradict and undermine their *theoria* and *praxis*. For this reason contemporary psychology in all of its forms cannot afford to ignore or hastily gloss over the critique presented by the exponents of the perennial philosophy, nor can it not take seriously its prognosis: the crisis and impasse of modern psychology.

> To explain man through [modern] psychology when what is really needed is a pneumatology or a "science of the Spirit", without which psychology—or the study of the soul—can only amount to the blind leading the blind because no matter how erudite or subtle our analysis will be we cannot escape the conundrum of the mortal attempting to define the Immortal; we cannot escape by our own means the narrow labyrinth of human observations and speculations unless we can appeal to a higher principle (p. 2).

CHAPTER ONE: THE WOUND OF DUALITY

Inseparable from the question of human identity is the essential longing for what resembles us most, although we are rarely aware of this process. This core impulse underscoring human identity is what the author indicates can lead us back to the Absolute and is what makes the human state the grandeur that it is. With this said, the search for wholeness in the world of multiplicity has its many trappings: "However, what is much less obvious is that, owing to the Fall, far from being attracted we can also be repelled by what most corresponds to us archetypally, as the medieval motif of the 'loathsome bride' illustrates, or the drama of the soul unwilling to give up its illusory freedom, fleeing the Spirit" (p. 19). Additionally, it is the obscuring of the heart-intellect or intellect (Sanskrit: *buddhi*; Latin: *intellectus*; Greek: *nous*; Arabic: *'aql*), the noetic faculty within the human individual which defines the human condition itself; it is this obscuring that gives rise to the wound of duality itself. "In primordial man or man of the Golden Age [*Krita-Yuga* or *Satya-Yuga*], the heart as a divine faculty was one before becoming polarized into heart and mind" (p. 25). This is why the traditional understanding throughout the ages has been that the seat of consciousness is in the heart and not the head; but as a result of the eclipse of the intellect, the understanding of these faculties became fragmented. Modern psychology, by not taking into consideration traditional cosmology and temporal cycles and its effects on the human psyche, is limited to the "accidental predicament of man in the modern world" (p. 31). Although contemporaries attempt to innovate anything and everything under the sun to expand consciousness, to escape the wound of duality, the author points out: "Just as man cannot create life, he cannot produce enlightenment, for the source of both life and enlightenment belongs to a transcendent order of reality; no man can approach the Real purely by his own means or purely on his own initiative" (p. 36).

CHAPTER TWO: WHO AM I?

Perhaps no question has been asked more continuously in the passing of time than "Who Am I?" "One of the greatest truths, and yet most fatal of illusions, is the notion that man is created in God's image or, in Buddhist terms, that every man has a Buddha nature, or in Vedantic metaphysics, *tat tvam asi*, "thou art That"—the "That" being the unnamable essence of Reality" (p. 39). And yet the inverse relationship is also true— you are *not* That, at least, as long as the identification with the empirical ego has not been curbed or integrated into what is higher than itself. While contemporary forms of spirituality make every appeal to suggest that everything is within you and while this is true in essence, it neglects the paramount recognition that: "There can be no immanence without prior transcendence" (p. 50).

A major stumbling block for modern psychology in all of its schools and forces—behaviorism, psychoanalysis, humanistic or transpersonal—is its apparent incomprehension of the existence of the noetic faculty within the human individual, which cannot but profoundly obstruct, if not derail altogether the inquiry of "Who Am I?" "Even though this doctrine of the 'Eye of the Heart' is the key of keys for understanding what man is, modern psychology finally knows nothing of it" (pp. 57–58). The author summarizes the interrelatedness of the Divine and the human: "In essence, the mystery of individuality touches upon a triple mystery: we in God, God in us, and God in Himself" (p. 59).

CHAPTER THREE: THE ICONIC FIGURE

In order for the human individual to contextualize him or herself within the Sacred, the representation of the Sacred needs to be included into all facets of the human collectivity. A striking and morbid feature of the modern and postmodern era is the virtual absence of the Sacred. While traditional societies in the premodern world were diverse and often spread out over large bodies of water and land, they nevertheless had a unanimous sense of the Sacred. Perry writes: "The sacred imprint of this prototype is projected onto society and assimilated by the masses in the measure that a collectivity can still do so post the Golden Age" (p. 61). While the iconographic figure takes on a human form and thus becomes a model for the true man or true woman, this model is also reflected in the theomorphic essence of each human being. To have a sacred symbolism reflected in the collectivity instills an integral psychology, which in a traditional society is rooted in principial knowledge that has very different implications on the idea of mental health than are currently represented: "Man's earthly wellbeing was always premised on, if not subordinated to, his everlasting wellbeing" (p. 66).

The author informs us, "To remove the sacred is to abolish at one fell stroke all true scale of perfection" (p. 80). This is why each civilization had its own archetypal symbolism that established a supra-individual ambiance, so that religion and spirituality could be made palpable in every activity done throughout one's day. Perry asserts: "Yes, indeed, 'The Spirit bloweth where it listeth', but this does not mean 'It bloweth just anywhere,' and certainly not at our beck and call" (p. 81).

CHAPTER FOUR: KINGDOMS AND NATIONS

Due to the large disgruntlement of the masses with both the Republican and Democratic parties in America—what has been termed by some the "Two Party Dictatorship", resulting in a cyclic choice from the lesser of two evils—the very principles underlying democracy are being called into question. Some propose that what is needed is to go beyond the bipartisan political paradigm and insert a third party option. In Europe, the social unrest is a very severe issue, as the masses are swayed to and fro in the attempt to back whichever political party promises to improve the current crisis, if not only to save the current infrastructures from total collapse. While there are many interesting discussions to be had in the various forums of the public domain, Perry is concerned with a much more urgent query given the corrosive political milieu, the very idea of government or temporal power and what its implications are for integral individuality.

Perry makes an interesting observation which will likely perplex contemporary minds when taken at face value: "God cannot be likened to a president or a prime minister, assuredly, but He can be likened to a king or an emperor" (p. 83). The author raises an imperative question which many today are also asking: "In what social setting can a human being best fulfill his integral vocation?" (p. 83). Perry presents an interesting quandary regarding the notion of civil liberties that is seldom pondered: "Freedom cannot be unconditional otherwise it is self-cancelling." And likewise: "Indiscriminate freedom benefits counter-forces that exploit its generosity against it" (p. 83). In the traditional or premodern world spiritual authority did not function in a vacuum, it also played an essential role in the directives of government as saints, wise priests, monks and/or hermits provided guidance to those in power. "The prevalence of such spiritual men deeply influenced the run of society in all epochs, and even of this one right up to the threshold of our modern world" (p. 90).

The author clarifies why it is so challenging for the modern and postmodern mind to comprehend the pervading sense of the sacred that existed in the traditional or premodern world and how the role of integral government assisted in these efforts: "The Divine imbued the air, so to speak, and all the social customs were laced with sacred formulas; buildings and homes were adorned with icons, possibly sacred statuettes or effigies, not forgetting sacred inscriptions, and people might wear amulets that had been consecrated or blessed at sanctuaries, or they might own talismans" (p. 91).

Some might suggest that the above is an exaggeration or a nostalgic position that seeks to make a utopia of the past and therefore regress to any era other than this one, but this is not the case, as Perry points out: "Traditional civilizations—all questions of their very real problems notwithstanding—were premised on the reality of the 'next world'" (p. 95).

It is the notion of unrestrained progress and immeasurable material comfort that in turn feed the endless torrent of consumption, besides underscoring blatant deficiencies as there is always more to be acquired. In the traditional world one found solace in the remembrance of one's transcendent origin, "My kingdom is not of this world" (John 18:36), coupled with the remembrance of its analogous immanence "The kingdom of God is within you" (Luke 17:21). The author offers a valuable insight: "Modern solutions rarely do more than displace ancient problems, or modify modalities, without solving the fundamental issue of the world not being Heaven" (p. 98).

CHAPTER FIVE: INDIVIDUALITY IS NOT INDIVIDUALISM

A predominant error in contemporary spiritual circles is that traditional methods of integration or self-realization obliterate individuality; now it does so if we are viewing individuality through the lens of the empirical ego because it itself is accidental and is not individuality in its truest sense. Integral individuality, as Perry informs us, is to participate in the transcendent itself, yet it does not conflate separateness with uniqueness as is often misunderstood. The notion of separateness becomes transparent when qualified by an integral spiritual vision which at the same time asserts that the human individual is unique *in divinis*; this is the unanimous understanding of transcendence and immanence and what this means for human fulfillment in light of the perennial philosophy.

The author informs the reader that the word "individuality" in the fullest sense rests on principle of indivisibility. Perry writes: "The mystery of existence is that each individual self can be 'one-self' in the virtually supreme sense in that each creature is insuperably absolute: unique, non-duplicable, occurring only once in eons of history, never to be repeated again, because that is why an individual exists" (p. 104). While individuality is an imperative aspect of the human condition it is also its greatest obstacle: "man, engrossed with his individual uniqueness, ends up competing with the Absolute Itself" (pp. 104–105).

"This principle of non-duplication of individual selves illustrates the inexhaustibility of the Divine Principle expressed through creation. Clearly, however, the illusion of uniqueness—making each one of us feel that he or she is an autonomous self in his or her own right—has to be an illusion" (p. 105). The diversity of human appearances are reconciled within the inner unity encapsulating all forms: "He it is Who did create all of you from a single soul" (Qur'ān 7:189). One of the most predominant misconceptions in present-day spiritual circles has to do with the Theravada Buddhist notion of "no-self," which does *not* conflate separateness with uniqueness, but is rather an inverse correlation of the notion of the Self that was meant to correct the errors of its time: "This doctrine is really a reverse variant of the doctrine of the One or sole-subsisting Self, the main difference being that instead of emphasizing the absoluteness of the Self (*Atma*), it takes the opposite point of departure by emphasizing the nothingness of individual experience" (p. 122).

With this said, the author also emphasizes that there is an intermediary reality between the doctrine of *anatta* and the doctrine of the Self alone is real, as he writes: "one would want to specify that an individual, upon attaining spiritual realization, certainly subsists as a recognizably distinct individual" (p. 123).

CHAPTER SIX: BEYOND GOOD AND EVIL

The author wastes no time in getting to the kernel of what this chapter presents—"to speak of individuation is to speak of choice, and to speak of choice is—vertically—to speak of good and evil" (p. 127). And the greatest of all paradoxes is that: "The Sovereign Good (the *Summum Bonum*) cannot have any real opposite since it coincides with Reality and hence with Totality; thus there is nothing, within the metacosmic realm, that is situated 'outside' of It" (p. 128). On the relative plane good and evil are opposites and necessarily so as the very premise of manifestation requires it, but on the Absolute plane all dualities dissipate for nothing can exist outside of the Absolute. With this said there are many abuses of the mystical understanding of the religions by New Age interpretations, which suggest that one can stand beyond morality. Although distinctions can be made in some essential respects between the exoteric and esoteric understanding of morality, the author states: "No human being can legitimately place himself outside the notion of morality as such" (p. 129).

Perry presents some noteworthy challenges to atheistic critiques of morality. "Even if atheists believe morality can be defined by man, they are still forced to borrow, wittingly or unwittingly, from a heritage of religious morality in order to put this morality into practice; one cannot, after all, reinvent the wheel: religion = morality" (p. 131). The very notion of a standard that in and of itself can degenerate is, as the author informs us, proof of the transcendent: "Corruption can only occur if there is something that is not corrupt at the origin. The very notion of morality, in fact, is proof of man's divine origin" (p. 131).

The idea that "man is fundamentally good" also requires one to see that it is not this or that individual man or woman that is good, but the theomorphic essence of the human individual that is "created in the image of God." While some might misinterpret Saint Augustine's (354–430) formulation, "Love God and do what thou wilt" and think that one is free of moral responsibility, it must not be unheeded that: "The pure cannot act impurely no matter what he does" (p. 142).[4]

CHAPTER SEVEN: SATAN IS NOT AN ATHEIST

What would a world void of transcendence look like? The author provides a glimpse into this bleak reality: "The truth is that a godless world could not long be sustained, for without at least some reference to the Divine, all values would turn to dust or become a matter of pragmatic, if not tyrannical, self-interest; and self-interest heedless of anything but personal needs would lead to the cutthroat disintegration of society" (p. 149). Perry magnificently illuminates the human conundrum when it comes to the affirming or negating of the divine Reality: "Strange to say it takes a measure of intelligence to deny God; that is, were it not for our God-given intelligence we would not know how to deny Him" (p. 149).

Perry perpetually affirms the transpersonal identity of the human individual as understood by the world's sapiential traditions: "Whether man understands this or not, or whether he likes it or not, man is forever *homo religiosus* and the day this is no longer so is the day the world ends" (p. 155).

---

[4] "If a man is Self-realized he cannot tell a lie or commit a sin or do anything wrong" (Ramana Maharshi, "Self-Enquiry," in *The Teachings of Ramana Maharshi*, p. 135).

CHAPTER EIGHT: CAPITAL PUNISHMENT

Very few will argue against the sheer volume of statistics that document the disproportionality of people of color incarcerated today in America, in what has been termed the "prison–industrial complex", and this goes especially for those sentenced to death row and those who are finally executed by the death penalty. What has baffled the public in recent years are the numerous instances where there is insufficient evidence proving that the crime was committed by the alleged perpetrator or even the contrary, that there was plentiful evidence indicating the person's innocence—and yet this did nothing to overturn the ruling. When innocent individuals can be executed by the same criminal justice system that is in place to protect them—what then is justice?

The author provides much food for thought regarding this heated and debated subject, but does so in a very contemplative manner, emphasizing the existential facets of the human condition that challenge the status quo. To begin with: "Justice cannot be properly defined without a proper definition of what constitutes the nature of man" (p. 180). Perry speaks to the materialistic psychology of modern and postmodern individuals, which refuses to understand the spiritual foundations of the human condition itself.[5]

At the crossroads of life and death there is a fascinating paradox: "If on the one hand there is something absolute about a human life... at the very same time there is something relative in a human death" (p. 188). Perry continues to highlight this ever so important dialectic: "How to do justice to these two dimensions without prejudicing either pole of this scale is the crux of the matter; in other words: how does one value human life without idolatry and how does one relativize human life without dehumanization?" (p. 188)

---

[5] "You attach too much importance to the body" (Ramana Maharshi, "The Guru," in *The Teachings of Ramana Maharshi*, p. 109).

CHAPTER NINE: ON AUTHORITY

Another impassioned theme of today is how to manage the increasing abuse of power and at the same time deter the increasing social entropy?[6] The traditional cosmologies of the world's religions correlate these corrosive facets with the final temporal cycle known as the *Kali-Yuga*. Due to the current unrest that is very much a globalizing phenomenon, one then wonders what authentic government is and what is its role in the day-to-day lives of human individuals? Perry refers to the transitions of the different types of government detailed by Plato, providing an interesting overview of where we currently are on this trajectory:

> Moving from theocracy, to aristocracy, then to timocracy, oligarchy, democracy, and finally to tyranny—this axis describing the declining transition of authority going from a truly enlightened rulership, then being appropriated by the noble classes, then by heroes, and later passing through the popular will, before ending in the hands of a tyrant, or a despotic regime (pp. 197–198).

Granted the term "elite" has many unfavorable associations attributed to it today, such as that of class privilege and exploitation, Perry reminds readers that the true elite should not be confused with the economic elite or the ruling class, because the term entails a spiritual prerogative. "For an elite to be an elite, it has to be anchored in spirituality" (p. 212). It is this intellectual elite that can reverse the engulfing confusion that marks this age, as the adage goes: "corruption of the best is the worst" (*corruptio optimi pessima*).

CHAPTER TEN: THE PRIMACY OF CHARACTER

Perry emphasizes that while the foundation of character is determined by a "few simple things" such as—"truthfulness, compassion, courage, loyalty, and patience"—these are not

---

[6] See René Guénon, *The Crisis of the Modern World*, pp. 100–116; José Ortega y Gasset, *The Revolt of the Masses* (New York: W.W. Norton & Co., 1993).

easily realized. Another interesting point that is mentioned in the book is the role of polarities in establishing sound character: "Character depends also on a polarity of virtues, a balance of positive and negative attributes, or energies if one will" (p. 219). By the terms "positive" and "negative", Perry is referring to the polarities in nature such as "hot" and "cold", "soft" and "hard", etc. and not to "defects".

We are told that in order to delve deeper into the meaning of character, free of biases, we need to return to "pneumatology—or the reflection of the Spirit in man—which has been our guiding principle from the beginning" (p. 226). The author upholds that without the Divine, character as such could not exist: "The loss of the sense of the Absolute cannot but undermine the whole notion of character" (pp. 242–243).

CHAPTER ELEVEN: THE FORBIDDEN DOOR

Amidst the barrage of practices offered in the spiritual marketplace to experience non-ordinary states of consciousness or expand consciousness through entheogens[7] or otherwise, many contemporaries may resent the idea that certain forms of knowledge are made available only for those who have made themselves eligible—that is for those with suitable preparation—as is definitely the case with esoteric or mystical knowledge. "The Divine requires both a ritual and moral preparation whereby the aspirant learns to 'die' spiritually" (p. 248). The author continues: "Self-naughting constitutes the preliminary basis for any sincere spiritual quest" (p. 248). While this flies in the face of New Age spirituality and will ap-

---

[7] See Whitall N. Perry, "Drug-Induced Mysticism: The Mescalin Hypothesis," in *Challenges to a Secular Society* (Oakton, VA: Foundation for Traditional Studies, 1996), pp. 7–16; Samuel Bendeck Sotillos, "Drug-Induced Mysticism Revisited: Interview with Charles Upton," in *Psychology and the Perennial Philosophy: Studies in Comparative Religion*, ed. Samuel Bendeck Sotillos (Bloomington: World Wisdom, 2013), pp. 130–154.

pear to be elitist, this is the way that principial knowledge has been transmitted or acquired since time immemorial.

Perhaps the entirety of this chapter may be summarized within the reflective words of the *sanātana dharma*: "Fostered by sacrifice, the god will grant the enjoyments thou desirest. He who enjoys these gifts without giving to them in return verily is a thief" (*Bhagavad Gītā*, 3:12—p. 245). An analogous point is made in the Islamic tradition: "Or do ye think that ye shall enter the Garden of Bliss without such trials as came to those who passed away before you?" (Qur'ān 2:214). Perry informs readers that no amount of consciousness expansion, whether it be "*chakra*-kindling"[8] or "*kosha*-breaching"[9] will bring the human soul one iota closer to the Divine. "Spirituality... is all about moral character and not about experiencing states" (p. 262). As it is all too easy for the human soul to mistake the psychic reality for the spiritual, the following heed of caution is necessary: "Indeed, it is much easier to open the 'forbidden door' than to close it once opened" (p. 269).[10]

---

[8] Hindu *chakras* are subtle centers in the human individual that relate to the many phases of spiritual development. It is important to note also that an analogue concept of the subtle centers or *chakras* may be found within the diverse spiritual traditions.

[9] "*Purusha* or *Ātmā*, manifesting itself as *jivātmā* in the living form of the individual being, is regarded, according to the *Vedānta*, as clothing itself in a series of 'envelopes' (*koshas*) or successive vehicles, representing so many phases of its manifestation; it would be altogether wrong, however, to compare these envelopes to 'bodies,' since it is the last phase only that belongs to the corporeal order. It is important to note, moreover, that *Ātmā* cannot, strictly speaking, be said to be actually contained within such envelopes, since, by its very nature, it is not susceptible of any limitation and is in no way conditioned by any state of manifestation whatsoever" (René Guénon, "Envelopes of the 'Self': The Five *Vāyus* or Vital Functions," in *Man and His Becoming According to the Vedānta* [Hillsdale, NY: Sophia Perennis, 2004], p. 67).

[10] See René Guénon, "The Confusion of the Psychic and the Spiritual," in

Perry emphasizes that integral spirituality is the rediscovery of simplicity: "If man could take pleasure in life's beauties, as God intended him to, no restless urge would goad him to pierce the veil of the five senses to seek out extra-sensorial states. He would find contentment in the plenitude of his spiritual possibility here on earth" (p. 270).

CHAPTER TWELVE: *HIEROS GAMOS* OR THE SACRED MARRIAGE
No book on the mystery of individuality would be complete if it did not address the theme of sacred marriage and its profound symbolism for traveling the spiritual path. In the manifest world of form, polarities are necessary for they provide equilibrium on the plane of manifestation, in fact without them the cosmos would collapse. And while polarities are necessary on the plane of manifestation they are reabsorbed into a principial unity that reconciles the coincidence of opposites. It is through traditional metaphysics that we can understand what is integral femininity and likewise integral masculinity. The common ground between man and woman, the author informs us, is their being *anthropos* or human beings, which takes precedence over their particular distinctions of male or female.

The Mystery of Individuality is a relentless, no holds barred exploration of the paradoxical nature of the human condition amidst the thrashing current of the modern and postmodern wasteland that has lost its vision in all regards, and more explicitly of what it means to be fully human. This work requires slowing down and centering oneself, and it may also entail suspending one's normative thought process, conditioned as it is by a hyper-cerebral outlook which fervently opposes anything that evades empirical verification. This does not however suggest suspending one's "critical thinking", but aligning reason with the transcendent source

---

The Reign of Quantity and the Signs of the Times (Hillsdale, NY: Sophia Perennis, 2004), pp. 235–240.

that fosters an awakening of intelligence. This book pushes us to go beyond the idols of relativism in order to enter another reality, an ancient reality, but nonetheless timeless and accessible—*here and now*. Those who make the effort to travel through its pages will certainly be rewarded.

25

*Men of a Single Book: Fundamentalism in Islam, Christianity, and Modern Thought**

This groundbreaking book analyzes unreservedly the bedrock of the modern and postmodern *Weltanschauung*, outlining its numerous pathologies, which are entangled in its collective mindset. This very phenomenon is what the award-winning Brazilian author Mateus Soares de Azevedo has perceptively phrased "secular fundamentalism", yet his examination goes beyond what is typically assumed by either "secularism" or "fundamentalism". The author expands upon what he has designated as "secular fundamentalism" by highlighting the various deviations that need to be accounted for as they have been unquestionably assimilated into the modern and postmodern perspective.

The concept of "fundamentalism" addressed in this book is used more comprehensively and broadly than usual. Marxism, Freudian psychoanalysis, Jungian analytical psychology, and science fundamentalism are included under the umbrella of "fundamentalism,"—not, of course, as religious fundamentalisms, but as expressions of this new concept of "secular fundamentalism".

In order to delve into what is meant by the terms employed by the author, one needs to examine inwardly the many

---

* Mateus Soares de Azevedo, Foreword by Alberto Vasconcellos Queiroz, Introduction by William Stoddart. World Wisdom, 2010, 148pp.

contemporary preconceptions that one takes for granted when living in an era engulfed in an anti-spiritual sentiment. Individuals of today need to keep in mind that "there has never been a civilization, throughout human history, without a religion" (p. 105)—except that of the modern West. At the apex of this inquiry is not the "clash of civilizations" as presupposed by Samuel P. Huntington and others who have assimilated this thesis—in this case, the mistaken notion is that Islam is against the West—rather, it is the decisive confrontation between two essential worldviews: that of the traditional world and that of the modern word. The first was recognized as the perennial norm, and the second severed itself from the *cosmologia perennis*[1] that was universal before its emergence.

This book is divided into two parts, the first of which, "Militant Fundamentalism vs. Traditional Religion", addresses in a discerning manner the myriad misunderstandings of Islamic spirituality in light of the Qur'ān and also illustrates the common ground between Islam and Christianity. It also provides an overview of Sufism, considered the heart of Islam, and which may very well play an instrumental role in offsetting the challenge of Wahhabism. The second part of the book, "Secular Fundamentalism", offers much insight into the key influences that have solidified the present-day mentality. A critical one in particular is the usurpation of traditional spirituality by modern psychology (most evident in behaviorism and psychoanalysis, but also found in humanistic and transpersonal psychology),[2] a side-effect of scientism that has diverted many: "It is true that while Freud boasted of the fact that he was an irreconcilable enemy of religion, Jung claimed 'sympathy' for it, while in reality emptying it

---

[1] See Titus Burckhardt, "Cosmologia Perennis," in *Mirror of the Intellect: Essays on Traditional Science and Sacred Art* (Albany, NY: State University of New York Press, 1987), pp. 17–26.

[2] See Samuel Bendeck Sotillos (ed.), *Psychology and the Perennial Philosophy: Studies in Comparative Religion* (Bloomington: World Wisdom, 2013).

of its deeper contents, which were replaced by the notion of collective psychism" (p. 87). This same scientism that the author has termed "science fundamentalism" wholeheartedly attacks spirituality while not taking full appraisal of, not to mention disowning, its own destructive tendencies, which far outweigh those of which it wrongly accuses religion:

> In the opinion of this trio of destroyers [Richard Dawkins, Christopher Hitchens, and Sam Harris], the religions have not brought anything positive to humanity; they are marked by intellectual insufficiency. Besides, according to them, they are a "risk" for our very existence.... One has to respond to their pseudo-arguments by pointing out that the great disgraces of the twentieth century were not caused by religion.... Modern dictatorships—"rational", "scientific", and violently anti-religious—persecuted and killed thousands of Christians, Muslims, and Jews in the epoch of the Soviet Union and Nazism, and millions of Buddhists and Taoists were killed in the "Cultural Revolution" of Mao Tse Tung's China (pp. 103, 106).

Readers familiar with William Stoddart, leading author, translator, and editor of Perennialist writings, will be very pleased to know that he has contributed a superb introduction setting down the book's imperative implication while enlightening the spiritual path for contemporary seekers. Stoddart begins his stimulating text thus:

> If one wished to sum up in one word the central evil of the modern [and postmodern] age, one could do so with the word "atheism". While this diagnosis might command ready agreement on the part of religiously-minded people, it might still, because it seems too abstract or too general, be regarded as a trifle facile. Nevertheless, I believe that, in one or more of its many guises, it is precisely atheism that is at the root of all modern evils. Atheism may be as ancient as fallen man, but the atheism that is with us today

has its direct origin in the ideas of the eighteenth-century "enlightenment"... (p. ix).

What is not understood in current discourse is that "Militant fundamentalism, then, constitutes a deviation of traditional and integral religion" (p. 9), and that such extremism cannot portray integral spirituality in any shape or form as it is axiomatically a departure from all revealed orthodoxies *in divinis*. And if we inquire into the perpetuation of many of these misconceptions, we see the corporate media syndicates with their so-called *pundits* at play, spinning their countless misconceptions: "Many in the mass media speak with full voice against 'fundamentalism,' but in a certain sense they are also 'fundamentalist' when they present journalist coverage that is in general ahistorical, superficial, and unilateral" (p. 11), writes Azevedo. The problem in advocating a political solution is that it, in turn, creates another problem, which places spiritual authority below temporal power: "The challenge in today's world is that politics now wants to superimpose itself on religion; it wants to oblige religion to follow her own ways, wants to place itself in the place of its 'master'" (p. 16).

With regard to the misguided notion that *jihād* signifies or is synonymous with "terrorism", the author dispels this notion with the following statement, which illuminates the universal implications of *jihād* or rather "spiritual warfare," as it is found in all religious traditions:

> What did the Prophet of Islam mean by this "greater holy effort" or "greater war"? The answer is the fight against pride and egoism which takes place in every human being's heart; it is the war on the ego and its vanity; it is the spiritual warfare.... The "greater *jihād*" is, or should be, the combat *par excellence* of the Muslims, and of the followers of all authentic religion.... Terrorism is not *jihād*.... The Qur'ān says: "Fight in the way of God against those who fight against you, but begin not hostilities. Lo! God loves not aggressors" (2:190) [pp. 20, 21].

Contrary to the conventional wisdom, "among the sacred scriptures of mankind, the Qur'ān is the most explicitly universalist" (p. 36). The implicit universal message of the Qur'ān is apparent for those who have eyes and ears to perceive it:

> It is worth noting that the Qur'ān preaches the legitimacy of the religions of the "People of the Book" (Christians, Jews, and later also Hindus), while the militants preach exactly the opposite, exacerbating politico-religious passions that denature their own faith and feed hatred. Militant fundamentalism believes that an unbridgeable abyss separates Islam from Christianity, but the Qur'ān teaches otherwise: "And We [God] also sent Jesus, son of Mary, to whom We conferred the Gospel and infused compassion and mercy in the hearts of those who follow it" (57:27) [p. 4].

It is with great clarity that the author elucidates that secularism and fundamentalism are *deviations which, in our present age, flock together* and give rise to "secular fundamentalism", a reduction projecting itself as a quasi-Absolute that cannot be:

> This secular and militant fundamentalism also has its (pseudo-) "orthodoxy" and its (pseudo-) "dogmas," which aim at being the exact opposite of religious principles. It is anti-religion-become-religion, but a "religion" that totally denies the Absolute—except its own passionately-voiced "absolute" claim that only the relative exists, that only the relative is "absolute" (p. 65).

The challenge that *Men of a Single Book* delivers is that while Truth is one, it has many expressions that cannot be reduced to a single credo, as Saint Thomas Aquinas (1224–1274) warned the faithful seven centuries ago. To understand this work is to go beyond the literalism and collectivism of the diverse revelations in their present state and thereby to recognize the spiritual counterfeits in order to dispel the shadows of what has become a sort of universal trance. As Stoddardt writes,

"We must be capable of the cardinally important intuition that *every religion*—be it Christianity, Hinduism, Buddhism, or Islam—*comes from God and every religion leads back to God.*"

26

*Of the Land and the Spirit: The Essential Lord Northbourne on Ecology and Religion**

Lord Northbourne (1896–1982), born Walter Ernest Christopher James, was the 4th Baron Northbourne of Kent, England. It is not commonly known that the wide range of people he influenced included such prestigious individuals as HRH The Prince of Wales and Wendell Berry. He collaborated with E.F. Schumacher (1911–1977) to bring greater awareness to sustainable farming practices and sustainable ecology as a whole. Nor is it frequently known that he was an adept practitioner of what he termed "organic farming" long before the environmental movement popularised this practice which has since become a norm in holistic or alternative farming circles.

In 1940, with astute clarity of vision, Lord Northbourne diagnosed the basis of the emerging disarray of the modern world that was encroaching upon the entire Earth, stemming from a fundamental dissociation from Nature. He consequently also underscored its cure—to embrace the interdependence of Nature, the terrestrial community and the sacred as an undivided whole. A vital facet of his life came to fruition when he was introduced to the perennialist or traditionalist

---

* Christopher James and Joseph A. Fitzgerald (eds.). World Wisdom, 2008, 256pp.

school via Buddhist author and fellow perennialist Marco Pallis (1895–1989), who contacted him after reading his first book *Look to the Land*, published in 1940. From this point on Lord Northbourne aligned himself with this perspective. Not only did he contribute to the perennialist writings with influential works that functioned as matchless introductions to this school of thought, such as *Religion in the Modern World* and *Looking Back on Progress*, but he also translated several axial texts from this school into English.

Of the Land and the Spirit is divided into five providential themes, containing many of Lord Northbourne's writings that have never before been published in book form: "Farming: An Ecology in Practice", "On the Value of Tradition", "Metaphysical Principles", "Art and Symbolism", and "Lessons from Life". Included in the Appendix is the private correspondence between Lord Northbourne and the renowned Trappist monk Thomas Merton (1915–1968).

The insightful Foreword by the esteemed author Wendell Berry sets the tone for this anthology by affirming the integral relationship of spirituality and ecology that is all too often unacknowledged, especially with the prevailing Cartesian-Newtonian paradigm of contemporary scientism coupled with the radical secularism of our age: "Those who take agriculture seriously enough and study it long enough will come to issues that will have to be recognised as religious" (p. viii).

These essays will thwart the apparatus of time within the reader in order to ground the perennial point of view that has always and everywhere been acknowledged. There are many beloved essays that will connect with the diversity of readers, such as "Agriculture and Human Destiny", "The Beauty of Flowers", "Religion and Tradition" and "Looking Back on Progress". Each of these essays, although unique and different from the others, contains an underlying reality vividly expressed in the Lakota affirmation *Mitakuye Oyasin*: "We Are All Related."

And yet the idea of the interconnectedness of all of life, although irrefutably true, is not an end in itself as is often assumed by proponents of the new paradigm or by holistic circles. The web of life necessarily implies not only wholeness, but a transcendent unity that manifests creation and is none other than a theophany, guiding this creation and reintegrating the human being within the terrestrial journey, as exemplified by the hermetic maxim "As above, so below."

One hears a lot of talk about the need for us to "build a better world" and we are pestered with conflicting policies, reforms, reorganisations and long-term plans meant to create this terrestrial Utopia. But if the word "better" does not mean "nearer to the Divine", all those manoeuvrings will lead to nothing but growing confusion and, in the end, to utter darkness.

We are extraordinarily fortunate to have this recent publication available and we cannot recommend it highly enough. This anthology belongs in the library of every seeker, as it presents an integral orientation that embraces the fullness of the human potential *in divinis* and what it accurately means to be human, which is inseparable from what is transpersonal or divine.

27

*On the Origin of Beauty: Ecophilosophy in the Light of Traditional Wisdom**

> Beauty is the splendor of the Truth.
>
> Plato

A striking phenomenon with regard to any mention of *beauty* is how oblivious contemporaries are to the truth of its origin *in divinis*. Yet it is not the physical eye that this reality remains opaque to but the "eye of the heart" or the transcendent Intellect which has become emaciated in the present age. Since time immemorial traditional civilizations and societies have intuited the sacred significance of beauty and perceived it as a direct manifestation of the spiritual world. This is why sacred science, found at the heart of all of the wisdom traditions, knew and understood that the natural world and all of its forms found on Earth corresponded to celestial archetypes. It is no longer debated that modern science has hit a dead-end for its destructive effects now apparent to all. And if we wait to observe how the reductionistic theoretical trajectory of modern science and its experiment culminates—there will be no you or I, nor environment waiting for its final triumph—the destruction of all that we know, the world itself will be achieved.

---

* John Griffin. World Wisdom, 2011, 304pp.

This volume contains a thought-provoking "Foreword" by Satish Kumar (b. 1936), Editor Emeritus of *Resurgence* magazine, founder and Director of Programmes of the Schumacher College, who unhesitatingly recognizes the frequently overlooked spiritual implications of the ecological crisis indispensable to any possible renewal. The book is divided into five fields of inquiry, each part containing two chapters.

PART ONE: WILDERNESS

The book begins with a personal anecdote of the author's early childhood recollections of encountering nature. In the summer of 1972 the author and two other siblings traveled with their father to see Lake Pedder in the heart of the Tasmanian wilderness before it was destroyed by a man-made flood in order to provide an impoundment for hydro-electricity. This singular event, which has remained with the author for some forty years, grounds the entire work, a veritable touchstone to the sacred—"the overwhelming presence of the spiritual within the natural world" (p. 24). The technological hubris that led to the demise of Lake Pedder is not an isolated phenomenon. Quite the contrary, it has become a common byproduct of living in the contemporary world, which allows readers to identify with the loss of their own or analogous "Lake Pedder".

The second section provides an important overview of *A Sandy County Almanac* (1949) by Aldo Leopold, a respected pioneer of environmental thought whose ideas have provided an enduring resonance with ecophilosophy.

PART TWO: ECOPHILOSOPHY

This section contains an overview of the emerging field of ecophilosophy which distinguishes itself from deep ecology and ecopsychology, suggesting that it is—"the last great Western philosophical response to an understanding of the human position *vis-à-vis* the world" (p. 47). Some suggest that the indigenous ways of relating to the environment, especially certain examples of ecological destruction, are equal to modern examples of environmental degradation. Yet these were an exception and not a rule.

> Although historical examples of "unecological" behavior can be found in all cultures (whether of primal peoples or more developed civilizations), destruction that is at once large-scale, is not done in ignorance of the consequences but often with full knowledge of them, and lacks any restraining wisdom, is a phenomenon only of recent centuries (p. 49).

Human conduct or behavior in the premodern epoch was always rooted in the underlying metaphysical principles of a spiritual tradition. There was no such thing as "secular ethics" or "secular morality", in the same way that nothing was perceived as separate from the sacred. Another important distinction regarding ecophilosophy is that the understanding of philosophy or the "love of wisdom" is taken from the ancient or classical interpretations referring to those who contemplate the cosmic order, its beauty, and strive to abide in this transcendent reality. However, such is not the case with modern philosophy which is relativistic and nihilistic and denies the transcendent order altogether.

The second section presents a synopsis of "deep ecology" (contrasted with "shallow ecology") and "transpersonal ecology", by way of highlighting the limitations as they do not fully incorporate the transcendent. With this said, they both identify with an expanded sense of "self" or "potentiality", yet these designations are limited to the psycho-physical and do not pertain to the spiritual domain. Griffin explores the origins of the environmental movement, thereby bringing much clarification to the subject. "It cannot be seriously denied that almost from the beginning in Christianity there were corruptions of the original teaching that come about due to its impact with temporal powers. Nor can it be denied that this 'weakness' provided an opening for the development of a secular science" (p. 85).

PART THREE: THROUGH A GLASS DARKLY

In the chapter aptly titled "Reductionism" the author outlines the core distinction between modern science and sacred science. The first relies on reason (*ratio*) which is incomplete unto itself, and the second relies on the Intellect (*Intellectus* in Latin, *Nous* in Greek, *Rūḥ* in Arabic and *Buddhi* in Sanskrit) which is a transcendent faculty within the human individual. We are reminded that "Rational consciousness is not perceptive; rather it interprets sensory data" (p. 96).

> The supra-sensory, transcendent, essential, or vertical dimension to reality was not open to investigation using analytical reason, but was known by means of the "faculty" of perception, originating prior to reason, that partook of the nature of this transcendence—the *nous* (Intellect) (p. 104).

While the idea of unmediated apprehension of reality sounds anachronistic to contemporary minds, it is this unitive means of perceiving that is unanimous within the sapiential traditions. With the disowning of traditional metaphysics, modern science erects a new metaphysics establishing in turn its own cosmology, ontology, empiricism and epistemology that are no longer connected to the spiritual domain.

The chapter titled "The Crisis of Modern Science" further elaborates on what has led to the entropic outlook that is destroying the ecosystem. Griffin provides an interesting synopsis of quantum theory and explores the notion that it has more in common with the mystical dimension than with modern science or its reductionistic elements. A synthesis between Eastern thought and modern science has been attempted, yet it was not to the benefit of modern science: "Quantum physics has in fact revealed an obstacle to the continuation of the methods of reductive science" (p. 129).

Seyyed Hossein Nasr (b. 1933) has wonderfully summarized the attempt to synthesize Eastern wisdom with quantum theory and why such efforts cannot bear fruit:

> *The Tao of Physics* does not really speak of Hindu cosmology or Chinese physics, but only mentions certain comparisons between modern physics and Hindu and Taoist metaphysical ideas...there are many profound correlations and concordances to be found between certain aspects of biology, astronomy and quantum mechanics on one hand and oriental doctrines of nature, of the cosmos, on the other.... But what has occurred for the most part is not...[a] profound comparison... but its parody, a kind of popularized version of a religious knowledge of nature (p. 129).

Griffin makes a valuable point which is often ignored: "It is the tragic assumption that the old truth is to be judged in the light of the new, and the terrible injustice of often propagating a view—quite untenable—that science deals with *all* of reality" (p. 136).[1]

PART FOUR: THE VERTICAL DIMENSION

The two chapters contained in this section are first "Descent" and second "Ascent". Griffin shares with the reader the challenging task of situating modern science in its rightful place. Rather than taking us forward into what is deeper or higher, it is doing the contrary: "To see modern science in

---

[1] It is worth adding the following quote by Frithjof Schuon (1907–1998) in the light of the above point: "A totalitarian rationalism that eliminates both Revelation and Intellect, and at the same time a totalitarian materialism that ignores the metaphysical relativity... of matter and of the world... does not know that the supra-sensible, situated as it is beyond space and time, is the concrete principle of the world, and that it is consequently also at the origin of that contingent and changeable coagulation we call 'matter'. A science that is called 'exact' is in fact an 'intelligence without wisdom', just as post-scholastic philosophy is inversely a 'wisdom without intelligence'" (quoted in John Griffin, *On the Origin of Beauty*, p. 138); the original quote can be found in Frithjof Schuon, *Light on the Ancient Worlds* (Bloomington: World Wisdom Books, 1984), p. 117.

terms of a 'descent' of consciousness is, of course, to exactly reverse the conventional image" (p. 152).

He informs the reader that while quantum mechanics or "new science" has expanded the vision of modern science allowing for a glimpse at the vertical or the spiritual domain, it does so by explicitly framing the limitations of the scientific paradigm itself. While modern science can measure and predict the physical forms of the manifest world, it cannot do so with the unmanifest world—that which is beyond or underlies the physical order. The central problem with modern science, beside its truncated vision that discredits the supra-sensible domain, is that it appropriates what is outside its designation. The author refers extensively to the work of Philip Sherrard (1922–1995), who wonderfully presents the quandary that modern science faces in light of integral metaphysics: "Nothing can be known except according to the mode of the knower" (p. 149). No matter how broad an outlook modern science adopts it is inevitably caught in a dualistic framework that it cannot escape, since consciousness is not a thing or an object that can be empirically studied: "The highest mode of consciousness, or consciousness in itself, is that in which there is no dualism between knower and what is to be known, observer and what is to be observed, consciousness and that of which consciousness is conscious" (p. 150).

PART FIVE: THE NATURE OF NATURE

From the standpoint of integral metaphysics, the world is sacred as it participates in the nature of the Divine. That nature itself is a *theophany* contrasts starkly with the modern and postmodern outlook which views nature as an object, a thing, separate and disconnected from everything else. Modern science's attempt to appropriate the whole of Reality demonstrates its infancy and naiveté, in contrast with sacred science which is rooted in the timeless truths: "After nearly 400 years of scientific analysis, it has remained impossible to explain what life is in terms of materialism" (p. 235). The traditional and primordial people universally acknowledged the primacy of the spirit, as it was the transpersonal that not only unified all of reality, but provided guidance in all matters of existence. Any attempt to study what the human being is or what the environment is, if devoid of the sacred, will always fall short and will inevitably be a distortion. The primordial peoples knew that nature and all existence was symbolic, and by knowing this symbolic language one could participate in the sacred.

At the heart of any discussion on integral ecology is sacred science, and without this common ground we are limited to the horizontal causality of the manifest world—whereas sacred science is informed by the vertical dimension of the supra-sensible that includes the horizontal order. If we are not blinded by the paradigm of modern science, we can see further into the remarkable beauty and grandeur of creation. In restoring the proper place of ecology and philosophy (the "love of wisdom") we need to turn to sacred science and its wisdom traditions.

On the Origin of Beauty grapples with the hard questions of how we got into this nightmarish scenario, which diagnostically looks very much like suicidal ideation, threatening the complete decimation of the natural environment and of all life forms. Yet this book radically differs from others, as it provides the compulsory understanding that underscores what brought it about, which is no minor task as this is inseparable from identifying the way out. What is necessary is a "paradigm shift" within modern science, not a revision or a makeover of the same thought process that brought about the current crisis. We urgently need a revival of sacred science that is situated at the heart of the perennial philosophy, which holds Beauty and Truth as inseparable and the Intellect as the transpersonal faculty within the human being that directly apprehends this Reality. There can be no remedy for the ecological crisis or any of the contemporary ills, for that matter, without the knowledge of the underlying causes which this book addresses.

28

*Beads of Faith: Pathways to Meditation and Spirituality Using Rosaries, Prayer Beads and Sacred Words**

> The Name pronounced even once is a benefit, whether one is aware of it or not. Prayer is not verbal, it is from the heart. To merge into the heart is prayer.
>
> Śrī Ramana Maharshi[1]

This new book, which comes with a DVD of the documentary film released previously under the same title, examines both the "outer" and "inner" meanings of the use and function of prayer beads that are instrumental in prayer, recitation, invocation, and meditation found throughout all of the world religions. The book begins by confirming that prayer beads have their origin in the divine, and simultaneously acknowledges the uses of prayer beads across spiritual traditions: "The use of prayer beads is not a practice recently invented or introduced, but is archetypal in nature, and common to every great faith tradition" (p. 9). It will interest readers to learn that the etymology of the word "bead" reinforces the transcendent function of prayer beads, taken from the Sanskrit *buddh*, which means "to awaken," referring

---

* Gray Henry & Susannah Marriott. Fons Vitae, 2008, 120pp.
[1] Quoted *ibid.*, p. 63.

to the Buddha or "The Awakened One," and simultaneously connected to the Saxon verb *bidden*—"to pray".

This work acknowledges the universal and perennial uses of prayer beads and guides the seeker into the sacred dimensions of varied faiths by introducing the spiritual methods employed with prayer beads. The allegory of terrestrial existence is likened to "a rope thrown by God to a drowning man," much like this "rope" of prayer beads comes from the spiritual domain and offers a spiritual method acting as a sacred *funiculus umbilicalis* or umbilical cord, connecting the practitioner to the divine through revelation "from Himself to Himself"—that is from the Divine to the Divine. The myriad practitioners are said to be as diverse as the paths leading up a mountain or points around the circumference of a circle traveling like radii to the center, to converge at the summit or the center, thus confirming the true purpose of human existence—union with the Self or the Divine.

This "summit", which is transcendent, is analogous to the "center" that is immanent, described in the text as it pertains to prayer beads "… the very act of pausing on a bead brings you back to the centre of where you are and *who* you are" (p. 10). Both the book and the DVD are filled with beautiful and contemplative imagery depicting the diverse ways that prayer beads are employed by spiritual practitioners of all traditions. The comparative approach of both mediums assists the reader in understanding each tradition via the wisdom found in the other.

The book begins with "The Universal Rosary" and then continues to explore the different uses of prayer beads through the world religions: "Catholic Rosaries", "Orthodox Rosaries", "Jewish *Tefillin*", "Hindu *Malas*", "Buddhist *Malas*", "Muslim *Tasbih*", "Native American Beads", and "Amulets and Meditation".

Prayer beads known as rosaries have been integral to the

act of prayer within the Christian West or the Roman Catholic Church since the Middle Ages. Some possible origins of the Catholic rosary, from the Latin *rosarium* or "rose garden," date back to the twelfth century during the Crusades, or in Moorish Spain, and stem from Islamic uses of prayer beads. Another origin is thought to be connected to Saint Dominic (1170–1221), who received the Holy Rosary from the Blessed Virgin Mary, as affirmed by Pope Leo XIII (1810–1903). It was during the sixteenth century that rosaries took the form in which they are known today. The rosary allows the practitioner to pray throughout the day no matter what activity he or she is being engaged in, thus creating a divine precinct within the heart. St. Augustine writes, "Do thou all within. And if perchance thou seekest some high place, some holy place, make thee a temple for God within" (p. 20). The text also explains the recitation of "Hail Mary" (Latin: *Ave Maria*), meditating on the Mysteries of the Rosary, and other key prayers.

Among the Eastern-Catholic and Eastern Orthodox Church contemplatives, the rosary is a woolen rope of knots (*komboskini; chotki; misbaḥa*) used to recite the Jesus Prayer or Prayer of the Heart. Quintessential to the Prayer of the Heart is the command of St. Paul, "Pray without ceasing" (I Thessalonians 5:17). The text also describes the wording of the Jesus Prayer: "Lord Jesus Christ, Son of God, have mercy on me," which is continuously repeated while integrating the breath, and can also incorporate prostrations that resemble yogic postures or *asanas*. In the film one can observe a monk of Mount Athos performing this practice of the Prayer of the Heart.

The Jewish tradition uses prayer straps known as the *tefillin* which are worn on the head and the arm. The *tefillin* contain passages from the Torah that when worn on the forehead and the arm closest to the heart sublimate the desires of the heart, body, and mind as mandated by King Solomon, "Bind them upon thy fingers, write them upon the table of thine heart"

(Proverbs 7:3). The text also explains the methods of praying with the *tefillin* in order to bind the words of God to man.

In Hinduism (*sanātana dharma*) prayer beads are known as *malas*, and are used to repeat a *mantra* or Divine names, a devotional practice known as *japa yoga* or *japa mala*. The purpose of repeating the Divine names is articulated by Swāmī Ramdas: "*Om* tunes the entire human being with the eternal music of the Divine, bringing the soul in direct contact with the in-dwelling and all-pervading Reality" (p. 64). The book elucidates the spiritual method of *japa yoga* as used by three spiritual masters of the Vedānta: Śrī Ramakrishna (1836–1886), Swāmī Ramdas (1884–1963), and Śrī Ramana Maharshi (1879–1950). The DVD takes one into the presence of some of the great spiritual masters and *sannyasin* of India, including also the sounds of their world.

The book describes how prayer beads or *malas* and chanting are used by the different schools of Buddhism known as the three "vehicles" or *yānas*—Theravāda, Mahāyāna, Vajrayāna. The text provides details on how one of the most widely used invocations is practiced: *Om Mani Padme Hum*— "O, thou Jewel in the Lotus, Hail"—and how constant repetition of this invocation offered to the *bodhisattva* Avalokiteśvara or Chenrezig can release the practitioner from the clenches of *saṃsāra*—the cycles of birth and death leading to liberation. There is also an introduction to Jain Malas at the end of the section. Some of the exquisite footage in the DVD takes us on a visit to Burma, to Pagan, a city of temples, and to the great *stupa* of Shwedagon Pagoda in Rangoon, and it also invites the viewer to enter the world of a Burmese Buddhist master among other sacred sites.

The Islamic tradition as well as Sufism, its mystical expression, refers to prayer beads as the *tasbīḥ*, which is reaffirmed in the prophetic traditions, "Repeat the *tasbīḥ*[2] a hundred times, and a thousand virtues shall be recorded by

---

[2] Here meaning specifically the phrase *subḥān Allāh*, "glory to God."

God for you, ten virtuous deeds for each repetition" (p. 90). In Sufism this process of remembrance or *dhikr* allows the seeker of truth to reside with God whenever and wherever God is remembered. A common recitation that is the first part of the *Shahādah* is: *Lā ilāha illā 'Llāh*, "There is no divinity but the Divinity," illuminating the quintessential Sufi doctrine of the "Unity of Being" or "Oneness of Being" (*waḥdat al-wujūd*). Found at the end of the section are useful pointers for praying with the *tasbīḥ*. The DVD takes us into the world of remembrance (*dhikr*), sound, and imagery of some of the great Sufi saints as well.

The uses of beads have a primordial origin for the indigenous peoples of the Americas. The Huichol Indians of Mexico, the Ojibwe of Canada, and the Iroquois of North America (Turtle Island) use beads as a spiritual vocation, which is similar to the use of the rosary. Beading allows the artist to experience the "heartbeat of creation" while simultaneously participating in the craft or sacred art that connects the individual with the spiritual realm. The various forms of traditional prayer are described, such as the sweat lodge (*Inipi*), the vision quest (*Hanblecheyapi*), and the act of praying with the sacred pipe (*Chanupa*).

The last section devoted to amulets and meditation draws attention to the ancient uses of beads not only as a form of religious devotion, but as a way of centering and quieting the mind to assist with worldly concerns and dispel fear.

The film concludes with a demonstration showing step by step how to make a rosary from rose petals by Brother Paul Quenon, a monk from the Abbey of Gethsemani in Trappist, Kentucky, who was a novice under Thomas Merton.

In order to better understand the world's religions in an age where diverse traditions are asked to peacefully coexist, we welcome *Beads of Faith* as an addition to other works dedicated to inter-religious dialogue. As this book acknowledges, it is through the "transcendent unity of religions"[3] that an authentic understanding and mutual respect for different spiritual traditions can take place.

---

[3] See Frithjof Schuon, *The Transcendent Unity of Religions*.

29

*Death as Gateway to Eternity: Nature's Hidden Message**

> This great, unborn Self [*Ātmā*], undecaying, undying, immortal, fearless, is indeed *Brahman* [Absolute].
>
> *Brihadāranyaka Upanishad* 4.4.25

Where do we go and what occurs when the physical body is no longer? This question is just as vital as asking where we have come from prior to obtaining this human form. Such existential and metaphysical questions have captivated the human mind the world over since time immemorial. Overall, contemporary life ignores the reality of any continuation beyond death and dismisses reminders of the impermanence of life. It prefers to give the impression that life on earth is permanent and that there is no reality save physical existence. This goes against the natural order and nothing could be further from the truth. It is in relationship with the whole of existence—with the mountains, stars, animals, plants and fellow human beings—that we can glean the meaning of the enigma of life and death. Enigma permeates the entirety of human existence, "We are born in mystery, we live in mystery,

---

* Hans Küry. Translated by Gillian Harris. Bloomington: World Wisdom, 2013, 128pp.

and we die in mystery."[1] All of time is contained in the present moment—what has been termed the "eternal now"—which connects the ephemeral to the eternal or time to the timeless. "In that supreme moment all moments are contained."[2] From this point of view, life and death are inseparable like two facets of one seamless Reality known to the ancients as a doorway—but a doorway to where?

The mystery of the present moment transcends the *spatio-temporal sequence of normal interpretations of chronological time*. It is through the timeless and universal wisdom found across the diverse cultures of the world that the phenomenon of life, death and the posthumous states beyond the physical existence of the body are illuminated. This wisdom is "the *philosophia perennis*—the primordial doctrine that transcends every articulated definition, lying behind all the diverse traditional forms and illuminating them from within" (p. 105).

The sapiential traditions ask of all human beings a central question that directs consciousness to a transcendent reality beyond the corporeal realm:

"When one realizes his own true nature he will be free from birth and death... if you free yourself from birth and death, you should know where you are. Now your body separates into the four elements. Where are you?"[3]

The author of this work under review, Hans Küry (1906–1987), was a Swiss writer who received a doctorate degree in English and specialized in the works of William Shakespeare. He wrote six books and several articles on a variety of literary, religious and philosophical themes. *Death as Gateway*

---

[1] Huston Smith, *The Way Things Are: Conversations with Huston Smith on the Spiritual Life*, ed. Phil Cousineau (Los Angeles: University of California Press, 2003), p. 30.

[2] Śrī Ānandamayī Mā, quoted in *The Essential Śrī Ānandamayī Mā*, p. 91.

[3] *Zen Flesh, Zen Bones: A Collection of Zen and Pre-Zen Writings*, ed. Paul Reps (New York: Anchor Books, 1989), p. 126.

to Eternity is the first work to be translated from his native German into English. Furthermore, it will interest readers to know that Küry was also a long-time friend and associate of Frithjof Schuon (1907–1998), a leading exponent of the perennial philosophy.[4]

If one were to undertake a survey of the lives of the saints and sages of the diverse sapiential traditions one would find a common theme that runs throughout their lives: they have all had a momentous experience or rather *metanoia* that has shifted their relationship to life and death by directing consciousness away from the ephemeral to the Eternal. This integral transfiguration of consciousness, comprised of both the psychological and spiritual dimensions, is described variously in the distinct traditions: it is encapsulated in the Prophet's saying, often cited by the Sufis, "Die before you die!"; and in the Gospel of John, Christ says: "Except a man be born again, he cannot see the kingdom of God" (John 3:3), or again in the Christian tradition, "It is no longer I who live, but Christ who lives in me" (Galatians 2:20).

Swāmī Ramdas (1884–1963) recalls a decisive encounter with death and its impact on his life on the occasion of the death of one of his close friends: "When circumstances force the soul to turn to its immortal, changeless existence, full of light, peace, and joy, it gets now and again glimpses of this supreme state, just as one gets flashes of light from the sun for a brief period whenever the clouds that cover it pass on."[5] Śrī Ramana Maharshi (1879–1950), in the summer of 1896 when he was seventeen years old, had a spontaneous experience

---

[4] See Hans Küry, "Hinweis auf Frithjof Schuon," in *Religion of the Heart: Essays Presented to Frithjof Schuon on His Eightieth Birthday*, eds. S. H. Nasr and W. Stoddart (Washington, D.C.: Foundation for Traditional Studies, 1991), pp. 177–188; Michael Oren Fitzgerald, *Frithjof Schuon: Messenger of the Perennial Philosophy* (Bloomington: World Wisdom, 2010).

[5] Swāmī Ramdas, quoted in *The Essential Swami Ramdas: Commemorative Edition*, ed. Susunaga Weeraperuma (Bloomington: World Wisdom, 2005), p. xxxiv.

where he was overwhelmed by a violent fear of death that lead to his recognition that: "The body dies but the Spirit that transcends it cannot be touched by death. That means I am the deathless Spirit."[6] The Spirit, hidden in all of the terrestrial forms, manifests as *līlā* or "divine play". This understanding of existence as manifesting the one and only spiritual Reality ascribes a new meaning to life and death, one that lies beyond all dualistic conceptions.

FIRST MEDITATION: OF JUDGMENT

Due to the mounting pressures of political correctness in the modern world, the notion of judgment itself is often rendered antiquated or even portrayed as deluded as each person is viewed to be autonomous and self-reliant, able to make decisions and be accountable for these decisions. The idea that judgment stems from an ultimate arbitrator of good and evil is often perceived in the present day as sheer nonsense. How then can we fully discern its meaning within the world religions and its import for our lives?

The oft quoted passage "Judge not, that ye be not judged" (Matthew 7:1–3) does not signify that all judgment needs to be suspended; accountability and discernment are fundamental to being truly human. At the same time, we might cite another passage that suggests that every human is accountable for his or her actions: "Every one... shall give account of himself" (Romans 14:12). Due to the hardening of the human heart caused by severing itself from the Divine, individuals find fault in others without looking into the substance of their own hearts. "God knoweth what is in your hearts" (Qur'ān 33:51), similarly, "He knew what was in their [the believers'] hearts" (Qur'ān 48:18). Divine Mercy is miraculous in its embrace, but accountability is not forgotten. According to the *ḥadīth qudsī*, "My mercy [*raḥmah*] takes precedence over My wrath [*ghaḍab*]."

---

[6] *The Teachings of Ramana Maharshi*, pp. 9–10.

Küry's book begins with an astute observation regarding the spiritual myopia of the present age and its predicament: "If many Westerners today find it difficult to believe in the immortality of the soul, the main reason lies in their living consciously only in quite superficial layers of human nature, in those layers which are indeed impermanent" (p. 3). The author contrasts this outlook with that of those who are centered on the spiritual domain and those who wish to awaken to the Real: "It is a different matter for the man who believes, prays, and concentrates on God; the vibrations of higher, celestial states touch him from within" (p. 3). The traditional world, prior to modernism and postmodernism, rather than being backwards, facilitated a way of life that was conducive to integrating the inner and outer dimensions of the human being, "traditional peoples... [had a] simple way of life, restricted to the bare necessities, [one that] already helps them to sever themselves more easily from external contingencies" (p. 4). Contemporary life, on the other hand, is not only unconducive to living one's religion, it actually robs one of silence, hindering the development of the inner life, leaving scant time for contemplation of the subtler realities. In this context, it is worth recalling the sacred saying within Islamic spirituality: "The first of his actions for which a servant of God will be held accountable on the Day of Resurrection will be his prayers" (*hadīth qudsī*). Metaphysically the act of sinning is to turn consciousness away from the Eternal and placing it on the ephemeral: "Forgetfulness of God is the greatest sin; His constant remembrance is the greatest virtue."[7]

The saints and sages of all of the diverse religious traditions affirmed the immortality of the human soul, holding that the Real was to be perceived in the eternal now of the present moment and not in what was to come. "The man plunged in God sees the paradisal and infernal states not as lying in the future, entering into play only after death; he sees them

---

[7] Śrī Ānandamayī Mā, quoted in *The Essential Śrī Ānandamayī Mā*, p. 132.

already now" (pp. 5-6). Metaphysically speaking, time exists eternally in the present moment, both past and future as well as what lies beyond the *spatio-temporal order*.

Correspondingly, "the 'posthumous' states cannot be categorized in 'temporal' terms... as is repeatedly testified, the dying man sees his whole life pass before him again, this overview indicates that he is entering simultaneity or non-temporality" (p. 6). What is unanimously affirmed is that what occurs posthumously hinges on what occurs in this terrestrial world. The states that the human soul must traverse posthumously are consequences of the soul's shortsighted, deluded thinking or misdeeds on earth.

The teachings of the sapiential traditions all convey the significance of the sacred scriptures to transmit in diverse ways how the Divine communicates Itself: "Heaven and earth will pass away, but my words will not pass away" (Matthew 24:35). It is through the vehicle of Tradition that the Divine speaks directly to the human: "Verily, verily I say unto you: He that heareth my word and believeth on him that sent me, hath everlasting life and shall not come into condemnation; but is passed from death unto life" (John 5:24). In connecting oneself to a true religion and living in accordance with its teachings, the human soul may return to its Divine origin, the One and sole Subsistent. "Who goes away—who else is it that arrives? What is the distinction between life and death? One who passes away, in fact, merges into the One who is ever-existent."[8] It is the identification with our transitory nature that brings about the fear of death; however, when we identify with our transpersonal nature, which is deathless, this fear dissipates. In its innermost depths, integral human identity is superior to the dissolution of the physical body and to the multiple lower states: "In my Father's house are many mansions" (John 14:2).

---

[8] Śrī Ānandamayī Mā, quoted in *The Essential Śrī Ānandamayī Mā*, p. 43.

SECOND MEDITATION:
OF THE RESURRECTION OF THE FLESH

Due to the diminishing presence of authentic religion and spirituality, contemporaries have a tremendous disadvantage from those living in previous ages, one that is not completely understood or directly perceived today. "The man living under the protection of a theocentric culture feels the nearness of God and becomes so attuned to the language of divine signs that he begins to understand them immediately, just as a child starts to understand human language by imitating its parents" (p. 26). In the purity of early childhood the radiance surrounding all sentient beings is perceived; this is why the religions refer to the childlike state as the optimal one for the spiritual path. It is worth recalling the following passage: "Verily I say unto you, Except ye be converted, and become as little children, ye shall not enter into the kingdom of heaven" (Matthew 18:3).

From a certain point of view terrestrial existence is defined by human birth, which is inseparable from duality; yet prior to the phenomenon of birth, duality did not exist for the human soul and therefore cannot define the human condition in the fullest sense. The human condition is paradoxical; on the one hand the soul originates and returns to the non-dual source, yet on the other hand it temporarily resides in a physical body bound to duality. With a non-dual consciousness human beings are not burdened by the judgment of good and evil, yet when consciousness is consumed by duality, judgment becomes unavoidable. The fallen state of *samsāric* existence is confined to dualistic consciousness and cannot avoid judgment as long as ignorance (*avidyā*) and illusion (*māyā*) continue to seduce and dominate the soul's perceptions.

The distinctions between the physical and the psychic and their connection to Spirit are essential in understanding what occurs with the dissolution of the human body. "For whom the body is a reflection of the Inward cannot take physical death for the perishing of the soul: a content of consciousness vanishes, but consciousness itself remains" (p. 30). Each human being has a distinct destiny, "there are as many destinies... as there are human beings" (p. 30).

THIRD MEDITATION: EARTHLY SIGNS OF HEAVEN

The third meditation explores the symbolic nature of the human condition. The author writes, "The divine Creation is a language.... The primordial, uncorrupted man reads the book of the world just as naturally as a revealed text" (p. 57).

> The world is like a dream of God, dreamed by Him in his capacity as Lord of the world; man's life, and the life of the other beings, are dreams within this general dream; the end of time is like an awakening from the world dream, the death of beings is like an awakening from their individual dream. Amnesia is a hallmark of the world (p. 51).

What then is the remedy for this forgetfulness? The remedy is to be found within religion and what binds the human being to a transcendent reality:

> The world is just a dream—this memory is religion (= re-binding)—or in other words the memory of the waking state (= divine Revelation). This consciousness of the dream nature of the world must be present in its center, as the all-governing principle, till the end (p. 51).

In essence, the human corresponds to the Divine; hence the prophetic dictum, "He who knows himself, knows his Lord" (p. 52). The inscription of the temple at Delphi "Know thyself" (*Gnothi seauton*) is a testament to this *gnosis*, as is too the following from the Gospels "The kingdom of God is within you" (Luke 17:21). Within Hindu spirituality it has been emphasized: "To realize God means to realize one's self."[9] It is through pure metaphysics or non-duality that the Divine may become known, but there is no "other" that realizes this truth

---

[9] Śrī Ānandamayī Mā, quoted in *The Essential Śrī Ānandamayī Mā*, p. 62.

for it is the Divine alone: "He knows Himself through Himself and He sees Himself by means of Himself."[10]

This is because "the inwardly-directed man recognizes other beings and his environment as reflections of realities that exist within him, behind the 'I', in the divine Self. The other beings and the environment are thus no diversion, but on the contrary, supports for concentration upon the true Center that lies behind his 'I'" (p. 53).

Küry asserts that animals function as messengers for what is experienced after death. He draws upon the symbolism of the eagle to make this point:

> The attitude of the eagle's flight is a symbol of the proximity of God; the acuity of its gaze, with which it espies the smallest living creature on the ground, is a symbol of the divine Omniscience; the breadth of its soaring and the rapacious grip of its beak and talons are symbols of the combination of all-inclusiveness and centrality in God (p. 57).

Black Elk or Hehaka Sapa (1863–1950), a remarkable sage of the Lakota Sioux, pronounced the following words when holding up an eagle feather: "This is *Wakan Tanka* (the Great Mysterious One); and it also means that our thoughts should rise high as the eagles do" (p. 57).[11] This gesture gives voice to the interconnectedness of humans with animals and the entire web of life. We must not forget that although human beings are "made in the image of God," they are also made of the earth: "And the Lord God formed man of the dust of the ground, and breathed into his nostrils the breath of life; and man became a living soul" (Genesis 2:7).

---

[10] Ibn 'Arabī / Balyānī, *Know Yourself: An Explanation of the Oneness of Being*, p. 19.
[11] Black Elk, quoted in John G. Neihardt, *Black Elk Speaks: Being the Life Story of a Holy Man of the Oglala Sioux* (Lincoln, NE: University of Nebraska Press, 1988), pp. xvii-xviii.

The environmental crisis not only impacts human beings but extends to all planetary life which itself originates from the spiritual crisis of contemporary humanity. The disappearance of many animal species in the present-day is not by accident as is outlined here:

> From this point of view, the extinction of so many animal species in our time is not unconnected with the equally evident impoverishment of inner spiritual possibilities in man. The gradual disappearance of the eagle from our regions is indicative; and the perishing of mighty species like the bison, the elk, the Atlas lion, etc. goes hand in hand with a dwarfism of the average human soul (p. 62).

In an age of spiritual darkness such as the *Kali-Yuga* or "Dark Age", individuals need to be aware that those on the path may need to conceal the inner gifts conferred to them in the face of a dehumanizing world, "The spiritual man [or woman] must hide his grandeur in order not to perish" (p. 66).

FOURTH MEDITATION: THE SOUL ON ITS PEREGRINATIONS
Diversity is reflected in the diverse religions: "Is there a more powerful expression of divine Mercy than the allotment to the diverse souls of precisely those bodies to which their wisdom is adapted?" The Divine discloses itself differently through the distinct religions and human types: "Veiled, according to their capacity of comprehension" (p. 80).

> Wandering in the labyrinth of the world; insatiable longing drives them from disappointment to disappointment, without curing them of the basic illusion: belief in an existence outside God.... In the case of very low beings, habit induces them to continue living out the same limitation in virtually endless succession—not on earth, but in other states corresponding to them (pp. 89–90).

One of the most important aspects regarding posthumous states is that the human being does not return to terrestrial existence in order to play out in an endless succession his or her human life on earth as is often assumed. "The doctrine of the transmigration of souls by no means presupposes a return to this earth, rather it can be linked to entirely different worlds imperceptible to the five senses" (p. 90). New Age teachings on reincarnation often put forward that human beings return again and again to earth to live as human beings, as if they could continue where they left off at the end of each lifetime—but this is not the case.

The root cause of the modern misunderstanding of reincarnation is the confusion between the psychic and the spiritual. According to Ultimate Reality or the doctrine of non-duality, Śrī Ānandamayī Mā (1896–1982) confirms: "There is no such thing as rebirth."[12] Similarly it is important to recall Śrī Śaṅkarācārya's (788–820) dictum in this regard: "In truth, there is no other transmigrant but the Lord."[13] This teaching categorically denies the possibility of the human individual reincarnating. When the phenomenon of death is looked at through a metaphysical lens, the relationship between the human microcosm—comprised of Spirit, soul and body—and what is commonly understood to be death, changes.

Due to the human being's limited understanding of the nature of things, he or she continues to suffer and be cast into the endless succession of rebirths:

> It is not the act itself that is the cause of this long chain of rebirths, but the tendency to perversion manifested in the sin committed, which can continue to have an effect in the soul even posthumously, so that the soul is, so to speak, magnetically attracted and ensnared in a correspondingly "alienated" world. If the sinner is able to purify his soul during his lifetime through sacred knowledge or through sacrificing his inferior instincts, the gates to higher and

---

[12] Śrī Ānandamayī Mā, quoted in *The Essential Śrī Ānandamayī Mā*, p. 124.
[13] Quoted in Ananda K. Coomaraswamy, *The Bugbear of Literacy*, p. 120.

more luminous kingdoms open to his soul after death (p. 91).

Likewise, rebirth into an animal body is due to the correspondingly dominating forces of the human psyche that it clings to. While the human psyche remains under the control of these forces, the soul cannot escape being reborn in the body of an animal or any other form for that matter.

What must not be forgotten is the pre-existing and ever-present Grace that is always available to human beings, regardless of their circumstances, "In principle God gives every living being no less than himself," however one needs discernment to apprehend this gift because "He gives himself cautiously, wrapped in forty thousand veils" (p. 94).

It is through continual remembrance and spiritual practice that the human soul can return to its Divine origin.

> Through constant, or at least regular, concentration on the Word of God (in the invocation of the divine Name in the traditional manner, in prayer, and in recitation of sacred formulas) the universal Center begins to shine in man's heart, and by following the rituals and laws revealed by God Himself, the circular paths upon which man moves outwardly, begin, at first almost imperceptibly, but then more and more markedly, to bend inwards, towards the Center, towards the Light in the heart (p. 97).

Śrī Rāmakrishna (1836–1886) reminds seekers that there is no distinction between the Divine and the Divine Names: "God and His name are identical."[14] In a corresponding manner, Ibn 'Arabī (1165–1240) writes: "There is but one Reality, which embraces all these attributions and relations called the Divine Names."[15]

With the current spiritual malaise of the *Kali-Yuga*, one of the boons is the gift of its sense of exile, a detachment which

---

[14] *The Gospel of Ramakrishna*, p. 222.

[15] Ibn al-'Arabī, *The Bezels of Wisdom*, p. 68.

allows the traveler on the path to consciously separate himself or herself from the phenomenal world so as to concentrate on the Divine:

> In empty worldliness and shadowy unreality, the soul filled with longing for God feels wretched, "in a foreign land," exiled, homeless. But with this feeling of alienation, sad as its cause may be, a precious jewel is given to the soul, a bitter but healing draught against the illusion of the here below (p. 106).

Death as Gateway to Eternity provides a litany of powerful spiritual reflections on the metaphysical nature of life and death. Even though the reality of death presents an inconvenient truth about the impermanence of all things, the contemporary world wishes to pretend that it does not exist. Regardless, death is a natural part of the web of life. When looked at within the context of integral spirituality, death takes on a different meaning, for our journey does not end with this human existence, but continues through a doorway into Eternity. The secular mindset that disavows transcendence and the sacred asserts that nothing happens when we die, but this belief contradicts the teachings of the sapiential traditions, for without death life itself would have no meaning and *vice versa*.

It would be impossible to live a meaningful life without the reality of death. By remaining steadfast to the message of the saints and sages of the world's religions and not giving in to the accelerating forces of angst and despair of contemporary life, we can find balance and an inner harmony: "Only strenuous effort, with a desperate 'despite it all!' will keep the general perplexity, despair, and apocalyptic mood under control" (p. 106). Living by these transcendent principles will guide not only how we live, but consequently how we die: "When the door opens for this poor soul at the hour of death, it is possible that, remembering its lifelong aspiration, it will— *Deo volente*—extend eagle wings and soar aloft to the goal of its longing" (pp. 106–107). Let us all hope that when the final breath of our human existence arrives, we will be able to consciously give ourselves to the process of death and say, as the Lakota Sioux, "*Hoka hey!*" or "I am ready." For our true identity is transpersonal in nature and is nothing less than the Eternal Itself: "Nor I, nor thou, nor any one of these, ever was not, nor ever will not be" (*Bhagavad Gītā* 2:12).

30

*Invincible Wisdom: Quotations from the Scriptures, Saints, and Sages of All Times and Places**

> In the present age [the *Kali-Yuga*], protective dividing walls have crumbled; the whole world has become our parish, and our gaze must now be universal.
>
> William Stoddart[1]

"Dear reader, have courage! Be not afraid!" explains William Stoddart, for "The sayings here anthologized are not outmoded, out-dated, or difficult to understand. Most of them are of a blinding clarity, they are universal and perennial; they combine a lofty vision with a homely wisdom that all can grasp" (p. xii). It is with these provocative and penetrating words that the author invites the reader to embark upon the otherworldly selections contained within this spiritual anthology.

Those unfamiliar with Stoddart's work will find that he is exceptionally qualified to assemble such a sublime collection as he has written numerous books on comparative religion and has spent a lifetime in profound reflection and serious practice

---

* Compiled by William Stoddart. Sophia Perennis, 2008, 128 pp.
[1] *Ibid.*, p. ix.

of the world's spiritual traditions, never straying from their universal summit.

Readers familiar with Whitall N. Perry's (1920–2005) seminal work *A Treasury of Traditional Wisdom* (1971, recently reissued as *The Spiritual Ascent: A Compendium of the World's Wisdom*), consisting of more than a thousand pages and praised as the "Summa of the Philosophia Perennis", will find the selections contained within the slim yet compelling collection *Invincible Wisdom* to be the *summum bonum*—a most indispensable and most accessible companion to the earlier work.

The selections within this anthology contain the kernel of the world's religions and wisdom, from traditions such as Hindu Quotations (*sanātana dharma*), Buddhist Quotations, Christian Quotations, Hermes Trismegistos, Confucius, Shankara, Mohammad and The Religion of the Sun Dance and Sacred Pipe. Other selections that will seize the eye of the reader contain: Kings and Queens, Democracy, Johann Wolfgang von Goethe and Unity in Plurality, Plurality in Unity.

The axial theme of this anthology could perhaps be best summarized with the fewest words possible by Nicholas of Cusa (1401–1464): "There is... one sole religion and one sole worship for all beings endowed with understanding, and this is presupposed through a variety of rites" (p. 92).

And yet there is perhaps no better dissimilarity to the invincible wisdom contained within this book as the following passage taken from the *Vishnu Purāna* dating back to the third century AD, describing verbatim what appears to be the disarray and collapse of the current social and spiritual order of humanity:

> Riches and piety will diminish daily, until the world will be completely corrupted. In those days it will be wealth that confers distinction, passion will be the sole reason for union between the sexes, lies will be the only method for success in business, and women will be merely the objects

of sensual gratification. The earth will be valued only for its mineral treasures, dishonesty will be the universal means of subsistence, a simple ablution will be regarded as sufficient purification....

The observance of castes, laws, and institutions will no longer be in force in the Dark Age, and the ceremonies prescribed by the Vedas will be neglected. Women will obey only their whims and will be infatuated with pleasure.... Men of all kinds will presumptuously regard themselves as the equals of *brahmins*.... The *vaishyas* will abandon agriculture and commerce and will earn their living by servitude or by the exercise of mechanical professions.... The path of the Vedas having been abandoned, and man having been led astray from orthodoxy, iniquity will prevail and the length of human life will diminish in consequence.... Then men will cease worshiping Vishnu, the Lord of sacrifice, Creator and Lord of all things, and they will say: "Of what authority are the Vedas? Who are the Gods and the *brahmins*? What use is purification with water? The dominant caste will be that of *shūdras*.... Man, deprived of reason and subject to every infirmity of body and mind, will daily commit sins: everything which is impure, vicious, and calculated to afflict the human race will make its appearance in the Dark Age (p. 82).

A note needs to be made regarding the Appendices and the Envoi of this work, for they formulate a profound compliment to the selections made throughout this anthology. "It must needs be that scandals come," "A Message of Hope" and "Think on these things" will not go unnoticed by readers as they both encapsulate the source of the spiritual eclipse that prevails in the current era and yet point to the cure of the modern and postmodern pathology.

In order to counteract the current angst of the world the author suggests the reader ponder over the following reflections:

Whatsoever things are true, whatsoever things are honest, whatsoever things are just, whatsoever things are pure, whatsoever things are lovely, whatsoever things are of good report; if there be any virtue, and if there be any praise, *think on these things* (Philippians 4:8—p. 107).

Stoddart reminds the reader in the Preface of this work that "Anthology, by definition, cannot be complete, but this does not mean that it must be arbitrary.... On the contrary, to the degree that the anthology is shaped by a guiding idea, the selection, far from being arbitrary, becomes a qualitative entity, and takes on a distinct and meaningful character of its own" (p. ix). It is this guiding idea, reflected within the pages of *Invincible Wisdom*, that has fashioned this work compiled during the span of a lifetime.

We welcome this work to the perennialist canon and hope that it will serve to point its readers to the timeless truths that exist everywhere and always, "Wise and useful quotations are of course endless, but a selection is what it is and, far from being arbitrary, this anthology, taken as a whole, amounts to a succinct, but powerful, affirmation of 'the True, the Good, and the Beautiful'. This is its purpose—and may it bear fruit" (p. ix).

Acknowledgments

1. *Introduction to Hindu Dharma: Illustrated*, by The 68th Jagadguru of Kanchi, introduction by Arvind Sharma, edited by Michael Oren Fitzgerald. Bloomington: World Wisdom, 2008. PUBLISHED IN *Sophia: The Journal of Traditional Studies*, Vol. 15, No. 1 (Summer 2009), pp. 151–158. ALSO PUBLISHED IN *Studies in Comparative Religion*, Web Edition 2009.
2. *The Original Gospel of Rāmakrishna: Based on M.'s English Text, Abridged*, revised by Swāmī Abhedānanda, foreword by Alexander Lipski, introduction by Swāmī Vivekānanda, edited and abridged by Joseph A. Fitzgerald. PUBLISHED IN *Sacred Web: A Journal of Tradition and Modernity*, Vol. 42 (Winter 2018), pp. 144–158.
3. *Timeless in Time: Sri Ramana Maharshi*, by A.R. Natarajan, foreword by Eliot Deutsch. PUBLISHED IN *Parabola: The Search for Meaning*, Vol. 44, No. 1 (Spring 2019), pp. 112–119.
4. *The Essential Śrī Ānandamayī Mā: Life and Teachings of a 20th Century Indian Saint*, biography by Alexander Lipski, Words of Śrī Ānandamayī Mā (translated and compiled by Ātmānanda), edited by Joseph A. Fitzgerald. PUBLISHED IN *Sacred Web: A Journal of Tradition and Modernity*, Vol. 41 (Summer 2018), pp. 101–115.
5. *Eastern Light in Western Eyes: A Portrait of the Practice of Devotion*, by Marty Glass. PUBLISHED IN *AHP Perspective* (April/May 2009), pp. 28–31.

6. *An Illustrated Introduction to Taoism: The Wisdom of the Sages*, by Jean C. Cooper, foreword by William Stoddart, edited by Joseph A. Fitzgerald. PUBLISHED IN *Sacred Web: A Journal of Tradition and Modernity*, Vol. 38 (Winter 2016), pp. 101–107.
7. *The Spiritual Legacy of the American Indian: Commemorative Edition with Letters While Living with Black Elk*, by Joseph Epes Brown, introduction by Åke Hultkrantz, edited by Marina Brown Weatherly, Elenita Brown and Michael Oren Fitzgerald. PUBLISHED IN *Shaman's Drum: A Journal of Experiential Shamanism and Spiritual Healing*, No. 81 (2009), pp. 59–60.
8. *Black Elk, Lakota Visionary: The Oglala Holy Man and Sioux Tradition*, by Harry Oldmeadow, foreword by Charles Trimble. PUBLISHED IN *Parabola: The Search for Meaning*, Vol. 43, No. 3 (Fall 2018), pp. 114–125.
9. *Samdhong Rinpoche, Uncompromising Truth for a Compromised World: Tibetan Buddhism and Today's World*, edited by Donovan Roebert, Bloomington, IN, World Wisdom, 2006. PUBLISHED IN *AHP/ATP Perspective* (October/November 2008), pp. 27–29. ALSO PUBLISHED IN *Studies in Comparative Religion*, Web Edition 2009.
10. *Honen the Buddhist Saint: Essential Writings and Official Biography*, edited by Joseph A. Fitzgerald, foreword by Clark Strand, introduction by Alfred Bloom, Bloomington, IN, World Wisdom, 2006. PUBLISHED IN *AHP/ATP Perspective* (December 2008/January 2009), pp. 26–27.
11. *Universal Aspects of the Kabbalah and Judaism*, by Leo Schaya, forward by Patrick Laude, edited by Roger Gaetani, Bloomington, IN, World Wisdom, 2014. PUBLISHED IN *Journal of Transpersonal Psychology*, Vol. 47, No. 1 (2015), pp. 142–148.
12. *The Rationale Divinorum Officiorum: The Foundational Symbolism of the Early Church, its Structure, Decoration, Sacraments, and Vestments*, by Guilielmus Durandus, Louisville, KY,

ACKNOWLEDGMENTS

Fons Vitae, 2007. PUBLISHED IN *Sacred Web: A Journal of Tradition and Modernity*, Vol. 38 (Winter 2016), pp. 109–114.

13. *Meister Eckhart on Divine Knowledge*, by C.F. Kelley, Cobb, CA, DharmaCafé, 2009. PUBLISHED IN *Sacred Web: A Journal of Tradition and Modernity*, Vol. 31 (Summer 2013), pp. 139–148.

14. *Christianity and the Doctrine of Non-Dualism*, by A Monk of the West (Elie Lemoine), translated by Alvin Moore, Jr. and Marie Hansen, Hillsdale, NY, Sophia Perennis, 2004. PUBLISHED IN *AHP Perspective* (August/September 2008), pp. 25–26. PUBLISHED IN *Self & Society*, Vol. 36, No. 4 (January/February 2009), pp. 45–47. ALSO PUBLISHED IN *Oriens: Online Journal of Traditional Studies*, Vol. 6, Nos. 1–2 (February 2009), pp. 1–2. AND IN *The Newsletter of the Association for the Advancement of Psychosynthesis* (February 2009), p. 4.

15. *What Does Islam Mean in Today's World? Religion, Politics, Spirituality*, by William Stoddart, foreword by Harry Oldmeadow, Bloomington, IN, World Wisdom, 2012. PUBLISHED IN *Temenos Academy Review*, No. 16 (2013), pp. 246–250.

16. *Know Yourself: An Explanation of the Oneness of Being*, by Ibn 'Arabi/Balyani, translated from Arabic by Cecilia Twinch, Cheltenham, UK, Beshara Publications, 2014. PUBLISHED IN *Sacred Web: A Journal of Tradition and Modernity*, Vol. 37 (Summer 2016), pp. 105–110.

17. *The Sufi Doctrine of Rumi: Illustrated Edition*, by William C. Chittick, foreword by Seyyed Hossein Nasr, Bloomington, IN, World Wisdom, 2005. PUBLISHED IN *Parabola: The Search for Meaning*, Vol. 43, No. 1 (Spring 2018), pp. 110–115.

18. *A Spirit of Tolerance: The Inspiring Life of Tierno Bokar*, by Amadou Hampaté Bâ, introduction by Louis Brenner, translated by Fatima Jane Casewit, edited by Roger

Gaetani, Bloomington, IN, World Wisdom, 2008. PUBLISHED IN *Journal of the Muhyiddīn Ibn 'Arabī Society*, Vol. 45 (2009), pp. 133–138. ALSO PUBLISHED IN *Education in the Light of Tradition: Studies in Comparative Religion*, edited by Fatima Jane Casewit, Bloomington, IN, World Wisdom, 2011, pp. 160–163.

19. *Introduction to Sufi Doctrine*, by Titus Burckhardt, foreword by William Chittick, translated by D.M. Matheson, Bloomington, IN, World Wisdom, 2008. PUBLISHED IN *Journal of the Muhyiddīn Ibn 'Arabī Society*, Vol. 44 (2008), pp. 93–96.

20. *The Underlying Religion: An Introduction to the Perennial Philosophy*, edited by Martin Lings and Clinton Minnaar, Bloomington, IN, World Wisdom, 2007. PUBLISHED IN *Journal of Transpersonal Psychology*, Vol. 41, No. 1 (2009), pp. 108–112.

21. *Pray Without Ceasing: The Way of the Invocation in World Religions*, edited by Patrick Laude, Bloomington, IN, World Wisdom, 2006. PUBLISHED IN *Parabola: The Search for Meaning*, Vol. 44, No. 3 (Fall 2019), pp. 110, 112–121.

22. *The Essential René Guénon: Metaphysics, Tradition, and the Crisis of Modernity*, edited by John Herlihy, introduction by Martin Lings, Bloomington, IN, World Wisdom & San Rafael, CA, Sophia Perennis, 2009. PUBLISHED IN *Parabola: Where Spiritual Traditions Meet*, Vol. 35, No. 3 (Fall 2010), pp. 114–121.

23. *Touchstones of the Spirit: Essays on Religion, Tradition and Modernity*, by Harry Oldmeadow, Bloomington, IN, World Wisdom, 2012. PUBLISHED IN *Network Review: The Journal of the Scientific and Medical Network*, No. 109 (Summer 2012), pp. 45–46.

24. *The Mystery of Individuality: Grandeur and Delusion of the Human Condition*, by Mark Perry, Bloomington, IN, World Wisdom, 2012. PUBLISHED IN *Journal of Transpersonal Research*, Vol. 4, No. 1 (2012), pp. 94–105.

Acknowledgments

25. *Men of a Single Book: Fundamentalism in Islam, Christianity, and Modern Thought*, by Mateus Soares de Azevedo, forward by Alberto Vasconcellos Queiroz, introduction by William Stoddart, Bloomington, IN, World Wisdom, 2010. PUBLISHED IN *Parabola: Where Spiritual Traditions Meet*, Vol. 36, No. 1 (Spring 2011), pp. 114–117.
26. *Of the Land and the Spirit: The Essential Lord Northbourne on Ecology and Religion*, edited by Christopher James and Joseph A. Fitzgerald, foreword by Wendell Berry, Bloomington, IN, World Wisdom, 2008. PUBLISHED IN *Resurgence Magazine*, Issue 258 (January/February 2010), p. 71.
27. *On the Origin of Beauty: Ecophilosophy in the Light of Traditional Wisdom*, by John Griffin, forward by Satish Kumar, Bloomington, IN, World Wisdom, 2011. PUBLISHED IN *Studies in Comparative Religion*, Web Edition 2013.
28. *Beads of Faith: Pathways to Meditation and Spirituality Using Rosaries, Prayer Beads, and Sacred Words*, by Gray Henry and Susannah Marriott, Louisville, KY, Fons Vitae, 2008. PUBLISHED IN *Parabola: Myth, Tradition, and the Search for Meaning*, Vol. 34, No. 1 (Spring 2009), pp. 116–122.
29. *Death as Gateway to Eternity: Nature's Hidden Message*, by Hans Küry, translated by Gillian Harris, Bloomington, IN, World Wisdom, 2013. PUBLISHED IN *Sacred Web: A Journal of Tradition and Modernity*, Vol. 39 (Summer 2017), pp. 169–182.
30. *Invincible Wisdom: Quotations from the Scriptures, Saints, and Sages of All Times and Places*, edited by William Stoddart, San Rafael, CA, Sophia Perennis, 2008. PUBLISHED IN *Sacred Web: A Journal of Tradition and Modernity*, Vol. 23 (Summer 2009), pp. 181–183.

Bibliography

Śrī Ānandamayī Mā. *The Essential Śrī Ānandamayī Mā: Life and Teachings of a 20th Century Indian Saint*, translated by Ātmānanda, edited by Joseph A. Fitzgerald, with a biography by Alexander Lipski. Bloomington: World Wisdom, 2007.

Bendeck Sotillos, Samuel. "Modern Psychology in the Light of Sufi Psychology: Some reflections." *Sufi*, No. 73 (2007), pp. 40–43.

———*Psychology and the Perennial Philosophy: Studies in Comparative Religion*. Bloomington: World Wisdom, 2013.

———"René Guénon and Sri Ramana Maharshi: Two Remarkable Sages in Modern Times," Part I, *The Mountain Path*, Vols. 51, No. 2 (April/June 2014), pp. 93–101; Part II, *The Mountain Path*, Vol. 51, No. 3 (July/September 2014), pp. 85–91; Part III, *The Mountain Path*, Vol. 51, No. 4 (October/December 2014), pp. 93–102; Part IV, *The Mountain Path*, Vol. 52, No. 1 (January/March 2015), pp. 93–104.

Biès, Jean. *Returning to the Essential: Selected Writings of Jean Biès*, translated by Deborah Weiss-Dutilh. Bloomington: World Wisdom, 2004.

Brown, Joseph Epes. *The Sacred Pipe: Black Elk's Account of the Seven Rites of the Oglala Sioux*. Norman, OK: University of Oklahoma Press, 1989.

Burckhardt, Titus. *Mirror of the Intellect: Essays on Traditional Science and Sacred Art*, translated and edited by William Stoddart. Albany, NY: State University of New York Press, 1987.

Casey, Deborah. "The Basis of Religion and Metaphysics: An Interview with Frithjof Schuon," *The Quest: Philosophy, Science, Religion, the Arts*, Vol. 9, No. 2 (Summer 1996), pp. 74–79.

Chittick, William C. *The Sufi Path of Knowledge: Ibn al-'Arabi's Metaphysics of Imagination*. Albany, NY: State University of New York Press, 1989.

The Cloud of Unknowing and The Book of Privy Counseling, edited by William Johnston. New York: Doubleday, 1996.

Cook, Francis Dojun. *How to Raise an Ox: Zen Practice as Taught in Zen Master Dogen's* Shobogenzo. Los Angeles: Center Publications, 1978.

Coomaraswamy, Ananda K. *The Bugbear of Literacy*. Middlesex, UK: Perennial Books, 1979.

——*Hinduism and Buddhism*. New York: Philosophical Library, 1943.

——"Paths That Lead to the Same Summit: Some Observations on Comparative Religion," *Motive*, Vol. 4, No. 8 (May 1944), pp. 29–32, 35.

——*Selected Letters of Ananda K. Coomaraswamy*, edited by Alvin Moore, Jr. and Rama P. Coomaraswamy. Oxford University Press, 1988.

——*Coomaraswamy, Vol. 2: Selected Papers, Metaphysics*, edited by Roger Lipsey. Princeton University Press, 1977.

Coomaraswamy, Rama P. *The Destruction of the Christian Tradition*. Bloomington: World Wisdom, 2006.

——"The Desacralization of Hinduism for Western Consumption," *Sophia: The Journal of Traditional Studies*, Vol. 4, No. 2 (Winter 1998), pp. 194–219.

——*The Problems with the New Mass: A Brief Overview of the Major Theological Difficulties Inherent in the* Novus Ordo Missae. Rockford, IL: Tan Books, 1990.

——*The Problems with the Other Sacraments: Apart from the New Mass*. San Rafael, CA: Reviviscimus Press, 2010.

Cooper, Jean C. *An Illustrated Introduction to Taoism: The Wisdom of the Sages*, edited by Joseph A. Fitzgerald. Bloomington: World Wisdom, 2010.

——*Yin & Yang: The Taoist Harmony of Opposites*. Wellingborough, UK: Aquarian Press, 1981.

Cutsinger, James S. *Splendor of the True: A Frithjof Schuon Reader*. Albany, NY: State University of New York Press, 2013.

al-Darqāwī, Shaykh. *Letters of a Sufi Master*, translated by Titus Burckhardt. Louisville, KY: Fons Vitae, 1998.

Meister Eckhart, *The Essential Sermons, Commentaries, Treatises, and Defense*, translated by Edmund Colledge, O.S.A. and Bernard McGinn. Ramsey, NJ: Paulist Press, 1981.

Fernando, Ranjit (ed.). *The Unanimous Tradition: Essays on the Essential Unity of All Religions*. Colombo: Sri Lanka Institute of Traditional Studies, 1999.

Ferrer, Jorge N. "The Perennial Philosophy Revisited". *Journal of Transpersonal Psychology*, Vol. 32, No. 1 (2000), pp. 7–30.

——*Revisioning Transpersonal Theory, A Participatory Vision of Human Spirituality*. Albany, NY: State University of New York Press, 2002.

Fitzgerald, Michael Oren. *Frithjof Schuon: Messenger of the Perennial Philosophy*. Bloomington: World Wisdom, 2010.

al-Ghazālī, Abū Ḥāmid Muḥammad. *The Alchemy of Happiness*, translated by Claud Field. Armonk, NY: M.E. Sharpe, 1991.

Glass, Marty. *Eastern Light in Western Eyes: A Portrait of the Practice of Devotion*. Hillsdale, NY: Sophia Perennis, 2003.

Grof, Stanislav. *The Cosmic Game: Explorations of the Frontiers of Human Consciousness*. Albany, NY: State University of New York Press, 1998.

Psychology of the Future: Lessons from Modern Consciousness Research. Albany, NY: State University of New York Press, 2000.

Guénon, René. *The Crisis of the Modern World*, translated by Arthur Osborne, Marco Pallis and Richard C. Nicholson. Hillsdale, NY: Sophia Perennis, 2004.

——*The Great Triad*, translated by Henry D. Fohr, edited by Samuel D. Fohr. Hillsdale, NY: Sophia Perennis, 2004.

——*Insights into Islamic Esoterism and Taoism*, translated by Henry D. Fohr, edited by Samuel D. Fohr. Hillsdale, NY: Sophia Perennis, 2001.

———*Introduction to the Study of the Hindu Doctrines*, translated by Marco Pallis. Ghent, NY: Sophia Perennis, 2001.

———*The King of the World*. Hillsdale, NY: Sophia Perennis, 2001.

———*Man and His Becoming According to the Vedānta*, translated by Richard C. Nicholson. Hillsdale, NY: Sophia Perennis, 2004.

———*The Reign of Quantity and the Signs of the Times*, translated by Lord Northbourne. Hillsdale, NY: Sophia Perennis, 2004.

———*Studies in Hinduism*, translated by Henry D. Fohr, edited by Samuel D. Fohr. Ghent, NY: Sophia Perennis, 2001.

The Symbolism of the Cross, translated by Angus Macnab (Hillsdale, NY: Sophia Perennis, 2001.

Gupta, Mehendranāth. *Srī Srī Rāmakrishna Kathāmrita, Vol. 2*, translated by Dharm Pal Gupta. Chandigarh, India: Sri Ma Trust, 2002.

Hadot, Pierre. *Philosophy as a Way of Life: Spiritual Exercises from Socrates to Foucault*, translated by Michael Chase, edited by Arnold I. Davidson. Oxford: Blackwell Publishers, 1999.

Huntington, Samuel P. "The Clash of Civilizations?" *Foreign Affairs*, Vol. 72, No. 3 (Summer 1993), pp. 22–49.

Hutchins, Robert. "Ten Simple Ways to Explain Transpersonal Psychology," *PDTP News* [Newsletter of the Proposed Division of Transpersonal Psychology in the American Psychological Association] (July 1987), pp. 9–12.

Huxley, Aldous. *The Perennial Philosophy*. New York: Harper & Brothers, 1945.

Ibn al-'Arabī, Muḥyī al-Dīn. *The Bezels of Wisdom*, translated by R.W.J. Austin. New York, NY: Paulist Press, 1980.

James, William. *The Varieties of Religious Experience*. New York: Penguin Books, 1985.

Jung, C. G. *Letters, Vol. 2: 1951–1961*, translated by R.F.C. Hull, edited by Gerhard Adler and Aniela Jaffé. Princeton University Press, 1975.

———*Psychological Types*, translated by R.F.C. Hull. Princeton University Press, 1976.

Laude, Patrick (ed.). *Pray Without Ceasing: The Way of the Invocation in World Religions*. Bloomington: World Wisdom, 2006.

Lewis, Bernard. "The Roots of Muslim Rage," *The Atlantic Monthly*, Vol. 266, No. 3 (September 1990), pp. 47–60.

Lings, Martin. *A Sufi Saint of the Twentieth Century: Shaykh Aḥmad Al-ʿAlawī, His Spiritual Heritage and Legacy*. Cambridge, UK: Islamic Texts Society, 1993.

——*Ancient Beliefs and Modern Superstitions*. Cambridge, UK: Archetype, 2001.

——*Symbol & Archetype: A Study of The Meaning of Existence*. Cambridge, UK: Quinta Essentia, 1991.

——*What is Sufism?* Berkeley, CA: University of California Press, 1977.

Lopez, Donald S. *The Heart Sutra Explained: Indian and Tibetan Commentaries*. Albany, NY: State University of New York Press, 1988.

Lumbard, Joseph E.B. (ed.). *Islam, Fundamentalism, and the Betrayal of Tradition: Essays by Western Muslim Scholars*. Bloomington: World Wisdom, 2009.

Margolis, Robert G. "At 'The Meeting of the Two Seas': An Introduction to Leo Schaya and His Writings," *Annals of Japan Association for Middle East Studies*, No. 13 (1988), pp. 399–418.

Maslow, Abraham. *Religions, Values, and Peak-Experiences*. New York: Penguin Group, 1994.

——*Toward a Psychology of Being*. Princeton, NJ: Van Nostrand, 1968.

Mudaliar, A. Devaraja. *Day by Day with Bhagavan*. Tiruvannamalai, India: Sri Ramanasramam, 2002.

Mukerji, Bithika. "Śrī Ānandamayī Mā: Divine Play of the Spiritual Journey," in *Hindu Spirituality: Vedas through Vedanta*, ed. Krishna Sivaraman. New York: Crossroad, 1989, pp. 392–412.

Nasr, Seyyed Hossein. *Islamic Philosophy from Its Origin to the Present: Philosophy in the Land of Prophecy*. Albany, NY: State University of New York, 2006.

———*The Philosophy of Seyyed Hossein Nasr*, edited by Lewis Edwin Hahn, Randall E. Auxier and Lucian W. Stone, Jr. Chicago: Open Court, 2001.

———"Reflections on Islam and Modern Thought," *Studies in Comparative Religion*, Vol. 15, Nos. 3 & 4 (Summer/Autumn 1983), pp. 164–176.

———*Sufi Essays*. Albany, NY: State University of New York Press, 1973.

———*The Need for a Sacred Science*. Albany, NY: State University of New York Press, 1993.

Nasr, Seyyed Hossein and William Stoddart (eds.). *Religion of the Heart: Essays Presented to Frithjof Schuon on His Eightieth Birthday*. Washington, D.C.: Foundation for Traditional Studies, 1991.

Natarajan, A.R. *Timeless in Time: Sri Ramana Maharshi*. Bloomington: World Wisdom, 2006.

Needleman, Jacob (ed.). *The Sword of Gnosis: Metaphysics, Cosmology, Tradition, Symbolism*. London: Arkana, 1986.

Neihardt, John G. *Black Elk Speaks: Being the Life Story of a Holy Man of the Oglala Sioux*. Lincoln, NE: University of Nebraska Press, 1988.

Lord Northbourne, *Religion in the Modern World*, edited by Christopher James 5th Lord Northbourne. Ghent, NY: Sophia Perennis, 2001.

Oldmeadow, Harry. *Black Elk, Lakota Visionary: The Oglala Holy Man and Sioux Tradition*. Bloomington: World Wisdom, 2018.

———*Journeys East: 20th Century Western Encounters with Eastern Religious Traditions*. Bloomington: World Wisdom, 2004.

Ortega y Gasset, José. *The Revolt of the Masses*. New York: W.W. Norton & Co., 1993.

Paine, Scott Randall (ed.). *A Catholic Mind Awake: The Writings of Bernard Kelly*. New York: Angelico Press, 2017.

Pallis, Marco. "Ossendowski's Sources," *Studies in Comparative Religion*, Vol. 15, Nos. 1 & 2 (Spring/Winter 1983), pp. 30–41.

Perry, Mark. *On Awakening and Remembering: To Know is To Be*. Louisville, KY: Fons Vitae, 2000.

Perry, Whitall N. (ed.). *Challenges to a Secular Society*. Oakton, VA: Foundation for Traditional Studies, 1996.

——*The Spiritual Ascent: A Compendium of the World's Wisdom* (new edition of the next title). Louisville, KY: Fons Vitae, 2008.

——*A Treasury of Traditional Wisdom*. New York, NY: Simon and Schuster, 1971.

Puhakka, Kaisa. "Transpersonal Perspective: An Antidote to the Postmodern Malaise." *Journal of Transpersonal Psychology*, Vol. 40, No. 1 (2008), pp. 6–19.

Śrī Rāmakrishna. *The Gospel of Ramakrishna: Originally recorded in Bengali by M., a disciple of the Master*, translated by Swami Nikhilananda. New York: Ramakrishna-Vivekananda Center, 1977.

——*The Original Gospel of Rāmakrishna: Based on M.'s English Text, Abridged*, edited by Swāmī Abhedānanda and Joseph A. Fitzgerald. Bloomington: World Wisdom, 2011.

Ramana Maharshi. *The Collected Works of Ramana Maharshi*, edited by Arthur Osborne. Boston, MA: Weiser Books, 1997.

——*Talks with Sri Ramana Maharshi*. Tiruvannamalai, India: Sri Ramanasramam, 1996.

——*The Teachings of Ramana Maharshi in His Own Words*, edited by Arthur Osborne. New York: Samuel Weiser, 1978.

Swāmī Ramdas. *The Essential Swami Ramdas: Commemorative Edition*, edited by Susunaga Weeraperuma. Bloomington: World Wisdom, 2005.

Reps, Paul (ed.). *Zen Flesh, Zen Bones: A Collection of Zen and Pre-Zen Writings*. New York: Anchor Books, 1989.

Rūmī, Jalāl al-Dīn. *Tales from the Masnavi*, translated by A. J. Arberry. Surrey: Curzon Press, 1994.

Said, Edward W. "The Clash of Ignorance," *The Nation*, Vol. 273, No. 12 (October 22, 2001), pp. 11–14.

Schuon, Frithjof. *Christianity/Islam: Essays on Esoteric Ecumenicism*, translated by Gustavo Polit. Bloomington: World Wisdom, 1985.

——*Esoterism as Principle and as Way*, translated by William Stoddart. Bedfont, Middlesex, UK: Perennial Books, 1990.
——*From the Divine to the Human*, translated by Gustavo Polit and Deborah Lambert. Bloomington: World Wisdom, 1982.
——*Gnosis: Divine Wisdom*, translated by G.E.H. Palmer. Bedfont, Middlesex, UK: Perennial Books, 1990.
——*Gnosis: Divine Wisdom. A New Translation with Selected Letters*, translated by Mark Perry, Jean-Pierre Lafouge and James C. Cutsinger, edited by James S. Cutsinger. Bloomington: World Wisdom, 2006.
——*Light on the Ancient Worlds*, translated by Lord Northbourne. Bloomington: World Wisdom Books, 1984.
——*The Play of Masks*. Bloomington: World Wisdom, 1992.
——*Spiritual Perspectives and Human Facts: A New Translation with Letters*, translated by Mark Perry, Jean-Pierre Lafouge and James C. Cutsinger, edited by James C. Cutsinger. Bloomington: World Wisdom, 2007.
——*Sufism: Veil and Quintessence*, translated by William Stoddart. Bloomington: World Wisdom, 1981.
——*Survey of Metaphysics and Esoterism*, translated by Gustavo Polit. Bloomington: World Wisdom, 1986.
——*The Transcendent Unity of Religions*, translated by Peter Townsend. London, UK: Faber and Faber, 1953.
——*The Transcendent Unity of Religions*. Wheaton, IL: Theosophical Publishing House, 1993.
——*The Transfiguration of Man*. Bloomington: World Wisdom, 1995.
——*Understanding Islam*. Bloomington: World Wisdom, 1998.
Shah-Kazemi, Reza. *Paths to Transcendence: According to Shankara, Ibn Arabi, and Meister Eckhart*. Bloomington: World Wisdom, 2006.
Smith, Huston. *The Way Things Are: Conversations with Huston Smith on the Spiritual Life*, edited by Phil Cousineau. Los Angeles: University of California Press, 2003.
Soares de Azevedo, Mateus (ed.). *Ye Shall Know the Truth: Christianity and the Perennial Philosophy*. Bloomington: World Wisdom, 2005.

Stoddart, William. *Remembering in a World of Forgetting: Thoughts on Tradition and Postmodernism*, edited by Mateus Soares de Azevedo and Alberto Vasconcellos Queiroz. Bloomington: World Wisdom, 2008.

Vaughan, Frances. "The Transpersonal Perspective: A Personal Account." *Journal of Transpersonal Psychology*, Vol. 14, No. 1 (1982), pp. 37–45.

Walsh, Roger. N. and Frances Vaughan. "The Transpersonal Movement: A History and State of the Art." *Journal of Transpersonal Psychology*, Vol. 25, No. 3 (1993), pp. 123–139.

Waterfield, Robin. *René Guénon and the Future of the West: The Life and Writings of a 20th-Century Metaphysician*. Hillsdale, NY: Sophia Perennis, 2002.

Wilber, Ken. "Foreword", in John E. Nelson, *Healing the Split: Integrating Spirit into Our Understanding of the Mentally Ill*. Albany, NY: State University of New York Press, 1994, pp. viii–xii.

Wittine, Bryan. "Assumptions of Transpersonal Psychotherapy," in *Paths Beyond Ego: The Transpersonal Vision*, edited by Roger N. Walsh and Frances Vaughan. New York: Putnam, 1993, pp. 165–171.

SOME OTHER MATHESON TRUST TITLES

Imam 'Ali From Concise History to Timeless Mystery
by Reza Shah-Kazemi, 2019

The Great War of the Dark Age: Keys to the Mahābhārata
by Dominique Wohlschlag, 2019

Breaking the Spell of the New Atheism in the Light of Perennial Wisdom
by Gustavo Polit, 2017

Weighing the Word: Reasoning the Qur'ān as Revelation
by Peter Samsel, 2016

Primordial Meditation: Contemplating the Real,
by Frithjof Schuon, 2015

Enduring Utterance: Collected Lectures (1993–2001),
by Martin Lings, 2014

Louis Massignon: The Vow and the Oath,
by Patrick Laude, 2011

Ascent to Heaven in Islamic and Jewish Mysticism,
by Algis Uždavinys, 2011

Orpheus and the Roots of Platonism,
by Algis Uždavinys, 2011

The Living Palm Tree: Parables, Stories, and Teachings from the Kabbalah
by Mario Satz, 2010

Christianity & Islam: Essays on Ontology and Archetype,
by Samuel Zinner, 2010

www.ingramcontent.com/pod-product-compliance
Lightning Source LLC
Chambersburg PA
CBHW022052160426
43198CB00008B/200